CHIEF DIVERSITY OFFICERS IN HIGHER EDUCATION TODAY

In this edited volume, diversity practitioners in the field of higher education speak about the transformative journeys that led them to become Chief Diversity Officers (CDOs).

Not always an easy path, chapter authors lay bare the challenges and successes of doing this important work in a society that is becoming increasingly hostile to their efforts. The narratives in this intriguing volume unpack the various pathways for DEI practitioners to practice their craft, step into the CDO role, and maintain a sense of self and wholeness while doing so. Full of wisdom and practical insights, this volume helps CDOs understand how to focus on educational priorities that champion access and affordability, equity and social mobility, belonging, and the promise of education, while building bridges across differences. Chapters conclude with key insights to reiterate major lessons from each author's journey, along with guiding questions for reflection.

Chief Diversity Officers in Higher Education Today is written for practitioners at all levels of higher education, but especially aspiring diversity, equity, and inclusion leaders. It's also an important resource for current CDOs in their efforts to support institutions seeking to fulfill their educational mission and strengthen the enrichment of undergraduate, graduate, and professional level scholars, faculty, and staff.

Carol E. Henderson is Vice Provost for Diversity and Inclusion, Chief Diversity Officer, and Adviser to the President at Emory University, USA, and Professor Emerita of English and Africana Studies at the University of Delaware, USA.

CHIEF DIVERSITY OFFICERS IN HIGHER EDUCATION TODAY

Narratives of Justice, Equity, Diversity, and Inclusion

Edited by Carol E. Henderson

09.11.2024

Ravi,

Continue to light the way.

In gratitude,

Carol

R Routledge
Taylor & Francis Group

NEW YORK AND LONDON

Designed cover image: Getty / Javier Rodriguez Jimenez

First published 2025
by Routledge
605 Third Avenue, New York, NY 10158

and by Routledge
4 Park Square, Milton Park, Abingdon, Oxon, OX14 4RN

Routledge is an imprint of the Taylor & Francis Group, an informa business

ISBN: 978-1-032-72487-4 (hbk)
ISBN: 978-1-032-71767-8 (pbk)
ISBN: 978-1-032-72488-1 (ebk)

DOI: 10.4324/9781032724881

Typeset in Galliard
by MPS Limited, Dehradun

Access the Support Material: www.routledge.com/9781032717678

for generations past, present…
and those yet to be

CONTENTS

PREFACE—SETTING THE TABLE: THE POWER OF OUR STORIES

Carol E. Henderson

So much has happened since the imagining of this volume over three years ago. I remember speaking into the atmosphere with a gathering of colleagues that I wanted to create an edited collection of narratives that would humanize the work we do as chief diversity officers. That would allow us to speak our truths about our everyday work and the importance of that collaborative work in mitigating inequities and/or barriers to student success and student flourishing. This collection would, likewise, share the work we do to aid our campus communities in fostering inclusive environments whose binding cords of goodwill, empathy, forgiveness, and mindful listening serve as the impetus for common decency and human respect. This volume would lift up those experiences and the various ways we enter this advocacy space—the pathways and tributaries we actuate to participate in an educational industry whose promise has always been fraught with visions of the haves and have nots; whose history is steeped in a culture and tradition of exclusionary practices that have not always made room for diverse people, cultures, and identities. The contours of that diversity include, but are not limited to race, ethnicity, immigration status, national origin, socioeconomic designation, gender, gender identity, gender expression, disability, sexual orientation, veteran status, neurodiversity, familial composition and/or pedigree, religious, spiritual, and philosophical affiliation, and/or belief systems.[1]

This is our truth as purveyors of this field. In this vocation, we know that higher education is still one of the few pathways in society that, with opportunity and support, allows for social mobility—a mobility that transforms families, neighborhoods, communities. It should not be for the privileged few. It should be available to anyone with the fortitude to take the educational journey. This elevated sense of awareness meets people where they are and ushers in a growth mindset that sees diverseness, not as a deficit, but an asset that enhances the college experience. From this vantage point, we understand that education is a social justice issue too; a human rights imperative; a necessary public good that changes lives and illuminates the wonderful complexities of the human experience in this nation. This conversation is germane to building a thriving and prosperous democracy. A democracy beautiful in its vastness—straining to actualize the ideals we hold dear. And our educational institutions should reflect the society we live in—in the true sense of the word.

It is this premise that we shepherd as stewards of the greater good. Diversity is our strength, a founding principle of our society that, as Heather McGhee reminds us, is our superpower. It has been since the country's founding.[2] While I could opine about the virtues of diversity as cultivator of innovation, critical thought, creativity, and healthy intellectual engagement—I will not. Colleagues more astute than I have done that *ad nauseum* in books, articles, podcasts, and interviews too numerous to list here. Samuel Museus, Shaun Harper, Sylvia Hurtado, Anthony Abraham Jack, Lori Patton Davis, Randal Pinkett, and Lisa Stulberg are noteworthy for their work on the saliency of diversity, equity, and inclusion in higher education. And colleagues such as Damon A. Williams, Katrina Wade-Golden, Tabbye Chavous, William B. Harvey, Paulette Granberry Russell, Earl Lewis, Edna Chun, and Eugene T. Parker III have discussed the import of the chief diversity officer as thought partners in this work.

The strength of this compendium rests in its focus on that collective work that refashions lives, and the practitioners who lead portions of it. Some of us were and still are faculty, committed to enriching the lives of student scholars both at the undergraduate, graduate, and professional levels, and of scholars on the postdoctoral track—all who will go on to impact, transfigure, and solve some of society's most challenging issues utilizing the disciplines of medicine, law, politics, theology, business, public health, and the arts and humanities. Others have entered this arena through student affairs, human resources, and other portals that provide insights into the disconnect between professed opportunities and lived realities in work and learning communities. Equity then becomes a tool to reassess, recalibrate, and recommit to providing an environment for all to work, learn, and flourish. In setting the table, these leaders tell their stories in their own voices. They are very clear on the challenges—and likewise the rewards—of engaging this work in this current climate. Their stories provide insight into that work, its importance in broadening access in the higher education landscape for students, faculty, and staff, and the costs of doing that work for the practitioners themselves.

This work can be exhausting.

The scrutiny under which we now lead takes your breath away. The current vitriol, animus, and inhumane gesturing codified in anti-DEI legislation and its attending communicatives mask other intentions that are adjacent to this work. As Eddie S. Glaude Jr. astutely observes, "it requires a tricky magic to transform DEI into the latest bogeyman ..." We are not the monster. We are not your Frankenstein.[3]

And yet we persist, clear in an understanding that our efforts are not immune to assessment and evaluation in order to do better—be better—within the whole of higher education. In this aspirational striving, we know, as Anthony Abraham Jack reminds us, that "access alone is not enough for fostering inclusion and generating mobility" (Jack, 22). That work must be accompanied by policy change, inspired praxis, and practice guided by the tenets of equity-mindedness. This is the work we do. We recognize that "proximity is not the same as interaction."[4] We must get proximate to the work to change the narrative; we must have uncomfortable conversations to identify the concern.[5] This work we encourage. We know that our institutional efforts must be intentional to have impact. That this work must be shared within the entirety of its infrastructure to be sustainable. It must be interwoven into the very fabric of our institutional milieu—it's operational edicts—to be fully realized. This is a mutual partnership we humbly facilitate. We know behind every data point and metric is a human story. It is those human stories that make this edited collection distinct. The narrative form is privileged in the gathering of thoughts presented here—the telling of our own journeys and the ways we pay it forward. These vignettes also create the mapping system for how we connect to other people's stories—their lived experiences. This is the wonderful binding cord that allows us, in this work, to change hearts and minds in service to humanity.

David Fleming proposes that *narrative leadership* utilizes the telling of stories not only as a means for "communicating vision and meaning," but also as a tool for interpretive listening. These actions, when combined, can inspire others on their journey to leadership excellence (Fleming, D. 2001).[6] As Fleming concludes, "stories are told every day at work. By listening, leaders can learn when and how to use those stories to communicate vision, values, and meaning." As leaders within the ecosystem of higher education, chief diversity officers and equity practitioners have a particular vantage point from which to support and enhance the educational mission of their institutions through the stories they hear and tell. And although each institution has a distinct ecosystem and environment CDOs function nimbly to accommodate, the goal remains the same: to guide the holistic development of civic-minded leaders who will go on to transform the world.

This collection is divided into three clusters: Pathways and Purpose, Impact and Transformation, and Perfecting the Pivot. In "Pathways and Purpose," writers chart their personal journeys in higher education, the benefits of equitable educational practices, and how these more inclusive practices helped to shape their lives and career paths.

In **"Wouldn't Take Nothing for My Journey Now," Sylvia Carey-Butler** meditates on her 40-year-plus journey through higher education as an administrator and equity practitioner. She charts the changing role of CDOs, and their ability to help build leadership capacity in areas of the institution that struggle to implement and execute fully their diversity, equity, and inclusion aspirations. Carey-Butler nestles her reflections in the leadership principles that have guided her work: open communication about current work at the institution and anticipated trends in the field; dissemination of data that informs the work; situational awareness to help one navigate the various levels and cultural microclimates of the educational organization; and collaboration because this work cannot be done alone. As she surmises, higher education systems have impediments that can be mitigated, and chief diversity officers sit in a unique seat in the institution to assist in that work. "You cannot have academic excellence without inclusive excellence," she writes. "Organizational excellence is underscored by the way diversity shows up and is welcomed and can contribute to the goals and mission of an organization."

In **"Feeding My 'Superpower' or Embracing My Spirit," R. Adidi Etim-Hunting** discusses how her superpower helped direct her to the purpose of her work in higher education. More than just a colloquial saying, Etim-Hunting's superpower grounds her in her equity work in DEIB. Nurtured in her Nigerian household and cultivated in her work as hall director and student affairs professional, Etim-Hunting believes that one must have empathy, an ear to listen, and a heart for service to advance the work of diversity, equity, and inclusion. Each of her past engagements within the systems and microclimates of Higher Education provided insight into the continuous collaboration necessary for building micro-inclusive communities of care. "I planted seeds of inclusion and diversity when opportunities presented themselves," she writes. While receiving praise in some circles of influence, Etim-Hunting also reiterates the difficulty of doing this work, and the obstacles she faced as a leader that had her doubt her ability to continue in her role as an equity practitioner. Those doubts were internal and external facing and chart the complicated pathways for some chief diversity officers in this space. "… the belief that my superpower was something that could kill me, forced me to question 'Is my work as a DEIB professional something I wanted to die for?'" That very real question, in this current climate, makes these narratives all the more important for determining your why in this work.

In **"Negotiating Your Non-negotiables," Sonia J. Toson** provides salient advice for self-care as an equity practitioner, while simultaneously proposing boundaries for effective execution of role responsibilities. She believes that work begins *before* one steps into the role. "One thing I know," Toson writes, "is that the most successful negotiations are won before they start." Framing her discussion in three components—preparation, planning, and practice—Toson provides a blueprint for not only determining what you personally need to meet the demands of the role; she likewise proposes a prework template for gauging the campus environment one is stepping into, determining what resources (financial, human, physical space, and other) are available to you to fulfil the expectations of the role, and what are the interpersonal dynamics of the unit and/or team you inherit. This last consideration allows for a pulse check of the morale of your department, and what intimate work needs to be done before the larger visioning of the unit begins. Determining your non-negotiables before you assume the position makes you an effective leader in the role and allows you to elevate and execute the work of diversity, equity, and inclusion with excellence.

The why of this work is evident in **Tamara A. Johnson**'s essay **"The Journey, the Struggle, and the Progress."** As Johnson explains, being a chief diversity officer was not part of her career plans. But in reflecting on her journey through the Higher Education space, considering her roles as assistant hall director, a graduate counselor, a master's student in the Human Resource Education Program, and a doctoral student in counseling psychology, Johnson realizes her skills' development as consultant, executive coach, conflict and crisis management, and student success advocate prepared her for her equity practitioner role. And although she aspires to mitigate institutional hurdles to create "the conditions, policies, programs and systems that maximize opportunities for all community members to engage, excel, and thrive," Johnson realizes this was the most challenging part of being a CDO. "The expectation to be 'all things to all people' is ever-present and unrealistic." But the consistency of the work does make an impact. Johnson provides powerful examples of opportunities granted but accessibility being limited. Her equity-minded approach to eliminating those hindrances activated an institutional network that made her a catalyst for change, and subsequently changed the experiences of students, faculty, and staff. As Johnson concludes, "despite the tribulations I experienced directly or vicariously that lend themselves to being fearful—it is a privilege to move fearlessly in service of justice."

The theme of equitable justice and systems change frames the second cluster of essays, "Impact and Transformation." While the previous section spoke to the various career paths one could take to become a resolute equity practitioner grounded in one's values and purpose, "Impact and Transformation" anchors the conversation in detailed personal case studies that leverage the CDO role to actuate microclimates of change in their circles of influence at their institution. In **"Dialogue and 'DEI': Two Sides of the Same Coin of Justice," Ed Lee III** explores the art of conversation as a mechanism for cultivating "organizational language leaders" who "model listening, grace, and discernment" as they design infrastructures of belonging for broader collaborative engagement. A former debate coach, Lee sees his current work as an academic diversity officer, existing in a liminal space. Navigating between the dean's office and the student affairs space, Lee works to "simultaneously shepherd and protect [the] institution's commitment to open debate and expression while crafting an enduring sense of belonging for [his] colleagues and the students [he is] entrusted with supporting." In this role, Lee sees himself serving dual functions. As a "cultural translator," Lee functions as a neutral listener who helps conflicted parties find a path forward in environments where communication is stilted. As bridge builder, Lee's role is to disrupt siloes and to cultivate inclusive spaces that restore the dignity of impacted parties and minimizes the zero-sum power dynamics that erode communication pathways. As Lee concludes, "diversity officers are situated organizationally to challenge established language rules that undermine a sense of belonging," reiterating an organization's values and commitment to the principles of equity and inclusion.

Lee's efforts at creating common ground when divisiveness and emotions are elevated finds kinship in the inclusive practices **Yves-Rose Porcena** speaks of in her essay, **"The Extraordinary Power of Kindness: Reshaping Organizational Culture as a CDO."** As a human resource professional, chief diversity officer, and equity practitioner, Porcena considers kindness a powerful tool to transform climate and culture when it is infused in the fabric of an organization's ethical and moral registry. She asserts that culture sets the people climate for an organization. Thus, kindness becomes a necessary companion to compassion when "the well-being of all employees is a priority." Centering the institutional ethos here allows institutions to unlayer the cumulative effects of biases, disrupt repetitive cycles of disconnect between perceived equality and lived inequities, and unveil "patterns, trends, and correlations" embedded in the institutional data that emerge upon evaluation. "Ultimately," she writes, "the pursuit of equity in higher education is intimately tied to the collective goal of fostering a more inclusive, enlightened, and kinder future for all" when kindness serves as the catalyst for that change. Moreover, in uprooting institutional practices that are not in alignment with institutional values, kindness becomes a way to "call-in" collaborators, not "call-out" leaders, managers, and higher ed professionals in that space. "Culture, whether overt or subtle, manifests in behaviors and consequently shapes the collective identity of an institution," writes Porcena. The chief diversity officer role, in this instance, is to help shape culture, understanding that people are necessary collaborators in reorienting campus culture.

In **"A Framework for the Sustainability of WOC DEIA+ Practitioners: A Queen's Collective," Alexis J. Stokes, Sherri H. Benn, Luz Janet Mejias, Angela Spranger, Caryn Reed-Hendon, J. Camille Hall, Ria DasGupta, and R. Adidi Etim-Hunting** explore the experiences of women of color equity practitioners who occupy these roles, and "how a mentoring network we call the Queen's Collective (QC) aids in our ability to thrive… ." More than just a recounting of the challenges of the work, this mentoring network speaks to the needs of distinct leadership development nurtured in safe and brave spaces. "… we aim to disrupt the hegemonic scope of knowledge production to account for the compounded complexities of gender intersecting race in the work of justice," they write. "It is essential for our stories as women of color in the DEIA+ space to be told." As a way of introduction, Melissa Harris-Perry's "crooked room" analogy serves as a powerful reminder in this essay of the ways some women of color contort themselves to accommodate others' vision of themselves. This phenomenon, situated at the intersectional crossroads of race, gender, gender identity, and sexuality, allows Stokes, et al. to direct particular attention to the paucity of scholarship written about WOC serving in DEIA+ roles. For them, the limited representation of WOC in senior leadership positions, coupled with the isolation and the effects on one's well-being created an opportunity for the Queen's Collective to emerge. Women of Color from across the country participate in this collective, developing and executing high-impact practices that seek to mitigate these outcomes. Their essay, organized around five principles, provides a glimpse into the strategic positioning necessary to successfully execute the responsibilities of these roles. Their holistic approach allows them to acknowledge their "whole" selves while serving others. "Remember," they write, "it is just, authentic, and courageous to maintain a relentless focus on the people in the organization you serve while not forgetting yourself." And it is in the "not forgetting" that one is empowered to continue the struggle of justice while dismantling the hierarchical systems and barriers that enable inequities and exclusive practices to thrive.

In the final unit in this collection, "Perfecting the Pivot," authors detail how they continue their efforts for justice, equity, diversity, inclusion, and belonging, albeit from different administrative and consultative roles. In these positions, they leverage the lessons learned as chief diversity officers and equity practitioners, finding other ways to activate justice work. Some authors also speak to the need to reimagine justice, equity, diversity, and inclusion initiatives given our current social and legislative climate.

In **"From Boardrooms to Breakthroughs: Perfecting the Pivot,"** TaJuan R. Wilson charts his journey as a first-generation student from a small town in Bearden, Arkansas to an executive managing director role in a higher education recruiting firm. In candid reflection that charts the significance of programs like Educational Talent Search (ETS) and Upward Bound in creating pathways to higher education, Wilson speaks of the importance of opportunity in shaping his life and career trajectories. Creating that opportunity for others is a guiding principle for Wilson as he moves into equity leadership positions in GEAR-UP, TRIO, and eventually, Chief Diversity Officer. While finding satisfaction in advancing equity and inclusive practices at a number of different institutions, Wilson also points to the contradictory nature of this work, particularly when the stated values of an institution are misaligned with actual practices—and resources. In such instances, his service as a chief diversity officer found him questioning the organizational mindset of one institution, so much so that Wilson resigns from one position due to the "fundamental disconnect between the organization's commitment to diversity and the actions it took." The nuggets of wisdom offered when one has to pivot in order to stay true to the values of justice, equity, diversity, and inclusion, and one's own moral compass, shape the remainder of the discussion in this chapter. As Wilson concludes, authenticity in one's leadership is the one true constant that will guide you in the pivot. It is shaped by one's core beliefs, and anchored in a resilience to stay the course despite the challenges that may lie ahead.

Benjamin D. Reese Jr.'s extensive career echoes Wilson's refrain that the work of justice, equity, and inclusion must be principled and central to one's leadership value system. In **"History of a CDO's Journey over 50 years,"** Reese traces the development of his equity awareness to childhood interactions in New York where, although he couldn't name it, he realized something was different on his trips to City Island with his childhood friend, Lenny, when he was not served until all white customers had been served. "My growing understanding of race in America and racial exclusion," writes Reese, "formed a springboard for my deepening analysis of the complex politics of racism in America." That understanding shaped Reese's advocacy for access to higher education opportunities for all students and grounded his career efforts for over fifty years. As did his doctorate in clinical psychology. Reese's ability to connect with individuals from different philosophical and ideological perspectives, such as CP Ellis, the former local leader of the Durham Ku Klux Klan, deepened his understanding "of the complexity of the human condition. People motivated by what I consider racist ideology, were often individuals committed to loving and meaningful family relationships." Such complexities would undergird the work Reese committed himself to in his roles as chief diversity officer, ombudsperson, and as director of The Institute for the Study of Culture and Ethnicity, a center he would go on to create in the division of The Fifth Avenue Center for Counseling and Psychotherapy in New York. "Managing differences ... requires skill in resolving systemic issues, but also requires a deep understanding and appreciation for the cultural context of individuals ... be they students, faculty, or senior level administrative managers of global programs." Reese's pivot allowed him to move through the academy in a number of roles, and within private industry focused on eliminating racial inequities wherever he found them. Setting expectations through service and leadership in NADOHE, The Journal of Diversity in Higher Education, and initiating the first NADOHE International Program broadens the lens of diversity, equity, and inclusion beyond institutional spaces and points up the global import of these efforts.

In **"Navigating Nepantla," Carolyn J. Morales** takes us on a moving journey through the DEI landscape centering her discussion in the Aztec language of Nahuatl. "There is an Indigenous term—nepantla," she writes. "It aptly fits the current state of DEI. It refers to being in the middle and existing in a state of in-between-ness," Morales explains. In this liminal space, "what-was" and "what-will-be" magnify the tensions of a future unknown. Morales leverages Gloria Anzuldua's theoretical lens to direct attention to the legislative, disciplinary, and social repositioning inherent in the DEI landscape to view the current context not "from a deficit lens," but as a constant reminder of "the cyclical and ever-changing nature of life." Instead, Morales poses, how can we view this pivotal moment as "a zone of possibility." Those possibilities require us to lean into this moment because "change inspires and requires innovation." Utilizing lessons gleamed from her many years in higher education, as both student and equity practitioner, Morales traces historical patterns in her own life as a Latine of Quechua heritage. Moving deftly between cultural tradition and life experiences, the poignant ebb and flow of life and death, grief and renewal, Morales points up the wisdom in it all as she grounds the why of equity work in the transformational potential of organizational and system change. She uses familial proverbs to reiterate the values of gratitude and service, family, and webs of care, and how these "offerings take the shape of programs, policies, and practice we craft, execute and assess that seek to redress persistent and long-standing social and structural inequities."

Anneliese Singh bookends this wonderful collection with her coda, **"We Can Build the World We Want to See: Reflections on the Roots, Branches, and Future of DEI Work."** More than just a recounting of the long legacy of justice work in the world, and its tributaries evident in the field of education, Singh answers the question, "how did we get here," and offers sage wisdom on a path forward not only for chief diversity officers and equity practitioners committed to this work, but for reimagining the field of DEI itself. Her ten principles guide this reorientation, rooted in the familial, cultural tenets of her leadership journey and personal story. Traversing such topics as the language we use to honor diversity, equity, and inclusion work to "being maladjusted" to advance the work, Singh encourages us to "reflect on the origin story and resulting branches of DEI work so that we can build a compass for what the future can hold for our field." In that work, we have the right to evolve as a field. "This is the power of cultural humility," Singh writes. "We should not abandon our creativity and vision in the process."

Singh's coda serves as a fitting refrain for the remnants of hope embedded in this assemblage of powerful and reflective voices. We find inspiration in our collective knowledge that what we do matters. We know that our society will continue to become more diverse. That fact will not change. And we have a choice, as a nation, and as a society, in how we respond to this beautiful inevitability in principle and in practice in higher education. And we must meet that reality with care and wisdom for the sake of our present and our limitless future. "We must emerge from this crisis in our republic with a new birth of freedom, rooted in the knowledge that we are so much more when the 'We' in 'We the People' is not some of us, but all of us," writes Heather McGhee. "We are greater than, and greater for, the sum of us." (289). Indeed, we are.

Notes

1 For further discussion of how one might define diversity, please see the resource guide at the conclusion of this collection.
2 Heather McGhee. *The Sum of Us: What Racism Costs Everyone and How We Can Prosper Together*. London: One World, 2022. P. 289
3 Eddie S. Glaude Jr. "DEI Is Not the Monster Here." *Time Magazine*. December 13, 2023. time.com. Accessed 1/26/24. 12:49pm.
4 Earl Lewis and Nancy Cantor, Eds. *Our Compelling Interests: The Value of Diversity for Democracy and a Prosperous Society*. New Jersey: Princeton University Press, 2016. P. 14.
5 Bryan Stevenson, in his work with his organization, The Equal Justice Initiative, has asserted that in order to change the world, we must get proximate to the work, have uncomfortable conversations, and change the narratives that sustain inequality and injustice. https://qcitymetro.com/2020/01/29/bryan-stevenson-4-steps-to-change-the-world/. Accessed 2/11/2024.
6 David Fleming. "Narrative Leadership: Using the Power of Stories". *Strategy & Leadership*. Vol. 29 no.4 (July/Aug 2001): 36.

ONLINE SUPPLEMENTAL RESOURCES

Some of the resources in this book can be accessed online by visiting this book's product page on our website: www.routledge.com/9781032717678 (then follow the links indicating support material, which you can then download directly).

- Leading with Conviction: Conversations with Paulette Granberry Russell and William B. Harvey
- Additional Resources

ACKNOWLEDGMENTS

No project of this scale and quality happens alone. I am indebted to a circle of colleagues, scholars, thought leaders, and educational practitioners who have made it their life's mission to extol the virtues of the common good. With this calling comes the responsibility of serving humanity with compassion, kindness, peace, and dare I say a sacrificial love. To my Emory community who embodies this work each day—thank you. You have created a space for me to flourish. To you I am forever grateful.

To the amazing contributors of this wonderful collection—I am because we are. This book is as much yours as it is mine. May this offering honor the spirit in which you gathered at this table of humanity—hopeful of the promise that is and is yet to be. Assured of a future that can hold all the people and all their dreams.

To my colleagues in the field: Paulette Granberry Russell and William B. Harvey—thank you for lending your voice to this project. It's all the better for it. To my CDO community who strengthens me every time we meet—I see you. May this small gift honor your perseverance and dedication to the greater good. To William T. Lewis, Sr., who helped me nurture the seed of this project over three years ago—I appreciate you. You model what service to humanity is with this work.

To my wonderful editor at Routledge Press, Heather Jarrow, who saw the promise in this project and allowed me to shape it in the voice of its writers—thank you for your guidance and sage wisdom from beginning to end. To Sofia Cohen, thank you for providing the technical support to get an idea manuscript ready. And to Kyanna Nusom, I so appreciate you. You have answered each question, guided every detail of our manuscript preparation during pre-production with grace and care. We recognize those efforts here.

To my women's writing collective—you know who you are—thank you for over a decade of scholarly engagement and thoughtful conversation. Your support is priceless. Your love is food for the soul.

To the incomparable Alicia Lane, who entered this project right when I needed her. Thank you for accepting my invitation to prepare this manuscript for submission. You have been a joy to work with. I look forward to seeing your continued impact in the world.

To my Delaware people—thank you for your love and support. To my mama, my son, Kelsey, my world-traveling sister, LaTonya, my brother-in-love Clem, and my nieces Lelycia, Tatyana, and Kiara—I love each of you very much. You ground my work as a scholar in the love of family. May the world continue to honor who you are as amazing humans destined for greatness. May it continue to make room for you to be.

Atlanta, Georgia

CONTRIBUTORS

Sherri H. Benn, PhD, currently serves as Tarleton State University's Vice President for the Lozano-Long Division of Global, Community, and First-Gen Initiatives, which supports students from 50 countries, 48 states, and 234 Texas counties. Benn serves as an executive member of APLU's Commission on International Initiatives.

Erica Bruchko, PhD, is the Librarian for African American Studies and United States History at Emory University. She holds a BA in History and a BA in Anthropology from the University of South Carolina, and an MA and PhD in History from Emory University. Erica is an active member of the Association of Research Libraries' African American Librarians' Interest Group and the Reference and User Association's History Section. She currently serves as Subject Chair of the African American Subject Funnel Project, a group that works with the Library of Congress to create and update subject headings related to African American history and culture.

Sylvia Carey-Butler, PhD, has over four decades of experience advancing diversity, equity, and inclusion inside and outside of the academy. She has worked at small private, large public, Catholic, HBCUs, and two-year institutions as well as the largest minority serving non-profit, the United Negro College Fund.

Ria DasGupta, EdD, is an equity practitioner in higher education and the arts. She is the director of EDIB Initiatives at The Juilliard School.

R. Adidi Etim-Hunting, MEd, is a scholar, executive coach, and leader, devoting over a decade to educating equity principles. Invited speaker at national and international conferences, Adidi also teaches Ethics in STEM, Mindfulness in Diversity, and Diversity Leadership. Adidi is currently serving as the Director of the DEIB Office for the Division of Development and Alumni Relations while pursuing a doctoral degree in Workforce Education and Development, emphasizing in diversity, inclusion, access, and equity at Penn State University.

Lisa FennFenn, MA, is the inaugural Senior Director of Belonging, Diversity, Equity, and Inclusion at Emory University Libraries and Museum. Before joining Emory University Libraries & Museum, Lisa served in several roles at Tufts University, including Director for Inclusive Strategic Initiatives and Program Director, Antiracism. Lisa held consulting positions over the span of 15+ years at Korn Ferry International, Global Novations, LLC, and J. Howard & Associates. Her perspective is informed by extensive experience consulting with a host of Fortune 500 companies on diversity, equity, and inclusion strategy. Lisa's educational credentials include a master's degree from Columbia University Teacher's College in New York City, and a bachelor's degree in Business Administration from Adelphi University on Long Island, New York where she is a native.

J. Camille Hall, PhD, LCSW, is the former Vice-Chancellor of Diversity and Inclusion and a licensed clinical social worker with 30+ years of experience. Her research focuses on risk and resilience in the Black community.

William B. Harvey, EdD, has a distinguished career in higher education, serving as a full professor at the University of Virginia, and North Carolina A&T University, among others. A renowned equity practitioner in the field of equity, diversity, and inclusion (EDI), Dr. Harvey helped to co-create the National Association of Diversity Officers in Higher Education (NADOHE) and served as its founding president. He was recently appointed rector of Danubius University in Galati, Romania in January 2021, becoming the first African American to head a European university.

Carol E. Henderson, PhD, is Vice Provost for Diversity and Inclusion, Chief Diversity Officer, and Adviser to the President at Emory University. She is Professor Emerita of English and Africana Studies at the University of Delaware. She is the author/editor of five books, the special issue editor of four journal collections and has published numerous essays in critical volumes and journals.

Tamara A. Johnson, PhD, is a proven leader in higher education, with special expertise in DEI, faculty development, and student affairs. She has led transformational change at several institutions in her more than 20 years of experience.

Ed Lee III, EdD, is the Senior Director of Inclusivity for Emory College of Arts & Sciences. With an emphasis on organizational communication, culture formation, and collaboration, Ed works with unit leaders to develop and facilitate DEI-related programs. Ed provides senior-level leadership for Emory's Barkley Forum for Debate, Deliberation, and Dialogue.

Luz Janet Mejias, MBA, began a sabbatical at the end 2023 to pursue consulting, writing, travel, and photography after 15 years in Higher Education Student Life and Equity and Inclusion. The most gratifying aspects of this work were the coaching of underrepresented students, pursuing creative ways to strengthen relationships and community, and creating educational content that impacted the status quo. She holds a BS in Organizational Management and a Master's in Business Administration.

Carolyn J. Morales, PhD, serves as the associate dean for belonging and community engagement and assistant professor of medical education in a school of medicine. Dr. Morales has more than 20 years of leadership experience operationalizing diversity visions into strategic plans within higher education.

Yves-Rose Porcena, DBA, is an organizational equity expert at Agnes Scott College leveraging knowledge and experience of global diversity to create workplace cultures that celebrate the unique strengths of every individual. She serves her communities as a board member on both local and international non-profit organizations.

Caryn Reed-Hendon, PhD, is the founding Director of Diversity, Equity, and Inclusion for Lawrence Technological University. Dr. Reed-Hendon's career in higher education administration spans more than 20 years, with a focus on equity, belonging, and mentorship in student affairs.

Benjamin D. Reese, Jr., PsyD, is the former Chief Diversity Officer for Duke University and the Duke University Health System; a clinical psychologist; and a global diversity, equity, and inclusion educator and consultant.

Paulette Granberry Russell, JD, is the current president of the National Association of Diversity Officers in Higher Education. She spent over two decades as a senior diversity officer and equity practitioner at Michigan State University, prior to this role. Granberry Russell's expertise in gender equity in STEM, affirmative action, and inclusive leadership. Her research and practice centers on dismantling structural barriers that prevent US higher education from reaching its identified mission, values, and goals.

Anneliese Singh, PhD, LPC (she/they), serves as Chief Diversity Officer and Professor at Tulane University. Dr. Singh's research explores racial healing, trans and nonbinary liberation, and South Asian American counseling and psychology.

Angela Spranger, MBA, MEd, is a former management faculty member who has served as the inaugural Diversity Officer at two institutions, as well as providing EDI consulting for organizations of varied sizes across the country. She is an engaging presenter, student mentor, executive coach, and the author of *Why People Stay: Helping Your Employees Feel Seen, Safe, and Valued* (Taylor & Francis/Routledge).

Alexis J. Stokes, EdD, is a DEI consultant and strategist with over 14 years of experience in establishing programs, policies, and practices that address systemic inequities and move organizations from words to sustainable action.

Sonia J. Toson, JD, MBA, CDP, serves as the Vice President of Organizational Effectiveness, Leadership Development, and Inclusive Excellence and Associate Professor of Law at Kennesaw State University. Dr. Toson has been a licensed attorney in the state of Georgia since 2001. Prior to academia, she spent eight years practicing law.

TaJuan R. Wilson, EdD, M.S., MPA, CDE, is a 15-year higher education professional and former CDO who now works as a Managing Director at one of the largest executive recruiting firms in the world. He is a proud first-generation college graduate and a proud native of Arkansas.

PART 1

Pathways and Purpose

1

WOULDN'T TAKE NOTHING FOR MY JOURNEY NOW

Sylvia Carey-Butler

Chapter Contents

Difficult Leaders

I begin with navigating difficult leaders. One year into a position that would launch my career in diversity, equity and inclusion, a new leader arrived on campus. I was disappointed the president who hired me had retired but cautiously optimistic that perhaps a leadership change would bode well for my role and unit. Nothing could have been further from the truth. I knew I was in trouble when I was told point blank, "I've read a book about offices like yours."

The second indication my department would be in trouble was when the leadership team was reorganized, and a thought-partners team was created. There were very few diverse voices at the table, and it was a relatively large university-wide leadership team. Reporting directly to the Provost,

DOI: 10.4324/9781032724881-2

I informed him I was disappointed I had not been invited to join the thought-partners team and that I felt strongly I should have been on it. I had learned the importance of self-advocacy especially when it came to inclusion. I wanted to be in an environment committed to ensuring everyone mattered. I was finally asked to join the thought-partner's team. The greatest takeaway from that experience was recognizing how important it was to speak up and stay grounded in my personal and professional values, especially those related to this work.

I have never been under the illusion that institutional leaders fully understand the lived experiences of all campus stakeholders, especially historically marginalized faculty, staff and students. Structural barriers to access, opportunity and full participation in higher education are far from being dismantled.

Structural barriers to access, opportunity and full participation in higher education are far from being dismantled.

However, I have always expected that leaders would be open to learning about the varied experiences of all campus stakeholders and have a willingness to face and address inequities. I wasn't being naive; I was being hopeful. However, one need only look at institutional leaders' career trajectories to garner insight into my flawed perspective. In the article "The Future of Leadership in Higher Education," Deloitte Insights (Clark 2017) stated that 56% of university leaders are traditionalists from academic ranks to the presidency. As such, their exposure to and understanding of DEI is often limited. CDOs must work to have an open, frank, and honest relationship with leadership who oftentimes have a steep learning curve around DEI. One way for CDOs to accomplish this is to ensure that DEI work is aligned with an institution's mission and that there's ongoing engagement with both campus leaders and key campus stakeholders.

The CDO must be cognizant of their leadership style when working with individuals who do not have the benefit of deep knowledge or commitment to DEI. A situational leadership approach may be appropriate. According to

Hersey and Blanchard (1993), a leadership approach is most effective when the leadership style can be adapted to diverse circumstances. The framework for Situational Leadership Theory allows one to identify the most appropriate method for problem-solving and decision-making. A CDO may draw upon one of the four areas, which include Telling (Directing), Selling (Coaching), Participating (Supporting), or Delegating. As the CDO, it is essential to utilize diverse strategies to accomplish the task at hand. As I reflect upon my career, I acknowledge the use of situational leadership to work within systems with diverse leadership personalities and needs.

One of the most important aspects of the CDO role is to assure that leadership is informed about current and anticipated challenges around DEI. Never let a leader be blindsided by events or information you know. Transparency is expected and must be honored. At the end of the day, if a CDO is not afforded access to and does not enjoy open communication with leadership, you will never be able to be successful in your role. A CDO must also be prepared to lead during difficult times. Institutions will often move from complacency to action in a crisis. Therefore, they need to remain ready to lead.

Analyze and know your worth and your perceived value within your organization. If ever in doubt, it may be time to find an institution with a leader that will be a partner in advancing DEI to ensure everyone matters at every level of the organization, all of the time. In the words of Kenny Rogers' "The Gambler," *you've got to know when to hold 'em, know when to fold 'em. Know when to walk away.*

Necessary Tools for Success

There is no doubt in my mind to be effective in advancing DEI, one must continue to educate oneself, be in community with like-minded colleagues, and use data to help tell the story of DEI on campus or within an organization.

The role of the CDO can be both daunting and overwhelming. To mitigate against the everyday internal and external assaults on your position, CDOs must be equipped with unassailable knowledge about DEI. Understanding the higher education and national landscape that impacts both the role and the work is important. This requires being in community with colleagues engaged in the work, staying current on the latest research, and attending relevant conferences, institutes, webinars, and taking advantage of professional development opportunities. Moreover, as a CDO, it is imperative to keep stakeholders engaged in the work. To this end, the collection and dissemination of data is a critical component of the work, and as such, annual reports and periodic campus and community updates are imperative to the work and go a long way in fostering an inclusive culture.

To create a culture of inclusion, higher education leaders must consider how their campus environments can adapt to meet the needs of today's highly diverse students rather than beginning with the assumption that diverse students must assimilate into existing environments with relatively narrow measures of quality. At the core of the principles of Inclusive Excellence is the tenet that inclusion, equity, and diversity should be put at the center of the University's mission, its use of resources, its development of offices, programs, departments, initiatives, and outreach, its hiring, and its academic programming. Building a supportive and inclusive environment is inextricably linked to institutional success. However, this is often not the case or is not understood. Somehow a heightened focus on DEI has translated into the weakening of institutions academic mission. Nothing can be further from the truth. I submit, you cannot have academic excellence without inclusive excellence.

... you cannot have academic excellence without inclusive excellence.

This also translates into the private sector as well. Organizational excellence is underscored by the way diversity shows up and is welcomed and can contribute to the goals and mission of an organization. Diversity is a driver of excellence in innovation, it enhances the learning environment and provides students the opportunity to interact with individuals from various backgrounds and experiences, thereby enriching their education.

Another important tool for CDOs is to understand organizational change. While organizational change theory may feel outside the scope of DEI work, it is an integral part of the work of DEI. DEI beckons the community to adapt, to change, to shift. It is important for CDOs not only to create environments that are transformational but to guide institutional leaders through organizational change with a DEI lens. As noted earlier, whenever there's either institutional or departmental leadership change, CDOs cannot assume that new leaders bring a comprehensive understanding of how DEI can help them achieve organizational success. When change occurs, the unknown can bring about uncertainty. I've learned to minimize self-talk, to ask questions to understand the impact change may have on both my role and the work. I try to look at the larger picture, but it isn't easy, especially if the changes were not expected. It can have a negative impact on how you see yourself or your approach to the work. I've been there. Perhaps the most important thing you can do is to ask yourself, what could you have done differently, what will you do now and what lessons have you learned? However, make room for the idea that a change may have had little to do with you and give yourself some grace.

Changing the Role of a CDO

As Raul Leon (2014) noted, The Chief Diversity Officer (CDO) position emerged as an executive-level role providing strategic guidance for diversity planning and implementation efforts for institutions and institutional leaders. We know today the role has evolved into far more. CDOs not only serve as institutional leaders' thought-partners but are often called up to address faculty and staff challenges, and collaborate to create a welcoming environment through programs and initiatives that historically may not have fallen under their purview. One can't help but understand how our institutions have become, quite frankly, a microcosm of broader society. So, whatever national or global issue that develops, rest assured, it will inevitably affect your work. The campus community will look to you for guidance and reassurance during times of crisis. Everyone will have a perspective on how you do your work and no matter what you do, someone's going to be upset or disappointed by the decisions you make.

Prior to my work in DEI, I held positions in access programs and Academic Affairs at several institutions. I began my work as a DEI professional in earnest in 2013. Although the scope of some of the positions I've held centered on equity or belonging, I was often called upon to participate in conversations, strategy sessions to address student concerns, or staff challenges. In fact, I was once asked by a human relations office to review applications to help identify applicants of color through affiliations with historically Black fraternities and sororities. My DEI work has led me to positions across institutional types (medium-sized public in the Midwest, large public in the South), to a highly selective institution in the East. I can honestly say I arrived at some of my positions with serious questions about institutional capacity and readiness to lean into the work of DEI. I have finally landed at an institution whose commitment and will is not performative. The year 2020 brought the nation to our knees with the murder of George Floyd and on the heels of Breonna

Taylor's murder and countless other Blacks who lost their lives to violence and bad policing. There was a shift in the national climate—a clarion call to face and fix the deeply embedded racism that permeates our nation and our institutions. Voices on the margin were amplified; institutional leaders suddenly found themselves leaning on the expertise and experiences of DEI leaders who had often been relegated to the margins of institutional decision-making. This resulted in the proliferation of CDO roles within institutions and organizations. It was a start, but we quickly understood that institutions could not have one point of failure, the CDO role. In essence, it would require leaders to fully embrace the guidance and expertise of the CDO to help make meaning of the times and develop solution-based strategies that could move the institutions to greater equity often spoken about in mission statements.

Address Institutional DEI Gaps

The role of today's CDO in higher education has shifted from a localized position creating welcoming and affirmative environments for diverse students, faculty, and staff to that of a thought partner to institutional leaders. Someone whose content expertise, who possessed credibility in diverse campus communities could lead the development and implementation of strategies to increase equity and inclusion and hold institutions accountable. The CDO role must ensure that DEI is and remains an institutional priority among a host of other formal and informal roles. To this end, the CDO, in many ways, has become a core and strong communicator of strategies to advance DEI, a key collaborator both internally and externally, and a strong strategist with the ability to address campus and national issues, helping academic leaders increase both DEI representation and retention, often having oversight of the institutions' Affirmative Action Plan (AAP) an essential tool in the recruitment and retention of faculty and staff. The AAP is prepared each year in compliance with the Office of Federal Contract Compliance Programs (OFCCP to ensure stakeholders are aware of how the AAP can assist in achieving departmental hiring goals). It reaffirms a commitment to equal opportunity employment for all employees and applicants for employment. It is an important tool for DEI leaders who are often charged with diversifying faculty and staff ranks.

Looking down the road and around the corner, never resting on laurels, as new initiatives, collaborations, and partnerships are developed and implemented, some CDOs must lean on experiences and connections to fundraise to build on their work. While some may bristle at the idea of fundraising to expand initiatives and establish partnerships that enhance the lived experiences of your institution's faculty, staff, and students, there is an immense reward in helping institutions build DEI capacity. As such, I posit that developing a close relationship with your institution's Advancement Office is critical to your success as a CDO. A promising practice and one that works for me in my current context is embedding a DEI advancement officer with a dotted line to the CDO. Doing so can prove to be transformative in external partnerships, especially with historically under-represented institutions.

Community Engagement

CDOs are often called upon to establish public and private partnerships. These partnerships can range from relationships with local authorities to create opportunities to shift perceptions of policing to establishing programs to support diverse populations. The CDO can bring an informed and unbiased approach to community building. In late 2017, and on the heels of conflict between police and the community, I was engaged to help build cultural competency for a small city police force. While it has been years since that experience, the immediate result of that collaboration with the local Chief of Police led to greater awareness and understanding of differences. In fact, it also led to a significant partnership with a very conservative political figure in that city that launched an initiative called "Unity in the Community," a family-friendly initiative highlighting the increasing diversity within the community. This initiative brought together educational institutions (K-12, higher education), local small businesses, and government officials highlighting the rich cultural diversity in the city. While a great deal of planning went into one day that celebrated all the ways in which the city was diverse, it helped to build connections across difference and establish important collaborations. One example is the relationship I was able to establish with the District Attorney who assisted me as I helped students of color, particularly African American males navigate the justice system who sometimes ran afoul of the law for minor infractions. It's my understanding it ended with the onset of COVID-19. This is one example of how partnership-building can lead to enhanced community engagement.

Changing Landscape

Shifting demographics, legal precedent, and state and local priorities are among the many variables that can impact the role of the CDO on campuses and within organizations across the country.

Shifting demographics, legal precedent, and state and local priorities are among the many variables that can impact the role of the CDO on campuses and within organizations across the country.

From the brutal killings of black and brown bodies, the more recent repeal of affirmative action, the legislative restrictions to DEI imposed by many state government officials, the DEI pendulum continues to swing. CDOs must remain steadfast in their commitment to the work. We must realize that as time and circumstances change, the work of DEI is constant and even more important. The power of inclusion stands the test of time. In the near future, the role of the CDO will only become more challenging, more trying and called into question. In fact, one only has to read online journals to see how often there are CDOs transitioning into and out of roles, or institutions reorganizing or eliminating elements of the role. DEI is not facing headwinds. It's in the middle of a hurricane!

Importance of Self-Care

Serve any time in a CDO role, and you will soon discover the emotional and physical toll it can have on an individual. Early in my career, an aspiring president who went on to serve as a president for almost two decades once said to me that "the higher you go in institutional leadership, the lonelier it becomes." No truer words have been spoken about leadership and how applicable they are to the role of the CDO. There is so much of what we do that must be confidential, and you often find yourself navigating very sensitive situations with colleagues around the leadership table. You will often question your judgment or have your judgment questioned. I say this because if you desire to become a CDO in higher education or the private sector, you better develop thick skin and a set of dorsal fins. It requires the activation of all of your senses and especially the use of emotional intelligence and strong discernment.

Daniel Goleman (1995) developed the Emotional Intelligence theory to help us examine the role of our emotional response in everyday situations. Goleman advocated that emotional intelligence is as important as IQ. CDOs often exercise the EQ in navigating difficult personalities and other internal and external challenges that impact the campus climate. One may ask, how does Emotional Intelligence support self-care? The theory articulates that your ability to recognize, understand, and manage your emotions will support effective relationship building, a critical factor in working with others. It is even more important in DEI leadership roles where your decision-making and/or judgement may be called into question. As one contemplates self-care, and the importance of mindfulness, finding peace with who you are and your work is important. Self-care requires you to be in tune with your physical, mental, social and emotional health.

Being a CDO has had an adverse impact on some CDOs. Anecdotally, several Black CDOs have left higher education and shared why they prefer the private sector. They suggest that they experience less pushback from organizational stakeholders in advancing DEI. Others have shared with me the challenge of balancing their mental health with the work, while some Black women discussed how stress has resulted in the loss of hair, and increased anxiety. In speaking to Black women CDOs in higher education and in the private sector, several have questioned whether the toll on one's mental and physical well-being is worth it. I submit, your physical health and well-being must be a priority. It's important to know your own limitations and to know when to access support. Regular exercise, staying on top of your health in the midst of your work is a gift you must give yourself. The CDO role requires a great deal of selflessness and it's easy to get caught up in the latest crisis, neglecting your own well-being. However, I have discovered that there is a deeper well to draw from when focused on the work of the CDO. I think about my work as a calling, my contribution to higher education. This is how I rationalize the amount of mental and emotional energy I spend in my role.

A Call of Service: A Witness to Idealism by Robert Coles (1993) provides a lens for individuals to examine how service work may fit into your life and the satisfaction this work can bring. This material resonates with me as I have often felt working in the field of education was my calling. I see a correlation between social and emotional health and work satisfaction. Coleman's work provides a window to the power of idealism to transform lives. It is often said that when you love what you do, you never work a day in your life. DEI brings tremendous satisfaction in knowing the impact you have on the lives of others. But what is sacrificed to do this work and do it well? As a DEI leader, how you think about and answer the aforementioned question will be important to how you approach and safeguard your well-being. I often say this work isn't for the faint of heart. Making your mental and physical health a priority is also about excellence. I once fell and seriously hurt myself on the job that resulted in major surgery. I was to be out of work for six weeks for recuperation. Two weeks later I was back in the office in pain but feeling that I had to be there, my team needed me. That experience taught me that what I modeled for my team wasn't commitment to the work but rather my expectation that they would do the same thing. That was not my intention. As a result, my healing was delayed and almost a decade later, I suffer pain from that surgery because I didn't take time for the physical therapy that was required.

There are things CDOs can do to ensure their well-being, which I believe is core to one's wellness in the role. The lack of attention to oneself and your personal needs will take a toll in the long-run physically or emotionally. One former CDO who had a stellar career at a large public institution with an excellent relationship with her university's president, walked away and never looked back. She said the work and expectations of the role was far too taxing. She felt she had already sacrificed so much with minimal impact. I offer the following insights having made them part of my practice as a CDO. These practices have served me well and helped me to stay focused on the work of DEI:

- *Understand your capacity and set professional boundaries.* It's often said you have to teach people how to treat you. You can't be on call 24/7 365 days a year. So, what does this require? Ensuring you hire well and implement standard operation procedures (SOPs) so everyone is clear about what to do in your absence or in your presence, so they do not always have to rely on your input and guidance. Of course, as appropriate. This will give greater agency to your team and other key campus stakeholders.
- *Write!* Writing to contribute your content expertise to DEI is important. Doing so will lend credibility to your role within the campus or organizational community. I'm not just talking about scholarship, I'm also talking about "journaling." There is something cathartic about gathering your thoughts and committing them to paper. It can serve as a reflective exercise as a leader that will have some utility as you navigate challenges on campus. I keep a gray journal with me most of the time and often when I'm frustrated, unsure about a decision or just in need of inspiration I will read and reread the things that I've written or nuggets that I've picked up along the way from others, especially leaders that I have

admired. It will also be useful for you to be able to reflect on your journey as you develop your team.

- *Make and maintain connections.* As a CDO you may often feel isolated in your work. Participating in communities of practices can offer emotional support. During my time at a large public university in the south, CDOs across a variety of institutional types came together informally on a monthly basis. We shared concerns, offered each other guidance or just a listening ear. This community of practice was so enriching for participants, it led to a very tight-knit community who came together one summer in a full-day workshop. The sustenance these gathering provided refueled each of us.

- *Mentorship still matters.* At every stage of my career, mentors have played a critical role in both my success and sanity. If you currently do not have a mentor/go to person, I encourage you to seek someone out. Having a voice outside of your current context to offer you advice and guidance will serve you well. Mentors have kept me from making profound mistakes as a DEI leader. I've had so many wonderful mentors along the way it's hard to single out just one. However, I will. During my tenure as Dean of Honors at Dillard University, then Provost Dr. Bettye Parker Smith was intentional about providing leadership guidance in a way that really resonated with me. She concerned herself with my development both as an administrator and an African American woman. Asked me hard questions about my career personal goals. Her straightforward guidance set me on a professional and economic path that has been transformative. Another example is the late Arthur J. Rothkopf, former president of Lafayette College in Easton, Pennsylvania. Just a year into my role as Assistant Dean of the College, he called me into his office to discuss my future. He encouraged me to get my PhD and offered me on campus housing as a way to save money, so I'd be better positioned to pursue a terminal degree. I followed his advice and never looked back. I never got the chance to thank him, but I think about him often and am eternally grateful for both his guidance and investment in my future. Mentors matter!

- *Take adequate time off.* Over the course of my career and especially during my former and current CDO roles, I've taken minimal time off. I either felt it wasn't prudent to be out of the office, or the projects I was working on needed to be finished within a certain time frame. What I've learned over time is that had I managed and planned better I could have taken the time off that I had earned. I would have also benefited from time away from the work, and everyone would have been better served had I done so.

Conclusion

The role of the CDO is essential to driving institutional commitment to DEI. I want to underscore that the work is not for everyone. As such, I strongly encourage leaders to be very intentional about developing such roles. If there is not a strong institutional and organizational understanding of and commitment to DEI and the role of a CDO, more harm than good can be done. While this may not be a popular thing to say, it's important to understand that just because someone has extensively researched and written about DEI, doesn't necessarily make them an effective CDO. Scholarship alone does not often translate into being a strong and transformative CDO. Leadership experience coupled with content expertise can be the margin of difference in DEI operational excellence.

No doubt, the role of the CDO is often challenging and currently facing unprecedented times. I firmly believe CDOs can stand in the gap in helping institutions fulfill their aspirations of equity and belonging. I am battle-worn but wiser. *I wouldn't take nothing for my journey now.*

Key Insights from *Wouldn't Take Nothing for My Journey Now*

- Transparency is a key component of creating a climate and culture of accountability and inclusive responsibility.
- Leveraging various leadership styles, such as situational leadership, can enhance the effectiveness of the CDO role.
- Data is a critical component of the work of equity and inclusion.
- Annual reports, community updates, and shared objectives foster an environment of engagement and knowledge transferal that supports the educational mission of an institution.

Things to Consider:

1 What are the "headwinds" that chief diversity officers and diversity practitioners face in this current moment?
2 What are structural barriers to access in higher education that administrators contend with? How do CDOs serve as thought-partners in the process to mitigate these concerns?
3 What is the changing role of CDOs in higher education?
4 How does leadership style contribute to the success or failure of CDO roles?
5 What are the four frameworks that support the effectiveness of situational leadership?
6 How does Carey-Butler connect organizational change theory to the work of CDOs?

7 What is the tension Carey-Butler points to regarding service and well-being in the career journey of CDOs?

References

Clark, Cole. 2017. Pathways to the university presidency: The future of higher education leadership. Authored by Jeff Selingo, Sonny Chheng, and Cole Clark, in *Collaboration between Georgia Tech's Center for 21st Century Universities and Deloitte's Center for Higher Education Excellence*. Deloitte University Press.

Coles, Robert. 1993. *The call of service: A witness to idealism*. Boston: Houghton Mifflin Co.

Goleman, Daniel. 1995. *Emotional intelligence*. New York, NY, England: Bantam Books, Inc.

Hersey, Paul, and Kenneth Blanchard. 1993. *Management of organizational behavior: Utilizing human resources*. 6th ed. Englewood Cliffs, NJ: Prentice Hall.

Leon, Raul A. 2014. The chief diversity officer: An examination of CDO models and strategies. *Journal of Diversity in Higher Education* 7 (2): 77–91.

Rogers, Kenny. The Gambler. Recorded 1978. Track 1 on *The Gambler*. United Artists Group, 1978, compact disc.

2

FEEDING MY "SUPERPOWER" OR EMBRACING MY SPIRIT

R. Adidi Etim-Hunting

Chapter Contents

I was once told that I possess a superpower, similar to the cultural superpower of heroes in comic books. I harnessed the power to get people to elicit their stories while simultaneously shifting their preconceived perception. I could be going about my business when I ask what seems to be a simple question, and suddenly find myself listening to a sensitive, private, and professional incident. With a calm and tender voice, free of judgement or guilt, I suggest an alternative perspective to their established conclusions, frequently amplifying the voices of those who have been marginalized or overlooked during the discussion. This "power" has been the narrative in my life and has happened for as long as I can remember. It was as if I had a natural gravitation towards all things diversity, equity, inclusion and belonging (DEIB), and I could never let it go nor 'bite my tongue' in the mist of advocacy.

Before I discovered my superpower and its potential towards a career, I honed my advocacy skills through my family. Growing up in a

DOI: 10.4324/9781032724881-3

multicultural household, my brothers and I found comfort in cooking and enjoying Nigerian cuisine more than American food. Our parents created a community of diverse "aunties" and "uncles" from various cultures worldwide. We embraced their food, learned about their beliefs and customs, and absorbed wisdom from their life experiences. Their stories of resilience in the face of cultural, religious, and sometimes ethnic discrimination became ingrained in my DNA. The inclusivity I learned from my family members and their experiences shaped my understanding and appreciation for equity and strong desire for advocacy. I attribute the development of my superpower to my parents' deliberate and thoughtful approach in raising my brothers and me.

I did not always see this superpower as usual. This is who I always have been, and I thought this was normal for most people. Even when I was an RA as an undergraduate student, I found an ease talking with people and learning more about their situation that I thought was normal for my peers. This ease guided me further in my life as I became a Hall Director while working on my master's. Though I did not always follow this internal guiding force of a superpower, I also did not take the time to consider what was happening within me. What I knew was that I enjoyed helping people to come to a place of empathy and care for those who may be different from themselves. It was something so natural to me, all the while integrating an equitable lens into my capacity to hear, counsel, and support. As a student I constantly engaged in DEIB initiatives through research, programming, and volunteer work, and thought that this was the extent of DEIB within the university. Unbeknownst to me, the convergence of my passion and innate strengths held the potential to forge a viable career path.

This revelation manifested during my tenure as a Student Affairs professional, a period when I lead a university-wide DEIB committee. While working a full-time job, which required nights and weekends, I simultaneously lead a DEIB committee under the vice president of student affairs. Though I enjoyed my job, I felt most alive when I was immersed in the work for the DEIB committee. I dedicated the majority of my time to the committee, and my thoughts became immersed in finding ways to integrate foundational equity concepts into my job. Initially modest and occasionally not meticulously planned, I planted seeds of inclusion and diversity when opportunities presented themselves. Instead of merely offering suggestions on planning details for the annual event, I advocated for the inclusion of secondary stakeholders, traditionally viewed as barriers, in decision-making meetings to proactively address and eliminate potential problems. Subsequently, I took charge of some of these meetings, no longer seeking permission but actively extending invitations to units that had never been granted a seat at the table despite consistently being affected by its decisions. These micro-inclusion actions fostered a deeper under-standing and respect between the units, establishing a continuous collabo-rative relationship for future events.

The fusion of my job and newfound passion through the committee unfurled a gateway, presenting the prospect of integrating DEIB into my career that my mind was unwilling to ignore. I actively pursued and welcomed opportunities to contribute and take the lead in committees, propelling myself and others toward DEIB initiatives. As I discovered more chances for collaboration within my job, I unexpectedly found myself under a spotlight that intensified with each leadership role, an experience I had not anticipated.

I flourished in the spotlight as I contributed to the creation of something substantial. As an early career professional, I accessed opportunities and privileges that many had yet to attain in their careers. Exhausting all available committee opportunities, I took the initiative to create my own, garnering significant support from some of my senior leaders and peers. However, simultaneously, I sensed an unspoken unease. Praises for my efforts were met with whispers of inadequacy. While I was actively fostering a more inclusive environment within my job, others were growing increasingly uncomfortable with the new ideas I provided and with my presence.

Some of the same professionals who had supported me days before were now adopting those ideas as their own. I had to cultivate a DEIB armor to shield myself from potential negative perspectives of those who resisted the inclusive changes I was implementing. While my university leadership role seemed incongruent with my lower management job title and power, I lacked the experience to comprehend how profoundly professionally unsafe this made me. It was not until later in my career that I realized my passion and committee leadership role could elicit jealousy, sabotage, deception, and more from my peers or leaders.

The job I once found enjoyable could no longer satisfy my desire for growth in alignment with my passion. Lacking job prospects that matched the leadership opportunities I sought at this university, I harbored a deep sense that I needed more than my current job could offer. During this period, a profound realization dawned upon me: my passion was not merely a fleeting interest, but a fervent calling demanding transformation into my primary vocation. I was convinced that this career direction was where my superpower had been guiding me, though uncertainty clouded my vision on how to embark on this journey.

Recognizing my success in committee work, I saw an opportunity to elevate my leadership role within the university. While unfamiliar with the term "Chief Diversity Officer," I advocated for transforming my leadership position into a full-time role—a novel proposition for the university. I dedicated portions of my one-on-one meetings with the vice president to articulate the vision of institutionalizing my committee work into a formal position, proposing direct reporting to them instead of the existing volunteer structure. I crafted a compelling business case outlining the reasons and methodology for the transformation of my committee into something innovative and groundbreaking for the university.

However, despite my unyielding advocacy for the creation of a potential position, I faced persistent resistance. Not towards the essence of the work, but rather its perception and execution within the university's structure. This resistance was rooted in the long-standing belief that DEIB efforts were viewed as supplementary initiatives, institutional obligations, and a way to meet legal compliance.

This resistance was rooted in the long-standing belief that DEIB efforts were viewed as supplementary initiatives, institutional obligations, and a way to meet legal compliance.

Even within student affairs, where various iterations of the diversity committee existed, it had typically been undertaken by a select few who incorporated it into their regular responsibilities. The prevailing sentiment was that diversity work did not necessitate a full-time position; it was something the university had managed successfully in the past with volunteers, as evidenced by past events and ongoing successes. The university's commitment to DEIB was demonstrated through the increase in diverse student populations, support of cultural centers and the establishment of new diversity center offices, all in aligning with current state and national laws.

Although I acknowledged the university's achievements and commitment, I recognized significant gaps that extended beyond the surface-level improvements seen through increased student diversity, financial resources, and a reduction in legal issues revolving around affirmative action. While advocating for the potential position, I often felt that my message was not sufficiently clear or comprehensive in conveying the imperative to transform this committee into a full-time role. Despite months of trying to develop a job description, I faced the challenge of creating a role for myself without any clear model to follow. Moreover, the limited number of existing DEIB full-time positions at the university were typically confined to roles overseeing specific student programs or offices. The prevailing reality was that individuals wanting to engage in DEIB work, beyond current positions, could only contribute through committee assignments. The concluding message I received was that DEIB committee efforts would persist in their current form, confined to the realm of committees or task forces, with no plans or provisions for expansion beyond this established status quo.

Invalidating My Validation

Even when confronted with the university's apparent reluctance to expand their DEIB efforts, the only available gateways seemed limited to existing roles within my university. While examining similar positions at my institution, none matched the vision I aimed to establish, but they seemed closer than what I currently was facing. The scarcity of open DEIB positions or new roles felt like navigating a fiercely competitive terrain reminiscent of "The Hunger Games." Attempting to secure these positions, coupled with the frustration of being unable to articulate my long-term career aspirations, proved devastating and disheartening. Despite understanding what my "superpower" was guiding me toward, I struggled to see a viable path to make it a reality. I experienced a sense of discouragement, convinced that opportunities aligning with both my superpower and my passion for DEIB were nearly non-existent.

Navigating through these challenging years in my career, I began to recognize how my professional safety was profoundly impacted by leading a university committee. While the chance to formalize my role remained elusive, I garnered consistent praise and additional responsibilities from senior leaders. However, a discernible tone of tolerance from certain leaders indicated a reluctance to fully embrace my efforts, and at times accept me as a leader. I had witnessed the competitive and sometimes hostile dynamics within academia. I observed colleagues dismissed for their efforts in DEIB, often due to politics, mistrust, or the notion that they had not "given enough time and labor to academia" to provide anything useful in the space. While assuming there might be more to their colleagues' stories, I understood the need to pay close attention to the politics and dynamics within the university to shield myself from similar treatment. I believed that steering a university DEIB committee would solely usher in opportunities, oblivious to the fact that it would also expose me to attacks, at times originating from the very community I sought to support.

I confronted a pivotal moment when I sought advice from a senior leader, whom I admired as a mentor and who had previously commended my superpower. To my dismay, their response shattered my expectations—they attributed my inability to advance beyond leading the DEIB committee to my superpower. It became evident that the same assertive efforts that propelled me into leadership positions were now acting as a hindrance to my future career.

It became evident that the same assertive efforts that propelled me into leadership positions were now acting as a hindrance to my future career.

I had successfully undertaken too much in too short a time, with what some perceived as insufficient experience within academia, to be deemed worthy of new career opportunities. The issue was not the quality of my work but rather how my efforts made certain professionals feel about their own work. In essence, I was advised to slow down and avoid overshadowing the contributions of others who had a longer tenure in academia. Moreover, if I had found myself facing the same hostility and exclusion that my predecessors had endured, it was a consequence of my own actions.

The opportunity to lead a diversity committee for the university had been my blessing and my curse. I found myself trapped with no visible escape route, unable to carve out a new career path, yet resolute in my determination to pursue DEIB work. Over time, I begrudgingly accepted this skewed perception of a DEIB career and tried to dampen the flow of ideas inspired by my superpower.

Yet, I found myself unable to quell the surge of my superpower, as it transcended its initial role of amplifying and fostering marginalized voices; instead, it evolved into the core of my personal and professional existence. The potency of my superpower was so formidable that I effortlessly infused inclusive practices without conscious effort. I was no longer willing to suppress my superpower for fear of jeopardizing future opportunities.

I uncovered avenues where I could authentically embrace the chance to contribute to this meaningful work, and derived fulfilment from actively seeking and participating in volunteer opportunities to offer DEIB support.

A persistent urge to delve deeper into DEIB continued to linger within me, pushing me to seek and learn more. I scoured available literature, utilizing the limited terminology at my disposal, and sought guidance from influential leaders on how to mold a career that was still taking shape in my mind. Frustrated with my own lack of clarity, I entertained the idea of venturing beyond my comfort zone outside of student affairs. The revelation came when I encountered a job posting for a university-wide Chief Diversity Officer (CDO) role at a smaller, less renowned university. Pulling on my graduate school researching skills, I delved into exploring the responsibilities of a CDO and diversity work outside of student affairs, discovering a realm of possibilities that filled me with newfound hope. Realizing that the position existed in other universities, I felt a step closer to having my proposal of expanding my committee leadership role validated. However, the journey to even come close to such a position in academia revealed that a PhD was an essential prerequisite. Although I had contemplated returning to school, I had never pinpointed the field or purpose until now.

During this time of research and exploration into the CDO, I stumbled upon the field of Organization Development. Here, I found a place where I could invite my superpower into a career and transform an organization through a DEIB lens. I quickly found a PhD program where I could take my superpower and a career path that took me one step closer to a position I had advocated for many years prior. Despite my strong bond to the institution and community, I realized I needed to align my career with the path my superpower illuminated.

A New Chapter

As I began my new role at a different institution, I found myself closer to the trajectory my evolving superpower was guiding me towards. Despite envisioning a hazy path to my *dream job*, I struggled to shake off the misconception that I lacked the qualifications for the kind of work my superpower was propelling me into. The role filled me with immense pride, and I excelled in it while innovatively intertwining DEIB initiatives into the very heart of the job's foundation. In this phase, a gateway of potential DEIB opportunities swung open, marking the commencement of a new chapter in my career.

I actively engaged and connected with numerous professionals across various levels of the institution, all deeply immersed in DEIB endeavors that surpassed the scope of my initial proposals at my previous institution.

Just a few years prior, I struggled to articulate the creation of a full-time position beyond the diversity committee leadership and chair. Now, I found myself encountering professionals in roles beyond anything I had previously deemed possible or even necessary within the university. I encountered individuals with extensive years of experience in the field alongside newcomers, all dedicated to the very work that I had yearned for long ago. These encounters not only expanded horizons within the institution but also revealed a wider network of opportunities beyond specific student programs and offices I was familiar with from my past.

I undertook a transformative journey to dispel the narratives surrounding myself and the DEIB in higher education, that I had previously encountered and absorbed. In this process, a wealth of possibilities unfolded within me on the realm of DEIB as a career path. This uncharted territory revealed a world I had been professionally oblivious to, where a community of like-minded professionals transformed their passions into thriving careers. I was unaware of the extensive diversity within the field of diversity jobs and career paths. For the first time, I experienced a genuine sense of belonging and envisaged the myriad ways in which my unique superpower could reverberate across multiple professions.

At this juncture in my career, my aspiration to become a CDO or attain a senior leadership role in Diversity was an unknown conviction I had held for several years, had now transitioned from a steadfast conviction to a tangible and promising reality. However, I remained entangled in the notion that I had not sufficiently "struggled enough" or "did not work enough in a specific area of the university" to warrant such a position. Despite dedicating more than a decade to an array of DEIB roles and opportunities, the persistent doubt of not being adequately skilled or knowledgeable enough for a full-time role continued to echo relentlessly. As a result, I had applied to several positions that held indirect relevance to CDO, dismissing any direct CDO opportunities, only to repeatedly hear that I was their second choice. This disappointment underscored the notion, embedded in my earlier career experiences with a mentor, that my proactive efforts had been excessive, ultimately casting blame upon myself for my career status. Despite finding encouragement in an environment with diverse DEIB professions and professionals, each with their unique experiences, I wrestled to extricate myself from the detrimental belief that only a specific elite echelon of professionals could attain the career I aspired to.

In retrospect, I came to recognize that the skills I had acquired over the years, coupled with the initiation of my PhD program, provided me with a clearer navigational path towards my desired career. However, while projecting confidence externally, an ongoing struggle with persistent doubt and negative thought loops restrained my personal growth. The reluctance to distance myself and forgive mentors and peers who had a detrimental impact on my inner thoughts stifled my ability to flourish. Further, expecting to uncover a well-defined, established path similar to others' journeys blinded me to the necessity for self-reflection and letting go of past negative experiences. Upon reflection, I can see how these challenges, rather than propelling me forward, impeded my ability to advocate for others and hindered my overall growth.

The Impact of 2020

The events, attacks, and murders of Black, Indigenous, People of Color (BIPOC) in 2020 has forever morphed the paradigm of what it is to be an *American* and whose *life* holds value within the society. Though there have been other social movements in America's history which have challenged the prescribed definition of an American and life, no events have dismantled the façade of equity, color-blindness, and a fare justice system as quickly or decisively as those in 2020. The murders of Breonna Taylor, Ahmaud Arbery, George Floyd, and countless others in 2020 resonated to the very core of the society's soul and spurred a national awakening and acknowledgment of the lived experiences of BIPOC.

In response to these events, including the COVID-19 pandemic and the global movement for racial justice, many corporations and industries publicly denounced racial inequality in their business models, and institutions of higher education slowly followed suit (Wilson and Tugas 2022). Universities issued statements of solidarity and commitment to equity and diversity. Presidents and chancellor administrators were pressured by their students, staff, faculty, alumni and donors, demanding change, action, and a rethinking of racial disparities on their campus (Ashcraft and Allen 2020; Kruse and Calderone 2020). Administrators published a litany of solidarity statements, emphasizing the role of higher education in fostering a more just and inclusive society. Universities pledged to take concrete steps to address systemic barriers, remove oppressive racially inspired elements on their campus, and support marginalized communities. A spark of hope was ignited, as universities were forced to grapple with their past, present, and future stance on access, inclusion, equity, and diversity.

As someone deeply involved in DEIB strategic plans and initiatives for years, I perceived these statements on TV more than what they appeared to the general public. These "promises" by universities were not the responsibility of the president or chancellors who issued them rather, the burden fell on others. These declarations conveyed a powerful message to university administrators, especially those working in diversity capacities like

CDOs and diversity committees. The message was crystal clear: "that you need to fix this" (England and Purcell 2020).

CDOs have historically used their platforms to advocate for marginalized groups, speak out on social justice issues, bring attention to systemic racism and other forms of oppression that affect faculty, staff, and students, among other matters. The global movements for racial justice that unfolded in 2020 elevated the visibility and significance of the roles of CDOs, along with similar administrative positions and committees. The work I had been led to by my superpower was now thrust into the forefront of the national dialogue. A deep sense of urgency, coupled with senior administrative support, emerged to strive for improvement and progress beyond our historical norms. However, these gestures made by university presidents, chancellors, and corporations, were received as hollow or as lip service to many in and outside of the BIPOC community, partly due to the lack of actionable changes provided (Ashcraft and Allen 2020).

As I observed the surge of newly established Chief Diversity Officer positions in 2020, and in some cases reestablished positions, I found myself uplifted that these roles were at last receiving the essential attention and long-overdue acknowledgment of their intrinsic importance. Furthermore, this renewed landscape presented me with prominent and widespread instances that aptly demonstrated the imperative nature of the work I had passionately advocated for over the years. No longer did I encounter the struggle of explaining the fundamental necessity of these roles to various audiences, as they could simply tune into current events and witness in real time why such positions were not only vital within higher education but also held significance beyond its borders. The role of the CDO, along with similar administrative positions, was not a panacea for addressing all deeply entrenched systemic DEIB issues. However, their impactful work has the potential to propel universities, corporations, and countries toward a more equitable and just society.

This transformation brought about a notable shift within DEIB career opportunities. While I was gratified by these advancements, a discordant undercurrent emerged within me. I observed my previous roles as a leader of chair of DEIB committees, undergo a metamorphosis into newly formed full-time positions, an evolution that left me both intrigued and unsettled. Concurrently, inaugural positions emerged with qualifications less extensive than my own, marking a notable shift of expectations compared to when I conducted a similar search five years earlier. Some of these roles demanded three to five years of direct experience, while others required a solid understanding of DEIB concepts and theory. Interestingly, the majority of these positions did not necessitate education beyond a bachelor's degree, with very few mandating a master's degree, and less than a handful requiring a PhD. Throughout this period, I shifted from a state of feeling underqualified and undereducated to being significantly overqualified, to the point where I encountered potential exclusion from certain roles because of the elevated level of education and experience I had acquired. I further felt disconnected from reality as I saw opportunities extended to individuals who, not too long ago, had cast doubt upon the very tenets of inclusive pedagogy or advocated limitations on access to gender-neutral facilities.

At certain junctures, it appeared as if CDO positions were being flung into the open like gifts hurled during Oprah's iconic "favorite things" episodes, available or appointed to anyone swift enough to grasp them. In the midst of these unfolding changes, I grappled with profound uncertainties surrounding the very essence of diversity-centric endeavors, and my superpower's trajectory, once a source of inspiration, now elicited feelings of resentfulness and disillusionment.

Rekindling My Superpower and Accepting a Community

My discontent over the tendency of Higher Education to conveniently overlook vital matters only to adopt them when they aligned with their own interests was a familiar sentiment, yet this instance felt uniquely unsettling. The proximity I had achieved, the profound transformations I had undergone, all guided by my innate power, imbued this situation with heightened significance. I found myself grappling with a pressing question: Could the internal drive channeled by my superpower inadvertently lead me to a cause that had morphed into a fleeting trend, exploited by academia and corporations? As I delved into the intricate web of complexities within this internal conflict, paradoxically, my engagement with the work deepened further.

In the process, the realization dawned that every profession undergoes oscillations, experiencing peaks and valleys, particularly those that have long been misconstrued and undervalued. Despite my ambivalence about certain trends within my field, I clung to a sense of optimism for the trajectory ahead. Rather than succumbing to resentment towards my present circumstances and the seemingly meteoric rise in the prominence of CDO roles, I harnessed that energy to intensify my pursuit of the path illuminated by my superpower. I once again, embarked on a journey toward personal evolution, as I gradually started releasing the grip of the past, embracing forgiveness, and developed the ability to interrupt the negative loop of doubt.

I discovered myself championing the cause with greater fervor than ever before, unlocking a deeper reservoir of confidence and engagement with the work. Upon witnessing others embrace roles that the events of 2020 had freshly awakened, I recognized that my potential exceeded the limitations previously imposed upon me, like when it was confined to committee assignments. The events of 2020 did not act as the sole catalyst. However, they played a pivotal role in steering me closer to the true calling of my superpower. I immersed myself in a multitude of DEIB-focused conferences, that had recently come to my attention, wholeheartedly embracing every opportunity that crossed my path, leveraging the new-found recognition sweeping through higher education and society.

I was blessed to be part of a sisterhood of seven dynamic, self-assured, and profoundly inspiring women of color, all actively immersed in DEIB endeavors at their respective institutions. Here, within this empowering Queen's Collective, they not only introduced me to a revolutionary and enlightening approach to the work, but they also revealed that the challenges I faced – the shadows of doubt, the demoralizing criticisms from those who ostensibly championed change, and the skepticism from those I aimed to uplift – were shared experiences. We all exchanged experiences, both positive and challenging, in our shared journey of doing this work. Their stories not only affirmed my own moments of success but also resonated with my moments of struggle.

Each of us discovered ways to learn and thrive from these experiences, refusing to wither in the face of adversity. They rekindled the flame of purpose ignited by my superpower, revitalizing the reservoir of untapped potential I possessed. In this sacred space, the Queen's Collective, we bore our triumphs and tribulations, our aspirations for the future and concerns of the present. Bound by the common thread of our values, we united monthly, casting aside our egos and designations at the threshold, fostering an environment of mutual support and camaraderie.

This collective not only fortified each member's determination but also reignited the sparks of confidence that had gradually, sometimes swiftly, been eroded by our individual institution. As a Collective we consistently reminded one another of our innate capabilities and prompted one another to rise above the limitations that others imposed. In the span of a year a quarter of us witnessed transformative changes, as we took on new professional positions. By a year and a half, I had undergone a metamorphosis, gaining an entirely new level of confidence that propelled me to relentlessly pursue positions I had once deemed out of reach, unless bolstered by a PhD. With unwavering support from the Queen's Collective, I approached interviews with a newfound confidence that had long lain dormant within me.

I felt both blessed and incredibly humbled to receive an offer for a DEIB leadership position within the university I was already working for. Positioned at a senior executive level within a division, my role granted me the professional authority to instigate change across a substantial portion of the university. In this leadership capacity, I not only directed and administered all diversity initiatives with a dedicated staff but also provided guidance to the vice president to whom I directly reported to. Within a matter of months, the university president entrusted me with overseeing initiatives that would impact all staff across the entire university. Finally, I had achieved the full-time position I had struggled to articulate and define all those years ago when I led a diversity committee at a different university.

As I shared news and ongoing success of my role to the collective, they enveloped me in an exuberant celebration, reminiscent of a ticker-tape parade. Within this space, I found solace, free from the concerns about my superpower or the need to conceal my insecurities. Here, I could authentically be myself without a shadow of fear. This Collective of sisters are not only pillars of support but also bridged a significant gap in my journey to embracing my superpower's calling.

Doubting My Superpower and Acknowledging Its Demand

Not long ago, a colleague posed a statement to a large group of primarily professional women of color, stating that the concept of possessing the superpower I identified with was a disgrace. They saw these types of superpowers not as an accolade, but as a notion to disassemble within one's own identity. My immediate response was a surge of indignation, coupled with a profound sense of anger and personal affront. Following the initial jolt, I chose to stay in the conversation as I wanted to understand their viewpoint on the superpower within the context of women, particularly black women, in higher education.

Their contention was that attributing a woman of color's superpower to the capacity to advocate and mobilize individuals toward a just resolution in higher education, paralleled the portrayal of the Black mammy figure prevalent in the 1830s and persisting thereafter. Rooted in the fabric of slavery's history in the United States, the mammy figure's fundamental role centered around tending to the needs of the white slave-owning family and their children. Mammies were not the superhero type we associate with today, instead, they embodied the figure ensuring that the intricacies of domestic life were managed and that the welfare of the children took precedence above all else. Mammies were seldomly granted their freedom, as they remained in servitude to the family until their death or were sold to another household to continue their duties until they died.

My peer's argument was that the mammy's *duty* and unwavering commitment to the family came at the expense of the black woman's own well-being. Moreover, asserting that a black woman's superpower revolves predominantly around tending to others' needs, especially within the realm of higher education that consistently upholds white-centric pedagogy, serves to prolong the stereotypical portrayal of black women. In other words, suggesting that my superpower revolves around attending to others within a predominantly white institution is essentially casting me in the role of a modern-day mammy.

While I did not align with every assertion my peers presented that day, and I noted a gap in their argument concerning the experiences of those who do not identify as women or Black in these roles, I could undeniably grasp and identify with the fundamental underpinning of their argument. The notion that being a woman, specifically a Black woman, entails having all-encompassing answers and solutions for everyone, all the while maintaining an air of gentleness and tranquility, was reality. I had personally encountered instances where this very ideal was expected for me, but not imposed on other women. The stark and alarming statistics, showcasing disproportionately elevated rates of hypertension, weight fluctuations, heart attacks, strokes, and an array of health issues among Black women in the United States, were indisputable truths I could not debate.

I anecdotally knew that these statistics were true for women in the workplace. I was acutely aware that health concerns, among a host of other challenges, disproportionately afflicted women who held the distinction of being the pioneering or solitary figure in roles of substantial authority, much like that of the CDO. Having grappled with some of these very health issues as a dedicated DEIB practitioner, it was a revelation I had not fully comprehended; that my proximity to the Mammy archetype was more profound than I had previously been aware of or acknowledged. I was forced to reconsider what my superpower was really doing within me or could do to me. This aspiration to embody a persona of limitless capability, comprehensive knowledge, and ceaseless support, fueled by my superpower, might paradoxically be the very force that kills us.

The complexity of my peers' argument gains further depth within the experiences of women of color in higher education, frequently holding to environments of solitude or relegated to a minority presence within respective fields. I understood, as a woman of color, how we are often compelled to substantiate our value and worth by bearing excessive workloads that surpass not only those of our peers but sometimes our supervisors as well. Numerous were the times when I concealed my personal struggles and projected unwavering strength to support others, *all the while lacking a comparable support structure to mend and rekindle my own spirit.*

To pull back on the belief that my superpower was something that could kill me, forced me to question; "Is my work as a DEIB professional something I wanted to die for?" I recall vowing to champion justice and confront inequities, summoning the words and legacies of trailblazers like the freedom-fighting sisters, Nina Simone, Adenike Oyetunde, and others. Initially, my response was an unequivocal "yes," as these luminaries had risked everything. However, I swiftly snapped back to reality, reiterating to myself that while my work holds paramount importance within the sphere of Higher Education, it is not the same. It does not require me to continually navigate life-threatening scenarios like the heroines I drew inspiration from, yet it can enact its own insidious toll. I required prioritizing my own well-being—physically, mentally, and emotionally—first, in order to cultivate personal and professional growth.

Gradually, I began to recognize instances in which I, along with my peers, unconsciously neglected our own fundamental needs while prioritizing the needs of others. *I began to acknowledge and embrace the reality that I could not continually be an anchor for everyone. I confronted the need to break free from the internal perpetuation of the mammy archetype, rejecting the compulsion to overexert myself to the point of exhaustion.* This was a time in which I went from a path of destruction, to unwavering grace, ultimately towards a deeper understanding my purpose.

Embracing My Spirit

From a young age, this intrinsic calling has been an unwavering impetus thrusting me toward advocacy in of myriad forms. This drive embodies an inner radiance, an inexhaustible energy that relentlessly propels me forward. While I derive fulfillment from my work and invest a significant part of myself in it, I believe that not every facet of my being is owed to the work. While I appreciate the significance of holding a DEIB role, I recognize that advocacy can extend beyond the confines of the job, and at times it necessitated being outside of a DEIB position. It is essential for me to maintain a balance where I prioritize my well-being, ensuring that the job does not consume all of me, and recognizing the importance of placing myself at the core of my endeavors rather than sacrificing my own needs for the sake of others. Daily, I engage in a resolute battle against the onslaught of negative self-talk and doubt, steadfastly replacing it with an unwavering voice of compassion and determination. I found a place, though not tangible, where I could experience inner tranquility without limitations.

I have ceased questioning my superpower, yet I now openly recognize and acknowledge the physical and mental impact the work can have on me. The question no longer revolves around the extent of my dedication to this work but rather whether I should categorize this compelling force as a superpower in the first place.

The question no longer revolves around the extent of my dedication to this work but rather whether I should categorize this compelling force as a superpower in the first place.

Transcending the conventional understanding of a superpower as a mere possession, it instead resonates at the very core of my being. I now see and accept it as the guiding spirit within me.

I perceive my spirit as a reservoir of unique knowledge and wisdom. Spiritual intelligence, intricately linked with emotional intelligence, signifies profound wisdom, compassion, and the capacity to sustain inner and outer tranquility, irrespective of challenging circumstances (Wigglesworth 2002). It explores the inner realms of the mind and spirit and their connection to existence in the world (Vaughan 2002). Moreover, it plays a pivotal role in cultivating a distinct and unwavering sense of identity, particularly within the dynamics of workplace relationships (George 2006). My characterization of this spirit intelligence is instrumental in not only acknowledging it, but wholeheartedly embracing it.

My professional accomplishments and hurdles have forged my resilience, elevated my self-worth and enriched the wisdom of my inner spirit. I was not forewarned by my mentors that engaging in this work would also catalyze profound inner transformation within me. By embracing my spirit, I have learned self-acceptance, allowing me not only to extend grace to those I am compelled to support but also to receive graciously. I am continuously embarking on a profound journey, and as time unfolds, I am gaining clarity about the person I once was, the person I am today, and the uncharted potential my spirit holds for my future.

Key Insights from *Feeding My "Superpower" or Embracing My Spirit*

- To do the advocacy work Etim-Hunting speaks of in her essay, one must be grounded in the personal conviction of one's purpose.
- One must be creative to design the future career-path they hope to see.

- One's superpower is their ability to have empathy for another person in need.
- Persistence pays off, even when you doubt your superpower.
- Having superpowers can come at a great personal cost.

Things to consider:

1 How does Etim-Hunting define her superpower? What is its connection to serving as an equity professional?
2 What resistance does Etim-Hunting discover in her professional circles that challenge her embrace of this superpower? What conclusion does she draw from this exploration?
3 What are micro-inclusion acts? How do these actions help to build community?
4 What barriers do secondary stakeholders face in the planning and execution of DEI initiatives?
5 What professional development disconnects does Etim-Hunting identify in her early efforts to become a chief diversity officer?
6 What is the importance of well-being in embracing one's (leadership) spirit?

References

Ashcraft, Karen, and Brenda Allen. 2020. "How Words Come to Matter: A Statement on Statements." *Management Communication Quarterly* 34 (4): 597–602. 10.1177/0893318920951643.

England, Jason, and Richard Purcell. 2020. "Higher Ed's Toothless Response to the Killing of George Floyd." *The Chronicle of Higher Education.* https://www.chronicle.com/article/higher-eds-toothless-response-to-the-killing-of-george-floyd.

George, Mike. 2006. "Practical Application of Spiritual Intelligence in the Workplace." *Human Resource Management International Digest* 14 (5): 3–5. 10.1108/09670730610678181.

Kruse, Sharon D., and Shannon Calderone. 2020. "Cultural Competency and Higher Education." In *Handbook of Social Justice Interventions in Education*, edited by Carol A. Mullen, 1–24. Cham: Springer International Publishing.

Vaughan, Frances. 2002. "What Is Spiritual Intelligence?" *Journal of Humanistic Psychology* 42 (2): 16–33. 10.1177/0022167802422003.

Wigglesworth, Cindy. 2002. "Spiritual Intelligence and Why It Matters." *The INNERWORDS Messenger.* 5. https://www.innerworkspublishing.com/news/vol22/intelligence.htm.

Wilson, Jeffery L., and Fred Tugas. 2022. "Institutions Can Say They Encourage Staff DEI Professional Development… … But the Individual Chooses to Embrace It." *SCUP* 51 (1): 108. https://www.scup.org/resource/journal-institutions-can-say-they-encourage-staff-dei-professional-development/.

3

NEGOTIATING YOUR NON-NEGOTIABLES

Sonia J. Toson

Chapter Contents

If I could share one of the most valuable practices in my journey as a chief diversity officer, it would be negotiating the non-negotiables that are necessary in the position. The role of Chief Diversity Officer (CDO) will require a great deal of you. It's important to make sure that you get everything you need as you negotiate your offer for the position. What are the things that you need professionally to be successful in the role? What do you need in your personal life to have joy and fulfill your purpose in the role? These are what I refer to as your personal non-negotiables.

Serving as a chief diversity officer is not for the faint of heart. When offering me the position, the president of my institution said "This job is

DOI: 10.4324/9781032724881-4

[a lot]. Take some time to think about it. Talk to some people. Talk to some of the parents serving on the Cabinet. Talk to other Black women." Why was she so candid? Why did she implore me to think carefully? I believe it is because she knew how demanding the role was and how much she would be asking of me, both personally and professionally.

In its 2023 State of the CDO Report, the National Association of Chief Diversity Officers in Higher Education (NADOHE), found:

- Many CDOs are under-resourced and understaffed. Nearly a third of them (32.2%) had annual operating budgets of $39,000 or less, and 44% of CDOs had between zero and two full-time-equivalent employees who report directly to them.
- More than a third of respondents could not agree that institutions provide adequate access to resources to perform their responsibilities as CDOs. One in ten felt strongly that they lack adequate institutional resources. (Also see Kyaw (2023).)
- Asked to compare their CDO role to their previous jobs, respondents were most likely to consider their job more or much more "stressful" than their previous position. In addition, positive terms like "fulfilling," "satisfying," and "rewarding" were highly rated choices alongside "overwhelming" and "upsetting." Few CDOs considered their work "manageable" or "predictable."

These findings demonstrate just how complex and taxing the role of a CDO is. Negotiating the right offer for such a multifaceted and demanding position requires a thoughtful approach and a strong sense of self-advocacy.

I did in fact follow my president's advice. I talked to all the people she suggested and a few more, including having an honest conversation with my daughter about how she felt about the possibility of me accepting the role. Through these conversations, research, and reflection, I gained key insight that was useful not only in making the decision to accept the work, but also in establishing the non-negotiable conditions under which I would accept the work.

In this chapter, I'll share a step-by-step process for negotiating the non-negotiables you need in order for you to thrive as a CDO. We'll dive into what to do before, during, and after the negotiation to set yourself up for success.

Pre-Game: What to Do before Negotiation Begins

Over the years I've spent teaching negotiations and coaching clients, one thing I know is that the most successful negotiations are won before they start.

... *the most successful negotiations are won before they start.*

How do you ask for (and get) everything you need to achieve your professional and personal goals as a CDO? The answer is simpler than you think. By being the most prepared. What you do before the negotiation is arguably the most important part of the process. This is your "pre-game." Your pre-game should consist of *preparation*, *planning*, and *practice* (Ury 2014).

Preparation

Preparation begins with determining what is necessary for you to flourish in the role, both personally and professionally. What are the things that are essential in your life that must not be compromised in order for you to perform the job of CDO in a healthy and sustainable manner? In other words, what are the absolute must-haves for you to perform the job with longevity as both a human and a practitioner? These are your unique and personal non-negotiables.

It's important to contemplate your needs from both the professional and the personal perspective; not just one or the other. To get the most out of your preparation, you'll need to engage in *research* and *reflection*. Research speaks to your professional needs, while reflection considers your personal needs.

Research

What commitment will you need from the institution to ensure you have the greatest opportunity for success in the role? You'll need to gather as much information about the role and the institution as you can. Information gathering is an integral part of any negotiation strategy at the planning stage. Research as much as you can to find out more about the position and the institution. The more information you have before the negotiation begins, the more likely you are to succeed. This approach is referred to as information-based bargaining (Shell 2006).

Start with gathering research about the position itself. This will help you determine what your true needs are in taking the position. You cannot determine your non-negotiables without being truly informed as to what you are taking on in accepting the position. Find out as much as you can about the institution and the role you are being asked to step into. Determine the organizational structure of the unit you will be leading. What resources are currently available to do the work? Are additional resources needed? Think broadly about this. Will you need more personnel, physical space, financial, equipment, or knowledge resources to successfully operate the unit? Do your best to probe these questions during the interview process.

Where are the gaps? What are the organization's expectations for the unit and for you as the leader of that unit? Once you have a sense of what will be truly required of the role, you can negotiate from an informed position. Knowing what you are walking into will help you determine your needs in taking the role. For example, if you are taking a role that involves standing up a unit, program, or initiative, the job becomes a more challenging endeavor. Likewise, if you are taking on a unit that is under-resourced in any way, the role is also a more challenging endeavor (Williams and Wade-Golden 2013).

You'll also need to know information about the current landscape and context in which you will lead. Are you walking into hostile territory? Is there a solid foundation from which to launch into a deeper level of work? It is useful to break down the current landscape into four categories:

- institutional context.
- regional context.
- national/international context.
- intra-unit context.

Institutional context refers to the context, particularly as it relates to diversity, equity, and inclusion within the university. Is the institution tolerant of, supportive of, or committed to the work of diversity, equity, inclusion, justice, and belonging? Each presents a vastly different environment, so it is important to know which one is applicable to the role you are considering. On the spectrum of DEI knowledge, development, and growth, where does the university as a whole lie? Is it still at the DEI awareness stage? Has it progressed to the stage of incorporating DEI into strategic priorities and resourcing the work accordingly? This information is directly relevant to the amount of work that the position will require and as such, is necessary information to have going into negotiations (Wong 2017). Ask forthright, honest questions of senior leadership at the institution to get a sense of the answers to these questions. Note both the verbal and nonverbal cues in their answers. Both can be revealing (Harvard Program on Negotiation Staff 2024).

The regional context refers to the context in the state or region of the country in which you will lead. Often there is a political climate in the region that will affect the role you're considering. Scan the news in the region. Note legislation that has been introduced, whether it passed or not, that speaks to DEI and the appetite for it in the region. Is the institution public or private? If public, is the institution part of a governing system? If so, the specific context within that system is important to know as well. If private, how does the board of trustees and donor base view diversity, equity, and inclusion? Does the board contain allies, detractors, or a mix of both? Is there support for the work you'll be doing? These are all questions that must be answered to make an informed decision about what the role will truly require.

The national context refers to the climate for diversity, equity, and inclusion in the country of practice. For example, in the United States, diversity, equity, and inclusion have been a particularly vociferous part of the discourse in recent years. The polarization and sometimes vitriol that is involved in the discourse can be daunting to a new (or even a seasoned) practitioner. Recent Supreme Court decisions related to university admissions and their future implications for diversity, equity, and inclusion make the work of a CDO even more daunting. Are you prepared to have your work be a part of this discourse in ways that may be unpleasant at best and defamatory at worst? Given the current political climate in the United States, practitioners and leaders must prepare themselves to be challenged in a variety of ways as they take the necessary steps to bring our institutions of higher education forward in this work.

Given the current political climate in the United States, practitioners and leaders must prepare themselves to be challenged in a variety of ways as they take the necessary steps to bring our institutions of higher education forward in this work.

Is the institution making the offer willing to support you and stand in the fight with you? Ask them directly with research-based specifics as to what that could look like. There are plenty of current events in the news to draw from for examples.

The intra-unit context refers to the actual unit or department you will be leading. What does the culture and morale in the unit look like? What resources have historically been allocated to the unit? What about the staff you inherit? Has there been a significant amount of turnover? Are there interpersonal dynamics that complicate working relationships and affect productivity? Do you have the right people in the right roles, or will you need to make personnel changes? Will your leadership style create culture shock?

Each of these contexts will present a unique landscape for the specific role that you are considering. Each distinct landscape requires a unique strategy and a nuanced approach that is specific to that work (Wong 2017). Armed with complete information about what the position will truly require the next step is to determine what you as a human will need to meet the demands of the role. The multi-level contextual analysis is an *outward* look at the position, while the analysis of what it will take for you as an individual to perform successfully in the role is an *inward* look that must be both reflective and honest.

Reflection

Deep reflection is so important for this part of the process. Based on all of the information you have gathered about the position, ask yourself, what do you need on a personal level to meet the required expectations and obligations of the role? What are your personal priorities for your life? Are you able to meet the demands of the job and still fulfill your personal priorities? For me, the most important things in my life are faith, family, self-care, and purpose. I am a single mother to a teenage child and also care for aging parents. This required me to determine whether I could meet my familial obligations and still fulfill the duties of my job. Things like transporting my child to and from school and extracurricular activities or taking my parents to doctor's appointments are difficult with a cabinet position that involves long hours, the management of several staff members, and a significant amount of both scheduled and unscheduled meetings. I knew that it would be necessary to outsource some help and call on my village to help with my familial priorities.

In addition, I determined that my specific role would require a great deal of me emotionally as a Black woman and a mother. The role requires a great deal of human interaction and emotional intelligence. It is emotionally laborious and mentally draining at times (Barrett, Chaddock, and Hathaway 2021). This said to me that it would be critically important for me to double down on my self-care protocols, given that this is one of my highest priorities. For me, this looks like scheduled time for prayer and meditation, regular exercise, regular appointments to ensure physical and mental wellness, and time to feed my soul by sharing meals and laughter with good friends. These components of self-care are all scheduled on my calendar regularly. However, that only happened because I negotiated and set expectations early regarding my time and my professional boundaries. Almost everyone at my university is aware that I have a daughter and she comes first in my life after God, without exception. When she needs me, I take time off.

I also needed to examine the role before taking it through the lens of faith and purpose. Looking honestly at the context and climate in which the role would be performed, would I be called upon to compromise my faith? Would I be able to walk in my purpose and serve a greater good by taking the role? For example, I believe that a core aspect of my purpose is to create equitable pathways and pipelines into careers in higher education for those who may not have access.

I believe that a core aspect of my purpose is to create equitable pathways and pipelines into careers in higher education for those who may not have access.

Given that, I had to find out what my scope of influence would be and if I would be trusted to execute organizational strategy. In other words, would I be trusted to put the right people in the right positions in my division? Would I be given the resources to grow and develop staff and help them gain the skills and core competencies needed to advance in their professions? Would I be provided with a respected seat at the table, thereby allowing me to speak someone else's name?

The answers to these questions all became critical components of my negotiation plan. What might this reflection look like for you? What are the must-haves that need to be in place in order for your personal life to work beyond the job itself? These are your unique and authentic non-negotiables, and they are different for each of us. Ask yourself, "What are my essential needs?" Is it time with your family? Regularly scheduled time to care for your mental health and wellness? Physical movement? A spiritual or meditative practice? A village of support? What are the things that make your life work and how can you obtain and maintain them in this role? Determining these items for yourself is a critical first step in negotiating an offer to serve as a chief diversity officer.

So, how do you figure out what your non-negotiables are? How do you accurately assess those personal and professional must-haves that will allow you to be successful as a CDO in this particular role? The first step is to realize that you have critical needs that go beyond the typical, "tangible" items that one negotiates as part of employment negotiations, such as salary, benefits, reporting structure, etc. When receiving an employment offer, people often focus solely on the compensation associated with the position. The best approach to position negotiations, however, is to contemplate all aspects of the job holistically, including your personal non-negotiables.

For example, do you need:

- flexibility in working hours so that you can exercise, meditate, or have time to meet family obligations? If so, set early expectations in the initial negotiations around your working hours, particular face-to-face/onsite working hours.
- plenty of sick days that can be used for both physical and mental wellness? If so, it may be important to negotiate extra leave time.
- to ensure that your family comes first? If so, then create space to be present for loved ones by setting early expectations about appropriate contact hours and windows of availability.
- time off to rest and recharge? If so, you can negotiate additional leave as well as a high enough salary to allow for wellness and travel.

So how do you ask for these items without seeming demanding or "extra" about it? First, remember that these items should be determined on your own during the negotiation planning process. Once you get to the negotiation phase, you are simply asking for what you need and leaving why you need it to yourself. Your employer doesn't necessarily need to know that you need extra time off for therapist appointments or lunch with friends; they simply need to know that you require an appropriate amount of time off given the nature of the position. Secondly, remember to be reasonable in what you're asking for. Asking for too much or for items that come at an unreasonable and burdensome cost to the institution will surely paint you as arrogant and demanding. If your personal non-negotiables fall significantly outside of the range of the typical asks for a CDO position, it may be wise to reexamine whether this is the right position or career for you.

If your personal non-negotiables fall significantly outside of the range of the typical asks for a CDO position, it may be wise to reexamine whether this is the right position or career for you

---

Another helpful tactic is to probe areas of importance to you during the interview phase, prior to being offered the position and negotiating your acceptance. For example, if self-care is important to you (and I'm hoping it is), then ask about that during the interview. Most interview sessions will end with time for you to ask questions of the interviewers. During that time, you might ask "What is your approach to employee wellness, particularly as it relates to senior leaders, who often have more demanding roles?" It is extremely helpful to hear this answer from the person to whom you'll be reporting directly. Note if there is a pause or an immediate response when you ask the question. There is a lot to be learned from the immediate reaction to the question itself (Harvard Program on Negotiation, 2024). Often the interviewer will answer and discuss how important wellness and work-life balance is. This gives you a good indication of their overall perspective on the topic and sets you up to negotiate for items that center around wellness, such as additional leave time or flexible working hours without it being a surprise or seeming unreasonable.

Planning

Now that you have settled on your non-negotiables, it's time to formulate your plan of attack. Planning is the second phase of your pre-game process (Ury 2014). Your negotiation plan should be based on the research and reflection from the previous step. Your plan should at a minimum include: your target goals based on personal and professional needs, the minimum you're willing to accept, multiple feasible proposals that include an emergency escape hatch, and a list of potential counterpoints with prepared responses to them (Shonk 2024). You may be thinking … "Whoa … that is a lot!" It is, but the position of CDO can be a lot, so we need to make sure we get a lot in our offer!

With all of those items in mind, you are able to craft a complete ask. Based on a true analysis of what the role requires, what you need to fulfill it, and the other party's needs and interests, generate proposals that meet both your needs and the institutions. Drafting multiple variations of your proposal will give you the greatest chance of being successful in the negotiation. Most people stop at only one or two potential proposals. The best negotiators generate multiple viable proposals, or MESOs (multiple equivalent simultaneous offers). Studies show that negotiators who deploy MESOs have an increased likelihood of successful outcomes in the negotiation (Leonardelli et al. 2019; Medvec et al. 2005; Shonk 2024). I typically prepare at least five different proposals when entering into a negotiation. Each proposal balances my needs with the institution's priorities and contains a balance of both tangible and intangible items. Each of your proposals should have a safety net that allows you to pivot away from the position when the time is right for you. I call it your "emergency escape hatch."

The emergency escape hatch is that strategic part of your plan that is forward-thinking. It contemplates the future moment when you are ready to pivot away from the role. Sometimes what is necessary in the role simply requires too much of us on a human level. This is particularly true in times of political or civil discord related to diversity, equity, and inclusion work or significant or institutional change or strife (Anderson 2023). DEI work is a journey and as such is filled with hills and valleys. It will always be a fight. It will always bring trouble, and while that trouble is what John Lewis would call "good trouble," it is trouble, nonetheless. There is no getting around the fact that trouble is exhausting; especially after you've spent years in the fight.

Furthermore, the work of diversity, equity, and inclusion will likely look a lot different as we move into the future. According to Michael Nelms, former chancellor of the University of Michigan-Flint, "The future of DEI at colleges and universities is unknown and uncertain at best" (Nelms 2023). Because of this, it is important to think ahead to the time when you might want or need to take off your armor and hand your weapons to the next generation of fighters. Part of your initial negotiations should involve creating what I call an emergency escape hatch. This is the exit strategy that will allow you to pivot when the time is right. There is no shame or failure in seeking other opportunities after serving in this challenging role. In fact, the role of CDO calls upon us to do and be so many things, we are well suited for a wide variety of opportunities after leaving the role. Negotiating viable "off ramps" as part of the initial negotiations is a wise endeavor if you are able to accomplish it.

There are a few options to accomplish this goal. If you come into the role with a faculty appointment, seek to negotiate the base salary that you would retain if you ever decided to leave administration and return to the faculty. Negotiating a high base salary that can be retained as a faculty member only ensures you won't be handcuffed to the CDO position for financial survival. Another option is to negotiate to expand your portfolio to include areas you might want to transition to in the future, such as compliance, leadership, human resources, research centers, etc. This makes transitioning to those areas easier if you choose to do so after serving as CDO. You can also negotiate membership in professional organizations and travel time to attend national conferences and events. This ensures consistent networking opportunities and allows you to cultivate a strong professional network that can be leveraged when it is time to transition from the role. Finally, you may choose to negotiate permission to engage in limited consulting engage-ments when time permits, provided they don't pose a conflict of interest. This will provide you with potential future employers if you choose to transition to another position, or a ready-made client list if you choose to transition to becoming a full-time consultant as an entrepreneur.

Now that you have a solid plan of attack, commit to it … in writing! Write down your plan, including all your alternative proposals. This is the weapon you will take into battle. You can be as general as jotting down a few bullet points or as specific as writing out a script for what you want to say. Your plan should encompass your reflection and the research you've conducted so that you can negotiate from an informed and specific position. Contemplate counterpoints or barriers to the things you're asking for and be prepared to respond to them. In other words, consider the potential of a no. Why might the employer say no to what you are asking for? Be prepared with an objective response grounded in research and logic; be sure that it considers the employer's goals and strategic priorities. Even in going after what you want, you must be reasonable. Rely on your research as you craft these responses.

It is important that this plan exists on paper and not just in your head. Once you have it in writing you can have it in front of you for reference while you're negotiating. This keeps you focused on your plan and accountable to yourself in asking for what you need. If the conversation gets tense or becomes tangential, you have your plan right in front of you to help refocus the conversation.

Practice

We've prepared, we've planned, and now it's time for the final step in your pre-game process: practice. Once you have that written plan, the key to a successful negotiation is to practice, practice more, and then practice even more (Boyles 2023). Study each piece of your plan and the logical reasoning behind it. Use it as a script and stick to it! Practice how you might pivot if things don't go according to your plan. I recommend reading your plan out loud alone, so that you can hear yourself asking for what you need with confidence. Then, practice using role play in a low stakes environment, for example with a friend or significant other. Finally, practice in a high stakes environment, with a colleague, mentor, or senior leader who often conducts these kinds of negotiations as a hiring employer. The more you practice, the more comfortable you will be during the actual negotiation.

Game Time: What to Do During Negotiation

In my work, I don't run into a whole lot of folks who love the act of negotiating. In fact, the opposite is true. They often dread it, which is how they end up retaining me. This is the part of the process that can feel like it puts a damper on what is otherwise an exciting next step in a person's career as a CDO. Negotiating firmly by confidently asking for what you want can be one of the most difficult and anxiety-provoking parts of the hiring process. I'll be honest, even as a negotiations' professor and coach, negotiating is not my absolute favorite thing to do and can still be very uncomfortable for me! If you're like me, once you're at the negotiating table (or these days, on a virtual call), anxiety starts to build. Your heart starts to beat just a bit faster. Your palms and forehead get just a bit "dewy." I can create a near fire-proof plan for a client any day of the week, but when it comes to my own personal negotiations, the task feels much more daunting. That being said, I've learned through research and practice how to push past that discomfort and handle critical negotiations confidently. Allow me to share some of my most successful tips with you to guide you on your journey to a successful negotiation.

- Immediately before the negotiation *take a slow, deep breath*. The effects of intentional breath on calming the nervous system are proven and reliable. A few deep breaths (as few as one to three) can ground you and refocus you on the matter at hand (The University of Toledo Counseling Center 2023).
- *Get comfortable with the discomfort.* Acknowledge that this process can be uncomfortable. Know that the discomfort and anxiety that often comes

with negotiation is a normal psychological response. The more we want the position, the less likely we are to ask for what we truly want. Asking for what we really want in any context involves vulnerability and therefore tends to be psychologically uncomfortable. We doubt our ability to influence others and are fearful of potential rejection leading us to be hesitant in asking for what we really want with confidence (O'Brien 2021). Combat this discomfort by getting comfortable with the possibility of receiving a "No" to something that you really want in your position as CDO. Practice hearing "No" so that you can take the emotional sting out of hearing it if it occurs in the actual negotiation.

Once you've dealt with the nerves, you can calmly execute your plan. You've prepared, planned, and practiced at the pre-game stage, now it's game time. You've already planned out and written down what you're asking for, now it's time to be precise in *how* you ask for it. At this stage, keep it simple and use three Cs to ensure flawless execution. At the table, be **clear**, be **concise**, and be in **control**.

Be Clear

Clear communication is imperative (Lester 2023). Sometimes nervousness or fear will cause us to be hesitant in our ask. When this happens, we may ask for what we want, but in what we would consider a "more palatable" manner (Warrell 2013). This results in a vague message that becomes lost in translation. Hesitancy may also come off as weak or unsure, which works against you at the negotiation table. The plan I insisted you write down before negotiation will help you in this moment! Refer back to your plan and state your proposal during negotiation as clearly as you have it written on the page.

Be Concise

I can't tell you how many clients I've coached over the years that have struggled with being concise in negotiations. The reasons for this are numerous. Sometimes nervousness and anxiety get the best of us. We ramble on and on in an effort to fill uncomfortable pauses that can come after we make our ask and we're waiting for a response. In addition, sometimes we use many more words than we need to in order to justify what we are asking and convey it as "acceptable" to the other party. However, if you are clear, direct, and your ask is reasonable based on the research from the pre-game stage, you don't need a lot of words. In fact, they can work against you. The more words you use, the muddier your message becomes. It also gives the other party more counterpoints and increased opportunities to wiggle out of what you're asking for. Finally, when you use too many words and end up veering well beyond the original point, the other party in the negotiation may view you as unfocused or scattered.

Control Your Emotions

When I'm teaching and coaching clients, we spend at least one to two weeks on the emotional aspects of negotiation alone because they have such a significant impact on negotiation outcomes. Failure to manage emotions can derail even the simplest of negotiations (Ury 2014). Certainly, negotiating an employment decision is strictly business, but we would be robots if emotions didn't creep in to some degree. The work of a CDO is a human-centered endeavor that is purpose-filled and incredibly impactful. Given that, it is not surprising that in fighting for what you need to carry this heavy load without sacrificing yourself, emotions might be stirred.

Emotions are a natural part of the human state, so it is futile to try to avoid experiencing them during a negotiation, especially one as purpose-filled and impactful as a university CDO. In fact, if you try to prevent any emotion from occurring in the process, you will likely come off as cold or incapable of handling the relational aspects of the job. The key is not to avoid emotions, but to notice and manage them. Notice the emotional reaction of the person you are dealing with (Harvard Program on Negotiations, 2023). Are they annoyed? Nervous? Seemingly uncaring? Distracted? Excited? Be aware of their emotions but don't let them throw you off your game. That might mean pausing before continuing. It could mean briefly acknowledging the emotion in the room but not dwelling on it. Get right back to your plan and stay the course.

At the same time, you may notice your own emotions surfacing during negotiation. That's ok! It could be that the decision-maker suggests a counter proposal that you find insulting or angering; you may panic if you're asked a question to which you don't have a response; you may experience frustration or even sadness upon hearing no to one of your proposals. If this happens, know that it is absolutely normal. You write your plan down for a reason and this is it! Take another deep breath, glance at your plan, and let it anchor you in this moment. Stay focused on what you need and why. Channel your inner Janet Jackson and control your emotions, don't let them control you! If you're able to handle the emotions, you have an excellent chance of getting what you need in your negotiation to thrive as a CDO.

Spin the Block: What to Do After Negotiation

Me vs. Me

Once you've worked hard to negotiate everything that is required to be successful in the role, how do you maintain the non-negotiables you determined were essential? In this work, there will always be a need to hold yourself accountable to your non-negotiables. When the pace is rapid and the work is taxing, we often forget the things that were important to us in the first place. We get caught up in the work and lose sight of the things that we determined were vital for both our professional and personal success in the role.

Personally, I've had moments when I became too busy with the demands of university administration that I let my self-care slip. I've gone weeks without exercising or spending quality time with friends and family. Failing to take care of myself is both dangerous to my health and compromises my ability to persist in doing this work. When this happens, I have to have a radically honest conversation with myself about my personal priorities, whether I'm staying true to them, and what I can do to get back on track as soon as possible. What I am describing is an internal negotiation that a CDO will consistently have with themselves in order to stick to their non-negotiables. Because it is so easy to get caught up in both the pace and the purpose-filled nature of the work, how do you hold yourself accountable to those aspects of your life and the role that are non-negotiable?

Accountability structures and partners are key in this area (Asare 2022). I make sure that my calendar reflects the things I have deemed priorities and are therefore non-negotiable in my life. My non-negotiables are written down and visible in my workspace both at home and on campus. My therapist and best friend serve as excellent accountability partners, reminding me to take time off and renew my mind through exercise and meditation. My colleagues provided further accountability by simply checking in on my mental health, well-being, and self-care practices and allowing me to do the same for them.

Consistent reflection and self-checks are also important. Scan to determine how you're feeling. Are you more often fatigued than rested? Do you find yourself increasingly unmotivated or without daily joy? What is the tone of your journal entries or prayer life? Is it hopeful and grateful, or has it grown apathetic, confused or bleak? These reflective self-checks are so important in determining our next steps while in the role. They may signal that it is time to renegotiate or exit the profession altogether.

External assessment also provides accountability. Be sure that you are being regularly assessed by both medical and non-medical practitioners (such as spiritual and clinical counselors). Professional caregivers are trained to see what we don't see. Even if our self-checks don't immediately reveal an issue, external professionals can help us stay accountable to what keeps us healthy and whole as we do the work.

It's Not Too Late

If you are reading this chapter after you've already accepted a position, it's not too late. You can always "spin the block" and reopen negotiations. While it is typically more difficult, you can still negotiate your non-negotiables after accepting a position. This will typically look like re-opening negotiations during regular 1:1 or evaluation conversations with your supervisor. The best tool you can use in this situation is to demonstrate a changed context or issue that necessitates renegotiation. Is there something different about the position, institution, or context that has changed since you accepted the role? The institution is unlikely to be moved by changes in your personal situation, so these renegotiations must instead leverage a changed organizational context. For example, has your portfolio expanded? Has one of the previously discussed contexts (institutional, regional, national/international, or intra-unit) shifted? Have the resources allocated to your unit become inadequate to meet the current needs of the university?

If you can formulate a basis for renegotiation, reopen the conversation with the current decision-maker. Discuss the changed context and the corresponding shift in needs for the position. Re-assess the situational landscape including the current needs of the institution and position your new request within that context (Williams & Wade-Golden 2013). For example, if the current focus of the institution is on student success, discuss how granting your request will help the institution achieve its student success goals. Ground your argument in data, research, and success metrics instead of subjective, personal criteria. It is critical to demonstrate how this request will result in a win for the institution or decision-maker, not just a win for you. Does it make the decision-maker look good? Does it increase the likelihood that the institution will meet its goals? How can you frame your ask in a way that makes clear the alignment between what you need and institutional priorities.

Armed with tools for before, during, and after negotiation, you now have the power to control your destiny as a CDO. Don't be afraid to use them! The work is taxing but worth it, so use these tools to set yourself up for the greatest success and longevity in your role. I am excited about your personal success story and am cheering you on from afar!

Key Insights from *Negotiating Your Non-negotiables*

- Pre-work is a necessary component of the negotiation process before accepting the role of chief diversity officer, academic diversity officer, diversity practitioners, or any other leadership role in higher education.
- Be clear on your personal priorities and how they may or may not align with the CDO role you seek.
- Consider creating a viable pathway for transitioning out of your CDO role and include it as part of your negotiation conversation.
- Reopen negotiations if position expectations change and your non-negotiables are jeopardized.

Things to Consider

1 What are the non-negotiables Toson speaks of in the pre-work section of her essay?
2 What are the findings of NADOHE's 2023 *State of the CDO* report Toson references in her essay? What do they reveal?
3 What are the four categories important for determining the cultural landscape of diversity, equity, and inclusion work at your institution?
4 What are the verbal and non-verbal cues of diversity, equity, and inclusion awareness CDOs should be mindful of as they consider a leadership role in this area?
5 What are some non-negotiables Toson discusses in her essay?
6 Take a moment to reflect on your non-negotiables as they relate to your current position. Have they remained consistent? If not, what changed? Is there an opportunity to realign your priorities with the expectations of the role?

References

Anderson, Jill. 2023. "The Future of DEI in Higher Education." Harvard Graduate School of Education. https://www.gse.harvard.edu/ideas/edcast/23/10/future-dei-higher-education.

Asare, Janice Gassam. 2022. "5 DEI Practitioners Share What Self-care Looks Like for Them." Forbes. https://www.forbes.com/sites/janicegassam/2021/11/24/5-dei-practitioners-share-what-self-care-looks-like-for-them/.

Barrett, Kimberly, Noelle Chaddock, and Gretchel Hathaway. 2021. "Addressing the Emotional, Interpersonal, and Professional Costs of Being a Senior Diversity Officer." INSIGHT Into Diversity. https://www.insightintodiversity.com/addressing-the-emotional-interpersonal-and-professional-costs-of-being-a-senior-diversity-officer/.

Boyles, Michael. 2023. "How to Prepare for a Negotiation." Harvard Business School Online: Business Insights Blog. https://online.hbs.edu/blog/post/how-to-prepare-for-a-negotiation#:~:text=Consider%20negotiating%20with%20friends%20or,you'll%20respond%20to%20each.

Harvard Program on Negotiation Staff. 2024. "Using Body Language in Negotiation." Negotiation Skills. Harvard Law School. https://www.pon.harvard.edu/daily/negotiation-skills-daily/negotiation-techniques-and-body-language-body-language-negotiation-examples-in-real-life/.

Kyaw, Arrman. 2023. *Report: Many CDOs are Under-Resourced and Understaffed.* Diverse Issues in Higher Education. https://www.diverseeducation.com/faculty-staff-issues/article/15546190/report-many-cdos-are-underresourced-and-understaffed.

Leonardelli, Geoffrey J., Jun Gu, Geordie McRuer, Victoria Husted Medvec, and Adam D. Galinsky. 2019. "Multiple Equivalent Simultaneous Offers (MESOs) Reduce the Negotiator Dilemma: How a Choice of First Offers Increases Economic and Relational Outcomes." *Organizational Behavior and Human Decision Processes* 152: 64–83. 10.1016/j.obhdp.2019.01.007. https://www.sciencedirect.com/science/article/pii/S074959781630557X.

Lester, Tonya. 2023. "How to Ask for What You Want." Psychology Today. https://www.psychologytoday.com/us/blog/staying-sane-inside-insanity/202304/how-to-ask-for-what-you-want.

Medvec, Victoria Husted, Geoffrey J. Leonardelli, Adam D. Galinsky, and Aletha Claussen-Schulz. 2005. "Choice and Achievement at the Bargaining Table: The Distributive, Integrative, and Interpersonal Advantages of Making Multiple Equivalent Simultaneous Offers." *SSRN Electronic Journal.* 10.2139/SSRN.732665.

Nelms, Charlie. 2023. Diversity, Equity, and Inclusion: Where Do We Go from Here?

O'Brien, Pamela. 2021. "The Power of Asking for What You Want, According to a Psychologist." Shape. https://www.shape.com/lifestyle/mind-and-body/how-to-ask-for-what-you-want.

Shell, G. Richard. 2006. *Bargaining for Advantage: Negotiation Strategies for Reasonable People.* Penguin Books.

Shonk, Katie. 2024. "Top 10 Negotiation Skills You Must Learn to Succeed." Harvard Program on Negotiation. https://www.pon.harvard.edu/daily/negotiation-skills-daily/top-10-negotiation-skills/.

The University of Toledo Counseling Center. 2023. "Deep Breathing and Relaxation." Anxiety Toolbox. The University of Toledo. https://www.utoledo.edu/studentaffairs/counseling/anxietytoolbox/breathingandrelaxation.html.

Ury, William. 2014. *Getting Past No: Negotiating in Difficult Situations.* Bantam.

Warrell, Margie. 2013. "7 Keys to Asking For What You Really Want (So You Get It!)." Forbes. https://www.forbes.com/sites/margiewarrell/2013/04/24/7-keys-to-asking-for-what-you-really-want-so-you-get-it/?sh=108d21261a56.

Williams, Damon A., and Katrina C. Wade-Golden. 2013. *The Chief Diversity Officer: Strategy Structure, and Change Management.* Sterling, VA: Stylus.

Wong, Kathleen. 2017. "Diversity Work in Contentious Times: The Role of The Chief Diversity Officer." *Liberal Education* 103, no. 3–4. https://eric.ed.gov/?id=EJ1161020.

4

THE JOURNEY, THE STRUGGLE, AND THE PROGRESS

Tamara A. Johnson

Chapter Contents

The Journey

I never planned to become a Chief Diversity Officer (CDO), but upon reflection, each of my academic and professional endeavors would serve to prepare me for the breadth and depth of knowledge, skills and abilities that would later be required for me to achieve success in this role. Frederick Douglass says, "if there is no struggle – there is no progress," which reflects my journey to CDO …

My interest in diversity was sparked as an undergraduate. I was accepted at the University of Illinois at Urbana-Champaign (UIUC) and was granted a President's Award scholarship. This scholarship covered 100% of my financial need—which was the only way I could attend since I was from a low-income, single parent household. Recognizing the low retention rates of students of color at UIUC, the Office of Minority Student Affairs proactively assigned me a Graduate Counselor (GC). My counselor was a Black, female graduate student attending UIUC, who met with me bi-weekly to monitor my academic progress and help me navigate the challenges I encountered. She

DOI: 10.4324/9781032724881-5

was a key contributor to my success during my first year in college as she taught me the strategies that would lead to my degree completion. My GC was relatable and knowledgeable. We easily connected because I could see myself reflected in her and she demonstrated a sincere concern for my academic success and overall well-being. Representation remains important across sectors, including higher education and I can personally attest to the significance. My GC reviewed my course syllabi and pointed out the "fine print," those details that I may have otherwise missed and reminded me about deadlines. When she received my poor mid-semester grades, she demonstrated a sense of urgency and provided a list of recommendations, including that I speak with professors. I never considered seeking professors during their office hours, but to my surprise, they were all quite receptive. This was the beginning of what would be a successful academic career for me.

After completing my bachelor's in psychology, I continued at UIUC as a master's student in their Human Resource Education program. What was most exciting for me was not the acceptance into graduate school—but that I was finally eligible to apply for a GC position! To my delight, I was selected, and I loved the role since it afforded me the opportunity to serve in the capacity that contributed to my success. I so enjoyed the position that it set me on a path to pursuing an advanced degree in psychology. I was admitted into a counseling psychology doctoral program and concurrently worked in residential life as an Assistant Hall Director (AHD), which covered my tuition and room and board (I was only responsible for covering the out-of-state residency fees). Having never worked in residential life, I had a steep learning curve, which was extra difficult as a new doctoral student. Looking back, the AHD role was critical in my development as a higher education professional. I learned the fundamentals related to fostering a living and learning environment conducive to student success, including community building, programming, professional development, conflict management and crisis management. My doctoral program required clinical hours, which I primarily completed at the university's counseling center. This provided me formal training in developing skills such as relationship building, assessment, and treatment planning.

A year-long predoctoral internship was required for my degree completion. Given my affinity for higher education, I continued my training at another university counseling center. Upon successful completion of my predoctoral internship, I officially earned my doctorate—the first person in my family (and, at that time, the only one) to achieve this level of education. A postdoctoral internship was also required for eligibility to sit for the licensure exam. Excited to combine my master's in human resources with my doctorate in psychology, I accepted a postdoc as an organizational development consultant with a government agency. This experience afforded me the opportunity to learn a completely different set of skills as I traveled nation-wide to assist with organizational change efforts. Consulting involved conducting assessments at the system, institutional, and departmental levels; providing leadership development and executive coaching; administering 360-degree assessments; facilitating employee workgroups; and leading strategic planning efforts. As amazing as this experience was, it solidified my passion for a career in higher education to ensure that I "pay it forward"—supporting the success of others in academia, specifically.

Although I was warned by many that if I left higher education, I would be unable to re-enter the field—I easily transitioned back as an Associate Director of Career Development at a highly selective private university. With a master's in human resources, a dissertation focused on the career development and racial identity of Black students and experience in consulting, a position within career services was a natural fit. My supervisor was an Executive Director who reported to a Vice President of Student Affairs (VPSA). During my interview for the position, I connected instantly with the VPSA because his doctorate was in organizational development, so we understood a common language given my postdoctoral experience. He invited me to schedule a time to meet with him if I was selected and accepted the role. After my start date, I did in fact, follow up with the VPSA, which started what would evolve into one of the most significant relationships of my career. He shared with me his wisdom and advice, suggested relevant readings, and sponsored my attendance at professional development activities. After about three years, I realized that I was ready for a position that offered more variety and challenge. Sometimes, you must be careful what you wish for, since shortly thereafter, the VPSA asked me to assume an interim position as Executive Director for Multicultural Student Affairs. Several colleagues and students questioned his decision since they were unclear how I could effectively transition from an associate director role in career services to an executive director role in multicultural affairs. This new position presented its challenges, but I appreciated that it offered the variety and challenge that I was seeking and allowed me to use *all* of the skills I gained from previous roles—the focus on building relationships and supporting students of color that I learned as a graduate counselor; the community building, programming, and conflict management that I was taught in residential life; the active listening and problem-solving I was trained in at the counseling centers; the change management and action planning strategies developed in consulting; and how to support students given the intersections of their personal interests, academic pursuits, and professional aspirations that I gleaned from my time in career services. The multicultural affairs role pulled all the pieces together and ultimately set me on the career path to CDO.

After spending almost five years in the multicultural affairs position, I accepted a position as Director of Faculty Diversity Initiatives at another highly selective private institution. This position was instrumental in helping me understand the systemic inequities relative to faculty of color. Most of my higher education positions were in student affairs, so working in academic affairs in the Office of the Provost was enlightening. Analyzing the quantitative/qualitative data in concert with directly hearing individual narratives about their experiences, proved invaluable for my career. This position equipped me with the integral knowledge and experience associated with the core academic affairs functions, which now coupled with my extensive experience in student affairs—prepared me for the ascension to my first CDO role.

The Struggle

As CDO, I have worked at three very different institutions—a mid-sized public university, a small private graduate degree-granting institution and a large community college. Irrespective of institutional type, I have found that the CDO role is among the most challenging positions within higher education.

Irrespective of institutional type, I have found that the CDO role is among the most challenging positions within higher education

Currently, we are in the midst of navigating a very tumultuous national landscape as we manage the elimination of diversity, equity, and inclusion (DEI) offices and positions, movements to ban Critical Race Theory, and the ramifications following the Supreme Court ruling against the use of race/ethnicity in college admissions. The aforementioned issues add another level of complexity to a profession that was already difficult. Additionally, the CDO position itself is largely undefined, with position descriptions spanning a full spectrum of expectations and responsibilities that may include functions traditionally associated with human resources, student affairs, and/or academic affairs. These roles also vary significantly depending on factors such as: historical context of inclusion/exclusion on the campus (Hurtado et al. 1999), the relationship between the institution and the surrounding community, campus size, geographical location, student and employee demographics, organizational reporting structure, allocation of resources, and support of the chief executive officer. Despite the differences that exist across institutions, my experience as a CDO has been relatively consistent. I attribute these consistencies to factors such as: each of my CDO positions reported directly to the president/chancellor; each institution had strong financial resources (although this did not necessarily translate to substantial DEI funding); all campuses were located in the Midwest; and the entire country is grappling with DEI so each institution represents a microcosm of our society at-large. Collectively, my experiences taught me priceless lessons as I navigated a variety of challenges as CDO.

Perhaps my most significant lesson learned as CDO is to "find the opportunity in the outrage," as Kyle from Chicago's WGCI radio station says! On a daily basis there are instances that I am literally saying to myself, "I can't believe …" or "Did they just say …" or "I know they did not have the audacity to …" or "Wait, they must not know who I *really* am because …" Fortunately, I have found that in most cases—there is, in fact, opportunity in the outrage.

I vividly recall a time when I reluctantly accepted an invitation from a faculty member to join her for lunch at her home. I had successfully coordinated with campus and city officials to resolve a complicated accommodations issue and she wanted to personally thank me. I raised an eyebrow since I typically do not visit colleagues' houses with whom I do not have a personal relationship and surely not for a one-on-one meeting (vs. a group gathering). However, I made the exception because I understood this was her effort to demonstrate appreciation. The lunch went fine until it was time for me to leave. Literally, as I walked to open the door, she stopped me dead in my tracks when she dropped a bomb, stating that "people" did not believe I *really* had a doctorate (which I had completed 14 years prior) and that "people" also believed I was only hired for this executive-level role because I was Black! Stunned in the moment, I found myself struggling not to bring out the fury that I felt within. This was a time when my training in psychology helped significantly, and I fell back on asking questions for clarification, like:

- Do "people" usually lie about their degrees here?
- Do "people" know that human resources verify credentials before employees start?
- Do "people" think that Black people aren't competent enough to hold executive-level positions?

In response, she essentially shrugged her shoulders as if she felt my questions were rhetorical, not warranting answers or perhaps she did not deem my questions worthy of answering. So, instead, she asked me questions related to where and when I obtained my doctorate. I was confused. Was she completely oblivious that her comments were racist and insulting? Was she trying to push me to my limit in hopes of confirming an "angry Black woman" stereotype? Was she attempting to catch me in lies associated with a delusion that I was misrepresenting my credentials? I could not discern her motives—but I thank God that, at that moment, a sudden calmness came over me. I answered her questions, asked her to share my information with the "people" who doubted my credentials, and I left her house. Later, when the announcement was released that I was leaving the institution, she sent an email saying how valuable I was and how much of a loss it was for the institution. She also invited me to a one-on-one farewell lunch. I did not reply.

As a result of this outrage, the opportunity before me was to deepen my collaborations for a more collective approach to improving campus climate. Since it is common for the CDO role to create a level of anxiety for fellow executive cabinet members because they are unsure of how this position will "interfere" with their areas, I typically start by focusing on my own portfolio and what is within my span of control. However, to truly impact the institutional culture requires having a deeper level of collaboration horizontally and vertically across the organization.

Systemic change is the most transformative—while also the most difficult to achieve. Accordingly, the biggest challenge that I face as CDO is addressing the systems that result in inequities. The expectation to be "all things to all people" is ever-present and unrealistic.

Accordingly, the biggest challenge that I face as CDO is addressing the systems that result in inequities. The expectation to be "all things to all people" is ever-present and unrealistic.

There is a huge spectrum of identities (e.g., ability, age, class, ethnicity, gender, national origin, race, religion, sexual orientation, etc.), a number of constituencies (e.g., students, faculty, staff, alumni, board members, employers, local residents, etc.), various initiatives (e.g., policies/procedures, trainings, programs, resources, etc.), different levels of impact (e.g., individual, group, system) and a plethora of DEI considerations. As CDO, every day I wear multiple hats as I navigate the complexity of higher education. My responsibilities include developing and executing a range of DEI initiatives; reviewing, creating, assessing and implementing policies; designing and delivering trainings on a host of topics; amplifying the voices of marginalized groups; advocating for essential services and resources; and collaborating across campus to integrate DEI into the fabric of the institution.

I consistently work to eliminate institutional barriers and create the conditions, policies, programs and systems that maximize opportunities for all community members to engage, excel and thrive. However, systems are inherently designed to maintain the status quo and those with the most power are often the most resistant to change. Farhang and Gould (2022) stated, "When we think about these systems, we see that those with the power to decide are often quite distant from those who experience the system's harms and burdens. Power—the ability to enact change in the system—is not justly shared. People who bear the brunt of broken, inequitable systems ... are the furthest from formal centers of power." Institutions have deeply ingrained traditions and established power structures that naturally resist efforts to overhaul systems, making it difficult to implement meaningful reforms. To that end, rarely have I had constructive conversations with colleagues that resulted in changing systems to become more just, without opposition.

I recall initiating a follow-up meeting with a fellow executive cabinet member to address student needs relative to food insecurity. The specific services being discussed fell within their portfolio and based on our initial discussion around this topic, I shared my perspective that they did not understand students with limited incomes. When I mentioned that sometimes students were waiting outside for our meetings to conclude so they could quickly consume the leftovers, my colleague responded by saying they had seen that before and minimized this as evidence of a problem. Given my direct reports and I had spoken personally with students experiencing food insecurity, I told my colleague that I felt their response was "cavalier" and did not demonstrate a sense of urgency regarding this matter. My colleague responded by saying that students waiting outside of our offices for food did not constitute valid data—but instead, when I cited statistics from an institutional survey we administered (which only 20% of our students completed), this source was deemed legitimate! I quickly responded by saying that there are some students who will never complete a survey—but may disclose personal details to us, and yes, we should also consider this data as legitimate. Only validating data reflected in formal surveys is such an elite approach that completely the other ways that students may articulate their lived experiences. In higher education, it is common to emphasize "data-driven decision-making,"—but we must not discount data received from direct conversations and observations. Such narrow thinking from those in positions of power, who as Farhang and Gould stated, "are often quite distant from those who experience the system's harm," is a disservice to our most vulnerable students. The steps necessary to modify the system/process to address the issues being discussed were relatively small on the scale of organizational change, so it should have been easy—although, unfortunately, it was not. While I willingly accept the responsibility for amplifying the voices of those who are most negatively impacted by institutional decisions—at times, the heavy lifting is exhausting.

Systemic change requires institutional leadership. While I have had a number of executive-level colleagues who were sincerely invested in supporting DEI change efforts, sadly, they often had a very limited understanding of DEI. This limited understanding is reflected in different ways, such as colleagues requesting DEI "checklists" or "toolboxes" that tend to result in performative acts as compared to the hard work that is required to achieve transformative change. Additionally, despite the importance of this work, DEI initiatives often compete with other institutional priorities. Surprisingly, it seems that my colleagues often believe that I can easily implement quick solutions to fix complex problems, with minimal financial and personnel resources to meet an unlimited list of needs and expectations. It is not enough for leadership to say that DEI is a priority—the operational and personnel resources must reflect this commitment. Without the appropriate financial support, the scope and effectiveness of DEI efforts are hindered.

Surprisingly, it seems that my colleagues often believe that I can easily implement quick solutions to fix complex problems, with minimal financial and personnel resources to meet an unlimited list of needs and expectations.

It is not enough for leadership to say that DEI is a priority—the operational and personnel resources must reflect this commitment. Without the appropriate financial support, the scope and effectiveness of DEI efforts are hindered.

Finally, when thinking about institutional effectiveness, measuring the success and impact of DEI initiatives poses a significant challenge. Traditional metrics such as recruitment numbers and demographic data may provide a partial picture of progress, but they do not capture the nuanced and qualitative aspects of inclusion and belonging. Climate surveys may provide the more qualitative aspects of the culture, but it is often difficult to assess which initiatives, strategies or programs contribute to the changes reflected in the data. As an example, cultural and educational programs such as those held during LGBTQ+ History Month afford us an opportunity to affirm and celebrate the diverse identities of our students, staff, and faculty. What is more difficult to gauge, though, is the extent to which this programming positively impacts the overall campus climate, the optimal number of programs to deliver, and the impact of such programs on those who are members of the community and those who do not share this identity. Additionally, progress is incremental and DEI initiatives take time to fully manifest. This creates an interesting quandary since everyone wants to see change happen quickly and institutional funding is often tied to the ability to produce results, but in this case—it is necessary to balance short-term expectations with the long-term realities of cultural change.

The Progress

I have been fortunate to play a critical role in leading impactful change efforts at the individual, departmental, and institutional levels. My experience working on various campuses in a range of departments has afforded me the ability to interpret situations from multiple vantage points and provide strategic leadership based on exposure to such different organizational and operational models. Success at each institution has looked very different, but across institutions, largely, I have been effective with establishing relationships, assessing institutional needs, and delivering results.

Among many things, Stephen Covey is known for his philosophy that "change moves at the speed of trust." In essence, he suggests that when trust is low, change takes longer, and that trust is key for high-performing organizations (Covey 2008). Although a simple concept, there is nothing truer—especially in the CDO role. Strong relationships facilitate institutional change at a much faster pace, period. I intentionally work to build relationships of substance, which I differentiate from transactional relationships. Relationships of substance are meaningful, based on an authentic connection and mutual respect, as compared to transactional relationships that are impersonal and typically limited to a particular scope or purpose. When relationships of substance are established, constituents share the real harm and pain they experience, what aids in their relief and recovery and what brings them joy. This allows me the ability to implement more impactful policies, programs, services, and resources. I consistently ask students, staff, and faculty for their feedback and ideas regarding ways to enhance their experiences and I retain an open-door policy. I also make every effort to remain easily accessible for students and colleagues to articulate their concerns directly to me.

I remember when a student worker in my department came to my office weeping because she was among the few selected to teach English as a second language abroad during the summer break, but she could not afford the airfare. In higher education, we often discuss eliminating barriers and ensuring that all students have equal opportunity and access. In this situation, the opportunity was granted but it was not accessible. This was a student of color from a single-parent, low-income household and even with her two part-time jobs, the expensive flight presented a huge barrier. She mentioned that she was referred to a few offices that were unable to assist her and she was devastated about the potential of missing out on what she described as a once-in-a-lifetime experience. She was inconsolable. Without hesitation, I contacted my counterpart in Foundations who secured funding for the student on the same day. In this situation, the relationship I established with the student led her to openly share her problem, while the relationship I established with my colleague allowed us to quickly resolve the issue. In the end, the student indicated that she had a phenomenal experience abroad. Although it is easy to consider this an isolated incident, as CDO, I work to always think systemically. In this example, because the student had access to me and I activated my network, this facilitated a speedy resolution. Recognizing the reality that other students may not have relationships with administrators in positions of power, the question becomes—how do we implement changes to the system/process such that access to those in positions of power is unnecessary? There are many options to answer this question, such as creating a special fund for the study abroad office to cover additional expenses for those demonstrating financial need. This is a small illustration of how we can implement systemic solutions for day-to-day problems to improve equity and eliminate barriers.

In my experience, the most marginalized desire a CDO who is a catalyst for change, while those with the most privilege are fearful of the change. The most marginalized regard me as successful to the extent they can see, feel, and experience change, while those with privilege regard me as successful to the degree they retain their comfort. I usually represent hope to the most marginalized, while I represent a threat to the most privileged. There is no word that truly captures the experience of managing this dichotomy—since arduous is an understatement. Despite this dichotomy, I focus on my staples of establishing strong relationships, conducting thorough assessments and implementing meaningful strategic initiatives, which are often successful.

At one institution, a committee created a DEI plan immediately prior to my arrival. I had never led the process of implementing a plan that I did not participate in designing, so this was a new experience. There were several items on the plan that I did not understand; some items that I understood, but I was unclear on what they were trying to achieve; and some items appeared more theoretical vs. practical. I appreciated the time and effort involved in developing the plan and I wanted to honor their hard work. Given this, I spent significant time with the authors to gain clarity and understand the spirit of each initiative. Those conversations were extremely helpful since my goal was not to performatively check items off a list to say they were completed. Instead, my goal was to implement a plan that achieved their anticipated outcomes and improved the campus climate. To achieve this goal, I had to understand the vision, the context that led to the items on the plan and the results they wanted to achieve. I also reviewed their recent climate survey results, relevant quantitative and qualitative institutional data and conducted an extensive listening tour that afforded me the opportunity to hear the voices of constituencies at all levels of the organization. With this information and insight, I made minor adjustments and proceeded to strategically execute the plan. Within my first year and a half, I successfully implemented over 70% of items as well as additional initiatives that I felt were important that were not included in the plan. My accomplishments included: adding DEI expectations into faculty and staff performance evaluations; implementing the requirement for all employees to complete a foundational online diversity training; creating a comprehensive DEI training program that granted certificates upon completion; launching a quarterly DEI newsletter; implementing numerous campus-wide educational and celebratory programs; creating unique banners that reflected a range of diverse identities to display on campus light poles; implementing awards to recognize students and employees for excellence in DEI; designing and opening a new identity space for students; hosting professional development programs for students and faculty of color; launching DEI alumni outreach initiatives; and increasing the racial diversity of employees within my area.

In this case, my approach involved respecting the expertise and wisdom of the various constituents, and in return, they were great collaborators who trusted me to execute the plan in a way that would yield their anticipated outcomes. It is powerful to experience the success that accompanies engaging constituents at all levels of the organization, integrating multiple sources of data to address climate concerns and the speed of change when there is trust.

In Closing ...

I did not know the journey I would embark upon would lead to the destination of CDO. While it has been a struggle to address systemic issues—the signs of progress inspire and propel me forward. Sometimes, I have found that the inspiration comes from the words that constituents have shared with me, such as an active member of the Black alumni association at a previous institution. Her comment was, "We were always confident that you would take care of our Black students and that we could trust you with making decisions in their best interest. We haven't felt that way since your departure." Her statement was particularly meaningful since that was the most challenging position of my career, and I am proud that my legacy includes centering the most marginalized. At that institution, data reflected that Black students had the lowest retention and completion rates and they also articulated witnessing/experiencing discrimination significantly more than their peers. Given this, it was essential to create a sense of belonging for Black students on that campus. I also understood that parents entrusted me with their children—a responsibility that is humbling and reminds me that my role is instrumental in creating safe learning environments that celebrate diversity and empower individuals to thrive.

My sister says, "you can't live by faith and by fear." I frequently tell others I am blessed that in doing this work, the Lord has not given me a spirit of fear. Despite the tribulations that I experience directly or vicariously that lend themselves to being fearful—it is a privilege to move fearlessly in service of justice. I have dedicated my life to this line of work because I believe in the importance of giving voice to the most marginalized; I believe in addressing institutional barriers that limit access and opportunity; and I believe in creating the conditions, policies, and systems that maximize possibilities for all individuals to excel. I have found that serving as a CDO is one of the most rewarding professions—particularly when I see the difference my work makes at the individual, group, and system levels. As we work to create more equitable and inclusive campus environments to yield successful outcomes across demographics, we must consistently evaluate and change the systems, policies, and practices that result in inequity.

As we work to create more equitable and inclusive campus environments to yield successful outcomes across demographics, we must consistently evaluate and change the systems, policies and practices that result in inequity.

I know that someone was around the table who proposed a President's Award scholarship that would literally change the trajectory of my life. Someone was around the table who had the courage to boldly suggest that a low-income student of color could successfully complete a college degree if the financial barriers were removed. Someone was around the table who resourced a program that connected me with a graduate student who looked like me to serve as a welcoming, knowledgeable, and caring resource who helped me navigate the complexities of college life. One of the reasons I so value my role as CDO, is because it affords me the opportunity to be that person around the table for others!

I am because we are—Ubuntu!

Key Insights from *The Journey, the Struggle, and the Progress*

- Funding, academic counseling, and proactive mentorship are critical elements for student success. For first-generation, low-resourced students, it is a necessity to aid in the transition to a higher education environment.
- Organizational development offers a unique vantage point to observe gaps and inconsistency in equity work at an institution.
- Horizontal and vertical collaboration across an organization is key in shifting campus culture and climate.
- Reluctance to reform organizational practices, structures, and policies in some institutional cultures stems from a reluctance to yield to the possibilities of a changed future and the responsibility of accountability.
- Traditional metrics may be ineffective in capturing the progress and success of high-impact belonging initiatives.

Things to Consider:

1 How did being an assistant hall director prepare Dr. Johnson for a chief diversity officer role?
2 What other academic positions and/or skill sets can one leverage to transition into a senior or chief equity role?
3 Johnson contends that CDO positions vary and are largely undefined as "position descriptions span [...] a full spectrum of expectations." What are some of the expectations she speaks of?
4 How important is the reporting structure in the success of the chief diversity officer role? Academic diversity officer role?
5 What can we glean from Johnson's discussion to "find the opportunity in the outrage," a common refrain from Chicago's WGCI radio station personality?
6 How does Johnson utilize silence as a navigation tool in a very painful and disparaging moment in her career?
7 How significant is data-driven decision-making in the purview of DEI leadership as one balances short- and long-term progress given the realities of campus culture change?
8 What is the tension Johnson notes between access and opportunity?

References

Covey, Stephen M.R. 2008. *The SPEED of Trust: The One Thing That Changes Everything*. Free Press.

Farhang, Lili, and Solange Gould. 2022. "Racial Justice and Power-Sharing: The Heart of Leading Systems Change." Medium. https://humanimpact-hip. medium.com/racial-justice-and-power-sharing-the-heart-of-leading-systems-change-45e4b53b9909.

Hurtado, Sylvia, Jeffrey Milem, Alma Clayton-Pedersen, and Walter Allen. 1999. *Enacting Diverse Learning Environments: Improving the Climate for Racial/ Ethnic Diversity in Higher Education.* ASHE-ERIC Higher Education Report. https://eric.ed.gov/?id=ED430514.

PART 2

Impact and Transformation

5

DIALOGUE AND "DEI"

Two Sides of the Same Coin of Justice

Ed Lee III

Chapter Contents

In 1998, the editors of *Contemporary Argumentation and Debate* invited me to write a piece discussing my experiences in the Atlanta Urban Debate League (AUDL), a partnership between Emory's Barkley Forum and the Atlanta Public Schools to expand debating opportunities in historically underserved communities (Lee 1998). The program's success in Atlanta would eventually galvanize a nationwide movement that produced similar leagues in New York City, Chicago, Dallas, San Francisco, Kansas City, and various other cities. That essay explored debate's ability to serve as a platform for the unheard and maligned to voice their interests and develop the skills to persuasively critique proposals that were inimical to their communal needs. The piece extolled debate's capacity to construct intellectually engaging spaces where students cultivated an interest in resolving our most intransigent social problems. I described my experiences in the AUDL as "my savior." While I would shy away from using such hyperbolic language today, the descriptor is not far off when I think about the lives and deaths of a few of my childhood friends. I opined that debate

DOI: 10.4324/9781032724881-7

"provided the opportunity to question the nefarious rites of passage (prison, drugs, and drinking) that seem to be uniquely debilitating to individuals in the poor urban communities" (Lee 1998, p. 95).

As I enter this conversation about the role of diversity officers in leading higher education's effort to be more just, equitable, diverse, and inclusive, I do so as a former debate coach who transitioned into a role focused on building inclusive communities in Emory University's largest college. My work at Emory College of Arts and Sciences (ECAS) is informed by the same desires that guided my musings in 1998. I seek to cultivate spaces where people can articulate their concerns and acquire redress. I am writing this piece at a time when many colleges and universities across the United States are struggling to find effective ways to respond to the trauma and social discontent unleashed on our campuses by the latest round of spectacular violence in the Israel–Palestine dispute. One cannot walk across Emory's campus without bumping into several sets of dueling chalked messages requesting the reader to bear witness to the drafter's unique pain and suffering. It is readily apparent that many of our students are riddled with fear, anxiety, and a desperate need to find an audience willing to listen to entertain their frustrations. Additionally, Emory has become a site for fervent student demonstrations targeting a new police training facility in Atlanta, Georgia. Some fear that it will further undermine the livelihood of our most vulnerable community members. "Stop Cop City" has become a mantra that encapsulates some of our students' deep apprehension about the unabated maldistribution of power and opportunities that inform policing, wealth allocation, and health outcomes for so many in the United States. These campus events and many others like them speak to an epoch in higher education when two of our most cherished and fundamental values, open expression and a commitment to create and sustain a sense of belonging, seem to be increasingly in conflict with one another.

These campus events and many others like them speak to an epoch in higher education when two of our most cherished and fundamental values, open expression and a commitment to create and sustain a sense of belonging, seem to be increasingly in conflict with one another.

While serving as an academic diversity officer in Emory's College of Arts and Sciences (ECAS), I still find myself traveling back and forth from the ECAS Dean's Office, where I support our DEI initiatives, to the student center that houses our debate and dialogue programs. I routinely travel from academic affairs to student affairs and back again. My work at Emory exists in a liminal space in other ways. It requires me to simultaneously shepherd and protect our institution's commitment to open debate and expression while crafting an enduring sense of belonging for my colleagues and the students I was entrusted with supporting.

My work at Emory exists in a liminal space in other ways. It requires me to simultaneously shepherd and protect our institution's commitment to open debate and expression while crafting an enduring sense of belonging for my colleagues and the students I was entrusted with supporting.

I see my work as that of a cultural translator bridging differing interpretations of the same moment and serving as trusted neutral working to illuminate opportunities for conflicted parties to find a common path forward. I am particularly interested in how efforts to cultivate more just and inclusive communities overlap with and are informed by the pursuit of effective interpersonal and organizational communication practices. Good communicators constantly assess the needs of their audience and adapt according. A keen awareness of the listener's unique needs, positionality, and perspectives is the hallmark of thoughtful and engaging communication. With that in mind, I sense the solution to many of our most explosive "diversity" challenges is more engaging and effective communication.

I hope my contribution to this conversation will do two things. First, I want to encourage other chief and academic diversity officers to serve as entrusted cultural translators willing to shuttle back and forth between unnerved and aggrieved communities as you lay the foundation for future encounters that feature empathetic listening and an exploration of common interests. Those are, indeed, critical components of a more durable sense of belonging. Second, I hope this piece moves us closer to achieving the just and responsive world that the much younger version of me wrote about in 1998 when I proposed, "Imagine graduating from high school each year millions of underprivileged teenagers with the ability to articulate their needs, the needs of others, and the ability to offer solutions. *I am convinced that someone would be forced to listen*" (p. 95, Italics added). I am increasingly convinced that one of the more critical roles of diversity officers is to listen. We are much closer to residing in the inclusive communities of our dreams when we are willing to serve as organizational language leaders actively modeling listening, grace, and discernment while creating the infrastructure for others to do so as well.

The rest of this paper unfolds in two parts. First, it explores my work as a communication scholar and practitioner increasingly focused on assisting local leaders as we develop communication norms and practices in their academic and cocurricular units that are fulcrums for creating convivial relationships and a sustained sense of belonging among racial and gender minorities. Second, the paper presents several conversation-based strategies I am using to help transform our academic departments into engaging and responsive environments built on mutuality and trust.

From Debate to DEI

In January 2021, I was invited to participate in a series of conversations with the Emory College of Arts and Sciences' department chairs. The agenda included exploring efforts to develop equitable and inclusive learning and teaching environments within their areas. This was part of a more significant effort to develop a culture of belonging and inclusion that improves the college's ability to retain women and racial minorities. During that time, I served as Emory's Senior Director of the Barkley Forum for Debate, Deliberation, and Dialogue. I was asked to join the meetings because of my experience as a conversation facilitator interested in the interplay between communication, culture, and diversity. At the time, my other projects included engaging the leadership of an academic department to improve the unit's understanding of how the dominant communication practices hindered the participation of women and racial minorities in reform efforts, hosting a monthly book salon, *Rapt By Others*, in Emory Campus Life that used memoirs to encourage engaged listening and a greater appreciation of cultural commonalities, and working with a mayor and city manager to create opportunities for their citizens to openly discuss the community's racist past and its impact on city's current demographic trends and politics.

My conversations with the ECAS department chairs revealed that, on balance, they desired to steward the development of more "equitable" and "inclusive" work environments even when they were unsure what that looked like or the role the chair should or could play in its development. For many, the fear of saying or doing something that could be interpreted as "superficial" or "window-dressing" was as strong as their desire to lead more diverse, equitable, and inclusive departments.

The following year presented several opportunities to continue those conversations in more focused ways. Working closely with a senior associate dean, I was encouraged to see my evolving role as that of an ethnographer noticing and documenting how faculty members were deferentially impacted by departmental norms, practices, and procedures. I also saw my role as something akin to Tett's (2015) cultural translator who works to bridge siloed organizational structures. Tett argued that a cultural translator serves as a trusted interlocutor who moves between organizational siloes and "explain[s] to those sitting inside one [part of the] department what is happening elsewhere" (p. 248). They are diplomats who operate with mutual respect for all participants while listening and, when called on, conveying their concerns in a forthright and honest manner.

Most importantly, creating hospitable encounters that preserved the dignity of disengaged and dejected community members was at the heart of my work of a cultural translator. A significant amount of my earlier work involved encouraging conversation partners to lean into their vulnerabilities as they explored their differences. That work made me sensitive to how low-level disputes can quickly escalate into recriminations, zero-sum power politics, and nonnegotiable demands for punitive actions when one's dignity has been sacrificed. My work then and now seeks to craft situations where silences and indignities are replaced with dialogue, mutuality, and affirmations.

My work then and now seeks to craft situations where silences and indignities are replaced with dialogue, mutuality, and affirmations.

I share Anderson's (2022) concern that the lack of earnest dialogue that preserves other's dignity can pave the way for the disputants "view[ing] one another as enemies who need to be silenced and defeated once and for all" (p. 69). Additionally, she lamented that when our relationships become dismissive and antagonistic "cooperation and consultation in defining the problems we face together, and in shaping policy solutions that take everyone's interests into account, is impossible" (p. 69).

At their best, my efforts opened the way for encounters that honored the needs and perspectives of the various parties, unlocked needling conversations, and served as a launching pad for deeper engagement throughout a department. Occasionally, my presence was interpreted as purely symbolic and part of an ongoing effort to obfuscate instead of addressing the "real issues" related to race and gender disparities. The odds of the former occurring seemed greater when our intervention strategies 1) focused on repairing proximate relationships, 2) crafted moments when department leaders spoke out in support of the organizational values, and 3) leveraged commonalities to defuse disagreements.

Mind the Microclimates

How we experience and remember our time learning, teaching, and working, whether we perceive it as thriving or languishing, is heavily informed by our consistent and ongoing interactions, or lack thereof, with a relatively small number of proximate students, faculty, and staff members who share a common goal to create, teach, and apply a specific body of knowledge. Those local relationships within each department will determine whether most endeavors succeed or fail. It is within those smaller units that are nestled within a larger college or university, the microclimates, that are most pertinent when discussing strategies for developing and sustaining inclusive intellectual communities and instilling a sense of belonging. In

Belonging: The Science of Creating Connection and Bridging Divides, Cohen (2022) concluded that we must remain mindful that "slight adjustments in the way we interact with people in our daily lives can do much to nurture belonging" (p. xiii). Conversely, slight adjustments in the opposite direction can usher in a regime of exclusion. Additionally, Byrd (2021) advocated focusing on the daily proximate relationships and local practices of exclusion to guard against an overall increase in campus diversity obscuring our view of local practices of exclusion and "pockets of underrepresentation and marginalization" (p. 134).

Ackelsberg et al.'s (2008) study of faculty experiences at Smith College refers to a microclimate as a small, relatively self-contained environment within which a faculty operates" (p. 84). They found that a faculty member's experience within their department, committee, or reading group heavily informed whether they believed the larger institution was welcoming, supportive, and committed to stated diversity goals. While acknowledging the limits of their focus on one small northeastern liberal arts college, they concluded that "daily behaviors at the level of the department can effectively undercut virtually any College-wide initiative" (p. 84). Mueller and Lawler's (1999) work on nested organizational structures supports the Smith College findings. They concluded that a person's most proximate unit within the larger organization, academic departments in our case, is likely to receive credit and blame when they evaluate their emotional relationship with the larger institution. Students, faculty, and staff members live in and are marked by their experiences within their local academic units. Our commitment to fostering a sense of belonging should focus on the daily interactions within these local units.

My personal experiences working with numerous faculty members in Emory's College of Arts and Sciences are consistent with what Ackelsberg et al. heard at Smith. Departmental interactions, relationships, and policies are a significant driver of faculty satisfaction, engagement, and retention. The inactions, and the occasional overt hostility, by a department leader were identified as reasons to dismiss efforts by Emory's Chief Diversity Officer and the Office of the President to ensure that the university is diverse, just, and inclusive. I feel the need to repeat that we rarely discussed aggressive or hostile behavior by a departmental leader. Our discussions were predominantly about frustrations with departmental thought leaders who were seen as well-meaning overall but unable to negotiate the identity issues cropping up in their department without minimizing, invalidating, and, at times, gaslighting their most impacted colleagues.

My work with each academic unit seeks to close the gap between the needs of the concerned faculty member and the response of departmental leaders. That includes occasionally needing to translate and recontextualize a colleague's concerns in a way that allows the organizational lead to better understand how historical and cultural experiences could be the source of the disconnection and discontent that the group is experiencing. My attempts to wade into our microclimates have led me to projects that required I separately interview community members at a time when they struggled to hold a faculty meeting without tensions flaring. That process allowed me to identify trends and commonalities that the group could not unearth without outside intervention. I have found that an inquisitive, trusted outsider is often better positioned to help the community appreciate how cultural slights can transform a localized disagreement into a spectacular and destabilizing moment of communal discontent.

I have found that an inquisitive, trusted outsider is often better positioned to help the community appreciate how cultural slights can transform a localized disagreement into a spectacular and destabilizing moment of communal discontent.

Efforts to sustain highly participatory and inclusive intellectual communities are easily undermined when community disagreements are unmoored from trusting relationships and shared spaces where dignity is protected while disparate needs are entertained.

My work in ECAS is increasingly focused on creating negotiated and tailored interventions that can transform our microclimates into sites of belonging. I hope more diversity officers start to focus on the quotidian, those nondescript everyday encounters or lack thereof, as they explore strategies for enhancing belonging and inclusion. It is in departmental meetings, seminars, and classrooms where the silences and joking slights first signal that the most marginalized members of our communities are, indeed, alone.

If You Hear Something, Say Something

Our history of discrimination and the maldistribution of educational opportunities, housing, and job training resources continues to reproduce a significant number of academic departments that are majority white and male. This is particularly the case when we consider those populating the leadership ranks of those units. These environments can be quite psychologically taxing for racial and gender minorities who perceive that their colleagues lack awareness of and/or are unwilling to respond to cultural slights, invalidations, and indignities that some must negotiate daily. A collective silence in response to statements, policies, and organizational norms that minimize or delegitimize the work or status of the few women or people of color in the department confirms their invisibility and relegates them to the status of "second-class citizens" (Sue 2016, p. 7). Sue's research on microaggressions powerfully described the anxiety and emotional exhaustion those silences impose on racial and gender minorities when they are the only people who seem to recognize their dehumanizing mistreatment:

> [M]any describe an emotional exhaustion of having to constantly deal with a never-ending onslaught of microaggressions and being placed in a no-win, damned-if-you-do-and-damned-if-you-don't situation. If a person chooses to confront the microaggression, energy must be expended in defending oneself, oftentimes with negative consequences. If a person chooses not to confront the situation, he or she must endure the affront in silence, often berating oneself for not having the courage to act on his or her convictions. (Sue 2016, p. 127)

Silence is disastrous for those most immediately harmed and for unit cohesion. Silence creates an increasingly toxic environment where race and/or gender becomes more salient for those who sense that their ability to thrive is undermined because of their cultural differences while others remain oblivious to the need to engage. While discussing avoidant behavior in the context of race talks, Sue argued that responding to a colleague or student's racial anguish with organizational silence is "offensive" and will be interpreted as an additional "microaggression that negates their racial identities and assails their integrities" (Sue 2016, p. 122). I understand that conversations about and across our cultural differences are uncomfortable and, potentially, threatening. However, avoidance will not resolve the issue. In fact, the longer the issue goes unaddressed, the more likely the delay will signal that animus toward those who dare to question established gender and racial hierarchies is the modus operandi of the department. Avoidance should be seen as an accelerant, not an answer.

We need more diversity officers who can mentor departmental leaders and equip them with the willingness and capability to quickly assess and acknowledge the concerns of aggrieved community members. This might require supporting the unit leader by giving them language and confidence to privately speak with concerned parties and publicly rearticulate the organization's values. It is imperative that we help our colleagues see this as an opportunity to reinforce their organization's commitment to cultivating a highly participatory, inclusive, collaborative learning environment when some perceive that it is falling short. This gesture, coupled with direct communication with the most impacted parties, can help prevent escalation.

While efforts by a diversity officer to break the organizational silence is less effective than a gesture of support from a more proximate colleague, we must be willing to serve as an imperfect substitute if a local leader is unprepared to respond to a colleague in duress. This is best done by listening to the aggrieved party, identifying their desired changes, and communicating those goals and the community's established commitments related to creating a more just, equitable, diverse, and inclusive work environment to the unit leader. This can and should be done in the context of reminding them that you are also available to support them in their development as an inclusive leader.

Second, we should take care to engage in a manner that steers the conversation away from obfuscating language and moral frames that may undermine the collective's understanding of the specific concerns at hand. This is not about tone policing or attempting to manage how the aggrieved chooses to process emotionally disturbing events. However, if our objective is to serve as a cultural translator and change behaviors or create the conditions for collaborative solutions, we must reconsider using inflammatory terms and phrases that are likely to be interpreted as insults as a substitute for exploring the specific policies or statements that are objectionable (Anderson 2022). While a proper understanding of the issues requires a conversation with the impacted parties, we should not expect them to translate their concerns into language that is understood by others. That is the work we should do as diversity officers.

One of the principal benefits of an approach that encourages precise identification of the conduct or procedure that the group needs to address is that it allows the community to more easily differentiate between malicious or "deliberate attempts to do harm" and suffering that derives from the "unjust consequences of decisions made long ago" (Anderson 2022, p. 83). Both require the community's attention and redress. However, the appropriate remedies are quite different. The former is worthy of condemnation. The latter is best addressed through education.

While some organizational changes are best pursued through a bottom-up strategy, diversity officers have a unique agenda-setting power when it comes to reforming communication norms and practices.

While some organizational changes are best pursued through a bottom-up strategy, diversity officers have a unique agenda-setting power when it comes to reforming communication norms and practices.

In *How We Talk Can Change the Way We Work*, Kegan and Lahey (2001) posited that all leaders are language leaders who "have exponentially greater access and opportunity to shape, alter, or ratify the existing language rules" (loc. 118). They conclude that the forms of engagement that a leader chooses to model and permit will "regulate the forms of thinking, feeling, and meaning-making to which we have access, which in turn constrain how we see the world and act in it" (loc. 177) As language leaders, diversity officers can inform the frame used to interpret events, use their platform to elevate a particular set of values, and provide space for aggrieved parties to articulate their concerns and identify strategies for redress.

As language leaders, diversity officers can inform the frame used to interpret events, use their platform to elevate a particular set of values, and provide space for aggrieved parties to articulate their concerns and identify strategies for redress.

More importantly, diversity officers are situated organizationally to challenge established language rules that undermine a sense of belonging. Statements and interventions by diversity officers that speak to the organization's values and their commitment to serve as an entrusted cultural translator can play a significant role in determining if others in the community opt for silence or restorative dialogue.

Bridging the "Us vs. Them" Divide

It is difficult for me to write about bridging the "us vs. them" divide without discussing my ongoing work with Emory's Barkley Forum for Debate, Deliberation, and Dialogue. Emory's support of debate began with the founding of the Phi Gamma Literary Society in 1837. Modeled after the British literary societies, Phi Gamma organized weekly debates encouraging students to deliberate salient and controversial issues. The Barkley Forum sustains this tradition by using debate, deliberation, and dialogue as instructional methods to preserve the established culture of debate, create structures needed for engaged conversations, and cultivate spaces for constructive exploration about and across our differences. Driven by a mission to create meaningful encounters that encourage students to seek and share knowledge, the Barkley Forum supports an intercollegiate debate program, the Atlanta Urban Debate League that you read about earlier, and The Emory Conversation Project.

During tumultuous moments on our campus when the need to bridge differences is most apparent, the Barkley Forum receives numerous requests to host public debates that can model appropriate and effective speech. While I agree that these tense moments require us to pause, listen, and reflect, my work creating and supporting the Emory Conversation Project, a program that works to shift the term of engagement by crafting situations where students are encouraged to find common ground while honoring their differences, points to a superior approach for bridging our cultural divides when emotions are high and we perceive our identities and personhood to be under attack. This is when we are likely to think that our personal needs are in direct competition with the desires of others and begin to embrace a zero-sum frame for viewing campus and world events.

My work creating structured and facilitated dialogues with the Emory Conversation Project serves as a template for several strategies I have used to bridge ideological and organizational divides found within some of our academic units. This bridge-building can be seen in my work as a hiring committee observer for faculty searches. In that role, I provide committee members with resources on implicit bias, attend candidate deliberations, and offer ongoing support to the committee chair as they develop meeting practices and processes that are fair for the candidates, feature open and inclusive discussions, and account for the institution's broader diversity goals. Additionally, I routinely serve as a communication and culture consultant for department chairs needing a thought partner as they negotiate interpersonal and organizational disputes. My engagement with department chairs tends to focus on identifying opportunities for strengthening connections by creating shared goals and developing strategies that allow them to be more effective language leaders. Finally, my work tends to feature discussions of common reads to establish a shared reference point and language. Whether it is a memoir-focused book salon in Campus Life or an ECAS reading group created to support staff members working to improve their "DEI" and "Communication" competencies, the goal is to craft situations where the participants will share their unique perspectives while remaining mindful of potential synergies and commonalities. Inspired by the numerous transformations I witnessed working with the Emory Conversation Project, my primary objective in ECAS is to craft moments that make it a little easier for people to rethink, reframe, and move forward together.

This strategy is supported by Cohen's research on belonging (2022). Cohen described "situation-crafting" as the intentional effort to "alter a situation, or people's perceptions of it, in ways that relieve tensions and make them feel appreciated and included" (p. 3). He advocates shifting our focus to crafting situations that encourage us to rethink our relationships and values because we rarely can will ourselves or others to change without a subtle but impactful nudge. Situation-crafting can serve as that nudge. Cohen argued that a willingness to connect with others and challenge our assumptions tends to follow those situations that present opportunities for us to navigate new lived experiences and entertain the problem from a different reference point. When we construct a tailored and timely intervention that prioritizes a shared goal, Cohen found that we are better positioned to initiate a "virtuous cycle" of belonging that mitigates the damage done by other threats to our identity and personhood (p. 47). He continued:

> [I]n an environment with genuine opportunity, they tend to have cumulative effects because they help people to see the situations they encounter as offering them more opportunity to exercise their talents, to build positive relationships, and to receive support and respect than they had expected before. These interventions can set in motion a virtuous cycle of positive reinforcement, helping people to progressively strengthen and protect their sense of belonging long after the intervention has ended. (p. 47)

Establishing positive relationships and a genuine commitment to a common goal produces a degree of mutuality that makes it easier to bridge "us vs. them" divides. Programmatic interventions and campaigns to improve our work and learning spaces are far more likely to succeed when they are built on a foundation of trusting and convivial relationships.

Appealing to broader goals can be a powerful check on politically and ideologically motivated reasoning. Extended engagement by people with diverse experiences and perspectives to achieve a shared goal can help to establish the framework and trust needed for them to negotiate more charged and sensitive issues. Ben-Porath (2023) argued that the existence of "a shared endeavor can help mend epistemic and perceptual fractures, in that it is built on trust and helps broadcast this trust through its network of participants" (p. 50). While writing specifically about the potential higher education scholars and practitioners to leverage their shared interest in teaching and learning, she forwarded that an effective strategy that reinforces dialogic habits while maintaining an inclusive community "requires sustained attention and a genuine commitment to a shared society, an assumption of general goodwill on all parts, and an ongoing dialogue" (p. 157).

Conclusion

Some people are surprised when I talk about my journey from being an active debate coach of a nationally competitive program to serving as the DEI lead in Emory's largest college. I see a connection between the two that is not always readily apparent to others. My success in creating more inclusive communities in ECAS is built on a foundation of debate, deliberation, and dialogue. My enduring commitment to supporting Emory as a cultural translator finds its roots in my training as a switch-side debater and dialogue facilitator. The telos of both is a more just world order. I will conclude this piece on diversity officers in the same way I ended the piece I wrote 25 years ago discussing debate. I wrote:

> Debate allows students to take control of their own educational destiny and make it a site of resistance. It allows those saddled with the baggage of poverty, racism, and sexism to construct their personal strategy for liberation. The Urban Debate League provides a space for us to learn what justice is because it forces us to learn from those disproportionately affected by injustice. (Lee 1998, p. 96)

I hope that my work as an academic diversity officer provides Emory with what the AUDL provided me. I want my work to be a site of resistance where we come together to achieve our shared goal to collectively learn about justice and bring it to fruition.

Key Insights from *Dialogue and "DEI": Two Sides of the Same Coin of Justice*

- Our current moment in Higher Education finds campus communities wrestling with the tension between our most cherished and fundamental values of belonging and open expression.
- Chief Diversity Officers should serve as cultural translators to bridge the divide in conflicted conversations to move towards a common ground resolution that supports institutional and communal values.
- To get to a more just and inclusive educational community requires difficult conversations.
- DEI practitioners are conversation partners in the work of creating opportunities for honest dialogue that encourages others to lean into their vulnerabilities to move from differences to shared humanity.
- Microclimates can build or disrupt a sense of belonging in localized intellectual communities embedded in academic departments, units, and/or disciplinary schools.

Things to Consider

1 How does Lee leverage the platform of debate to persuasively connect to the purposed role of academic diversity officers?
2 What are the critical components of a more durable sense of belonging Lee speaks of in his essay?
3 What issues does Lee name in his essay that US colleges and universities find themselves struggling with in our current moment?
4 What does Lee mean when he speaks of "organizational language leaders?" What are the benefits of such practices?
5 What has Lee learned about the escalation of low-level disputes and its effect on impacted parties? How do DEI professionals help to facilitate resolutions that serve the community and can lead to restorative practices in academic departments and units?
6 What is the unfortunate by-product of interventions viewed as purely symbolic in contested departmental disengagement?
7 Why does Lee ask us to "mind the microclimates" as we consider the work of inclusion and equity?

References

Ackelsberg, Martha, Jeni Hart, Naomi J. Miller, Kate Queeney, and Susan Van Dyne. 2008. "4. Faculty Microclimate Change at Smith College." In *Doing Diversity in Higher Education*, edited by R. Brown-Glaude Winnifred, 83–102. Ithaca, NY: Rutgers University Press.

Anderson, Elizabeth S. 2022. "Can We Talk?: Communicating Moral Concern in an Era of Polarized Politics." *Journal of Practical Ethics* 10 (1). 10.3998/jpe.1180.

Ben-Porath, Sigal R. 2023. *Cancel Wars: How Universities Can Foster Free Speech, Promote Inclusion, and Renew Democracy.* 1st ed.: University of Chicago Press.

Byrd, W. Carson. 2021. *Behind the Diversity Numbers: Achieving Racial Equity on Campus.* Harvard Education Press.

Cohen, Geoffrey. 2022. *Belonging: The Science of Creating Connection and Bridging Divides.* W. W. Norton & Company.

Kegan, R., and Lahey, L. 2001. *How We Talk Can Change the Way We Work.* Jossey-Bass.

Lee, Edward. 1998. "Memoir of a Former Urban Debate League Participant." *Contemporary Argumentation & Debate* 19: 93–96.

Mueller, Charles W., and Edward J. Lawler. 1999. "Commitment to Nested Organizational Units: Some Basic Principles and Preliminary Findings." *Social Psychology Quarterly* 62 (4): 325–346. 10.2307/2695832.

Sue, Derald Wing. 2016. *Race Talk and the Conspiracy of Silence: Understanding and Facilitating Difficult Dialogues on Race.* edited by 1st: Wiley.

Tett, Gillian. 2015. *The Silo Effect: The Peril of Expertise and the Promise of Breaking Down Barriers.* Simon & Schuster, Inc.

6

A FRAMEWORK FOR THE SUSTAINABILITY OF WOC DEIA+ PRACTITIONERS

A Queen's Collective

Alexis J. Stokes, Sherri H. Benn, Luz Janet Mejias, Angela Spranger, Caryn Reed-Hendon, J. Camille Hall, Ria DasGupta, and R. Adidi Etim-Hunting

Chapter Contents

Introduction

Melissa Harris-Perry applied the theory of the "Crooked Room" experiment to the meta struggles of being Black and a woman. Harris-Perry's findings are a powerful allegory that reveals the impact of one's

DOI: 10.4324/9781032724881-8

environment on one's orientation to "reality." In the study, participants were placed in a crooked chair, in a crooked room and told to align themselves upright. A significant number of the participants regarded themselves as straight but only relative to their surroundings; however, not everyone did this. Some participants managed to get themselves more or less upright regardless of how crooked their surroundings were. This may seem perplexing but, this is not illogical when one considers the powerfully ubiquitous nature of White-man hegemony. The participants who tilted themselves, even as much as 30 degrees, were simply aligning themselves with an environment, which was equally as tilted.

Harris-Perry's examination of the intersectionality of race, gender, and gender roles under the auspices of hegemony and the use of the Black female experiences as an analytic category, challenges the research lenses that construe reality through White male identity (Harris-Perry 2011). Although the participants in the study cited by Harris-Perry were not Black women, the experiment's grand metaphor showcases the experiences of Black women and, we suggest, women of color equity practitioners writ large. In this chapter we explore those experiences – our experiences – of women of color (WOC) occupying diversity, equity, inclusion, and accessibility (DEIA+) practitioner roles in higher education and how a mentoring network we call the Queen's Collective (QC) aids in our ability to thrive in our own versions of this crooked room. The goal of this chapter is not to solely highlight the challenges but to shed light on how we have developed a mentoring structure that serves our professional and personal needs as WOC DEIA+ practitioners and hopefully can serve as a model for those who come after us.

In March 2021, several hundred people gathered in virtual spaces for the national conference, "Dismantling Structural Racism: Transforming Higher Education," sponsored by the National Association of Diversity Officers in Higher Education (NADOHE). Eight women of color in attendance, though separated by material reality, found themselves connected, drawn together by a simultaneous cathartic epiphany. The catalyst of their mutual intrigue was reciprocated interest in the minimal attention given to the experiences, scholarship, and perspectives of women DEIA+ practitioners.

Patricia Hill Collins states, "Anti-racist politics that do not make gender central are doomed to fail because someone will always be left behind. If either women or men remain subordinated, then social injustice persists" (Collins 2004, pp. 6–7). With this notion top of mind, "The Queen's Collective." We intentionally chose this nomenclature to celebrate both the power and dignity of women of color in DEIA+ work and the power of community. Queen (kwēn) is a noun defined as "Something personified as a woman, that is foremost or preeminent in any respect" (Word Reference, n.d.). Collective (kə'lektiv) is an adjective denoting "a number of persons or things considered as one group or whole". As a noun, it is defined as "a collective body; a cooperative unit or organization" (Merriam-webster, n.d.).

Drawing on "the Crooked Room" concept, Harris-Perry posits that Black [wo]men exist in a sort of vacuum and until enlightened to the pretense of their environments, may be encouraged to mentally assimilate with and into whatever their surroundings may be (Harris-Perry 2011). Hegemony makes this true for almost all of us, even without our awareness. Deborah Waire Post (1990) states that in her very first year of law school, she learned how easy it is for women to adopt the attitudes of men, while also unearthing a surprising discovery. The "crooked" reality makes room for members of the affected group, in this case, women, to strengthen or create a space where that sense of community can be built on their shared experiences. This is what the Queen's Collective has cultivated, a shared community where DEIA+ professional women of color can be their whole selves and define their experiences and voices juxtapose highly politicized micro and macro cultural environments. Ergo, "the most important and valuable contribution of counter-hegemonies is the solutions they offer" (Post 1990, p.155).

For the Collective, the solution is a community that addresses the unique experiences of WOC DEIA+ practitioners and invests in career mobility, sustainability, as well as our overall well-being.

For the Collective, the solution is a community that addresses the unique experiences of WOC DEIA+ practitioners and invests in career mobility, sustainability, as well as our overall well-being

---

And like Harris-Perry's *Sister Citizen* project, we aim to disrupt the hegemonic scope of knowledge production to account for the compounded complexities of gender intersecting race in the work of justice. It is essential for our stories as women of color in the DEIA+ space to be told.

Women of Color

When we say Women of Color, who do we mean? We celebrate that we are a collective of WOC DEIA+ practitioners. We recognize that race and gender are interconnected and cannot be separated as discrete aspects of self (Collins 2004). This is especially true for us in the DEIA+ field. Our race and gender influence our lived experiences including how each of us approach our DEIA+ work and how we have encountered resistance or obstacles in this space. Thus, having a space that centers our experiences as WOC has proved to be crucial to our development and overall well-being. It has helped us to make sense of experiences we have had throughout our careers.

We have each had varying experiences when joining spaces designed for WOC. At times these spaces did not account for the varied perspectives in the room and individuals had not done the work to understand how their social identity can impact their understanding of power and privilege. Edwards and McKinney posit that Black women's lived experiences are distinctively different and are not interchangeable. They go on to say that the term "WOC" negates racial identity in the service of racial unity (Edwards and McKinney 2020). However, we believe racially diverse women can harness their collective and inclusive power to break down barriers and bridge intractable divides. We choose to use the term WOC because the beauty of the Queen's Collective is we have each engaged in the introspection needed to give space to all our experiences while also not co-opting discussions that focus on the unique lived experiences of the different racial groups amongst us. According to Loretta Ross (2011), the term was coined in 1977 at the National Women's Conference when other minority women joined a group of Black women in support of their "Black Women's Agenda." It was "a solidarity definition, a commitment to work in collaboration with other oppressed women of color who have been minoritized" (Ross 2011, 1:31). The Queen's Collective strives to build upon this work.

Challenges

We would be remiss to not share some of the challenges we have experienced throughout our careers. From a lack of mentors who share our identities and chosen field to not seeing ourselves reflected in the ever-growing scholarship on the field of DEIA+, challenges are omnipresent in our work, and are often the generative source of our camaraderie.

Isolation of the Work

We have been cautioned that if we want our career to grow, we should brace ourselves for it to be lonely "at the top." Although there is a sense of weight and isolation that comes with most leadership roles due to the responsibility, confidentiality, transparency, and direction needed to lead a cohesive organization, never has this statement been more impactful than in the work of Equity and Inclusion.

The caveat we must understand is that the experience of isolation in DEIA+ work is not unique to leadership, as it can occur in different functions and at different levels of hierarchy. However, women, particularly women of color, face a dual challenge in the workforce, as they experience not only isolation but also the added burden of limited representation in leadership positions.

The complexity of our roles is often missed by those who are not familiar with the everyday nuances that impact what we do, and the issues that can create conflict in matters of a highly sensitive nature. As a DEIA+ professional, one must build trust, credibility, and reliability, while also holding empathy, discretion, and safety. We must speak the truth in a way that listeners will receive it, understand policy and its stretch (or lack thereof), speak encouragement and life into the discouraged and sometimes defeated, and also mediate change and agreement within groups that can hold extremely different views.

We must speak the truth in a way that listeners will receive it, understand policy and its stretch (or lack thereof), speak encouragement and life into the discouraged and sometimes defeated, and also mediate change and agreement within groups that can hold extremely different views.

We sometimes find ourselves stuck between protecting an organization while also advocating for its members.

> *We sometimes find ourselves stuck between protecting an organization while also advocating for its members.*

Our roles require us to build meaningful partnerships, and to do it all in a positive, supportive stance while wearing a cloak of sometimes isolating confidentiality.

We each learned quickly that the "entry point" through which we approach the work determines the spaces and networks to which we have access, and the critical nature of any resource gaps (Spranger 2022). Operating through rugged terrains of resistance, lack of collegiality, uneven support, trust, and potential hostility arising from vocal opponents, DEIA+ professionals can quickly develop a sense of defeat and futility in pursuing our initiatives (Coopwood and Lewis 2017; DasGupta 2019; Pemberton and Kisamore 2023). Coopwood and Lewis (2017) found that workplace pressures and circumstances silence DEIA+ professionals from sharing their experience, which can deepen the feeling of solitude.

This isolation is not gender specific, as some may be inclined to believe, but it can be amplified for WOC as we are often the only individuals at the leadership table with our identities. The common obstacles women in leadership experience such as a lack of acknowledgement of our contributions, being interrupted in meetings, and the policing of our clothes, speech, and behaviors is not absent from our experiences. These experiences can begin to erode an individual's well-being as we often operate in isolation without a network for support, chipping away at our emotional wellness and long-term viability in the field.

Impact on Overall Well-being

While our experiences, professional titles, levels of authority, power, and institutional affiliations may vary greatly, a common thread amongst us all is the profound impact these roles have on our physical and mental well-being. As DEIA+ professionals our primary aim is to cultivate an environment that is welcoming and inclusive for the communities we support. These roles necessitate a relentless focus on people, as we navigate advocacy within a system that was established without due consideration, and at times, with intentional exclusion of the very populations we are dedicated to support. In addition, our efforts to challenge the status quo can disrupt established norms leading to friction with certain stakeholders who may be committed to DEIA+ in words but resistant to the change. This unrelenting state of affairs leaves many with a prevailing sense of stress and anxiety, adversely affecting mental and physical well-being.

Amidst our dedication to supporting others, we frequently overlook the importance of reflecting upon our own well-being and mental health. This phenomenon is frequently observed in professions that place a strong emphasis on supporting others, as compassion fatigue can gradually emerge, resulting in burnout, heightened stress levels, and physical and cognitive exhaustion. Moreover, alongside those who may not endorse the work, there is the paradoxical possibility that the very individuals we work to support, can become adversarial towards the profession if we are perceived as symbolic, "window dressing," and "fixers" for the institution (Johnson 1974; Ashcraft and Allen 2020; England and Purcell 2020) or " … another 'Band-Aid' tactic to appease critics and onlookers" (Wilson 2013).

Many DEIA+ roles were created without sufficient consideration for long-term professional sustainability, and often developed with unrealistic expectations and responsibilities (Brown 2017). Consistently engaging in reactive measures, university controversies, political and legal constraints, and the evolving needs of the community we serve, we often find it infeasible to take extended breaks from work. Consequently, it is not surprising that the average tenure in a position is 3–5 years (Coopwood and Lewis 2017). More recent data indicates that the average tenure of DEIA+ professionals continue to compress.

Excluded from the Scholarship

As the landscape for DEIA+ in higher education expands, a growing body of literature addresses the experiences of the administrators who lead the work (Arnold and Kowalski-Braun 2012; Stanley 2014; Stanley et al. 2019; Wilson 2013). Yet, within this research, the opportunity is lost to examine the experiences of WOC who likely make up the majority of DEIA+ practitioners in colleges and universities. The only existing demographic study to date cites that, in the United States, higher education chief diversity officers (CDOs), or executive-level administrative DEIA+ professionals, are 87% people of color and 58% women (Williams and Wade-Golden 2013). Barring select research efforts, the unique challenges these practitioners face, and subsequent efforts to address them, seldom appear as topics in the scholarly realm (DasGupta 2019; Marana 2016; M. L. Nixon 2013; Monica L. Nixon 2017).

This dearth of scholarly attention to understanding the contributions of WOC DEIA+ professionals is similarly reflected in the academic conference arena, even where discussion of the DEIA+ profession is the objective. For example, in 2022 and 2023, since the formation of the Queen's Collective, only four of the concurrent sessions at the NADOHE annual conference have addressed the experiences of WOC. Our experiences are captured in length on social media, in blogs, and editorial pieces and we do not diminish the value of those contributions. We instead argue that they further defend the need for greater representation in the scholarly literature that will be used to influence the policies, practices, and structures around DEIA+ work.

Lessons Learned

It was these shared challenges that made each of us raise our hands when Dr. Benn asked who would like to connect outside of NADOHE. Pulling from the African Proverb "It takes a village to raise a child," the Queen's Collective is grounded in the value of community. Through our varied experiences, we have learned that without a community of support, we will not only face professional burnout but stunt our professional growth in this field.

We have learned that without a community of support, we will not only face professional burnout but stunt our professional growth in this field.

We will change the system together, not in isolation. In the words of bell hooks, *"For one of the most vital ways we sustain ourselves is by building communities of resistance, places where we know we are not alone"* (hooks 2015).

The building of community and relationships can have a significant impact as one develops their sense of identity and approach to the work. Professional learning communities, faculty writing groups, peer networks, and professional organizations are some of the ways academics have worked to build community and establish their support network. These high-impact practices can increase sense of belonging, collective growth, collaboration, and self-care (Majorana et al. 2023). As we have developed the Queen's Collective, we have reflected on how we build a professional learning community that centers the unique experiences of WOC CDOs and other equity professionals in a holistic way. The framework described in this chapter is grounded in several principles we have learned throughout our careers and time together and produces a space where we are seen, safe, and valued (Spranger 2018).

Principle One: Mentoring Framework, Establishing a Shared Goal

Our shared goal has been to bring more attention, awareness, and support to WOC (like ourselves) who do DEIA+ work in higher education. When Dr. Benn brought up that the experiences of women of color DEIA+ professionals are not reflected in conference sessions (like the one we were all virtually attending at the time) or scholarly works, it resonated with each of us enough that we felt compelled to answer her call. We established our commitment then, and have solidified it since, seeking to become the place where that energy and attention to our work, struggles, and ingenuity would come to the fore.

Principle Two: Decolonizing Approach

We knew it was vital that we create a mentoring network that differed from the traditional mentoring structures we had all participated in. These structures did not meet all our personal or professional needs over the years. Traditional mentoring models involve matching a junior person with a senior person in their respective field or organization to provide career guidance related to achieving goals and being successful in an organization or field (Felten et al. 2013). This structure is based on a culture of assimilation and hierarchy that purports one can only learn from those with more years in the field or a higher-ranked position. It maintains the status quo of power dynamics within organizations and can serve as a gatekeeping mechanism. In addition, traditional mentoring tends to be one-directional, limits the definitions of success, and doesn't allow space for cultural ways of being in academia (Alarcón and Bettez 2017; Jones, Wilder, and Osborne-Lampkin; Núñez, Murakami, and Gonzales 2015; Gaëtane and Brooks 2011).

Peer mentoring and mentoring networks provide a supportive space for WOC in the academy and have had a positive impact on retention and overall well-being (Alarcón and Bettez 2017; Jones, Wilder, and Osborne-Lampkin; Núñez, Murakami, and Gonzales 2015; Kelly and Fries-Britt 2022). However, many of the mentoring examples in the literature focus primarily on faculty WOC, of the same rank and within the same institution. This excludes the experiences of administrators in academia and only perpetuates the myth that faculty and administrators don't have shared experiences and a more senior person cannot learn from a junior person. We know one's journey to becoming a CDO can vary with some transitioning from a faculty role and others having a pure administrative background. Therefore, we wanted to further challenge the hierarchical structure of academia by creating a mentoring network that spans academic roles and institution types, is intergenerational, and is mutually beneficial. We have built upon the work of Jeannette Alarcon and Silvia Bettez, who stated, "peer mentoring can occur among faculty of distinct ranks as long as the approach involves 'coequal' and 'mutual' or reciprocal relationships" (Alarcón and Bettez 2017, p.27). By applying this approach, we have created a space where we as equity practitioners in higher education can pour into one another's professional and personal development. The Queen's Collective is grounded in the values of collective decision-making, openness to multiple perspectives, and inclusion of all voices.

Principle Three: Celebrating the Diversity amongst Us

In the Queens' Collective, women who have served as faculty and administrators connect across institution types from business schools and smaller colleges to the Big 10, Ivy League, and performing arts institutions. The Collective reflects the diversity of US geographic regions (Northeast, Southeast, Midwest, and Southwest are all represented), institution types, and job titles.

We each hold graduate degrees; six hold doctoral degrees and a seventh is completing her dissertation. We all come to this work from varying backgrounds, with some doing full-time DEIA+ work as "post-George Floyd" appointees for three years since that catalyst event in Minneapolis (Gaudiano 2022). Others have worked in diversity and inclusion functions, with or without the formal title, for over 25 years. At least two of the women in the Collective were appointed to roles as DEIA+ leaders in their academic institutions; and most of the members (five of eight) have served or currently serve as inaugural DEIA+ officers.

As with diversity officer roles across the country, the titles and levels of responsibility and authority vary, and range from Vice President reporting directly to a University President to being the director of a center (Williams and Wade-Golden 2013). The diversity of our collective adds to the strength of our community. It allows us to learn about best practices outside of our peer institutions, hear fresh perspectives, and gain a greater understanding of what is happening at all levels of an institution through a DEIA+ lens.

Our meetings touch on every aspect of the work from office structure to our approaches to self-care and mindful leadership. Budgeting, strategy, career progression, personal and institutional responses to the rapidly changing socio-political landscape, and the pressures of avoiding toxic stereotypes such as "Strong Black Woman" or "superwoman" (Allen et al. 2019) and "Angry Black Woman" have all appeared on the Queen's Collective agenda (Motro et al. 2022).

As previously mentioned, we gathered with the goal of expanding the body of womanist research around the work of DEIA+ but that shared goal quickly grew to include pouring into the whole person. We still recognize that for many of us (especially those who also hold faculty appointments) there is a need to write and publish, in the hope of creating job security and flexibility in our academic fields. However, we choose not to subscribe to the societal and academic pressure that says your value is in your production. Rather we remind each other that we are valuable just as we are, and we can redefine productivity in a holistic way that acknowledges contribution beyond publication and material output.

Principle Four: Acknowledgment of the Whole Person and Redefining Productivity

For many of the reasons we highlighted earlier, DEIA+ work is lauded as some of the most difficult to undertake in corporate and non-profit organizations. Hence, our renewed sense of urgency in changing what contribution to the work and productivity looks like for practitioners. We are continuously constructing and fostering spaces that empower others to embrace their authentic selves. However, it is rare to encounter individuals intentionally creating similar spaces for us as professionals. Organizations such as the Nap Ministry, is an example of how many Black professionals are creating spaces for respite and self-care amidst being overworked and overextended. The Nap Ministry creates "sacred spaces where the liberatory, restorative, and disruptive power of rest can take hold" (Organization of Multitudes section). The Queen's Collective aims to provide that safe space for ourselves. With global uncertainty, instability within the university and political landscape, and a constant attack on DEIA+, we have cultivated and nurtured a community where the protective barriers shielding our egos crumbled away, allowing our genuine selves to emerge and be fully present within the group.

During the early stages of this group, we made a collective decision to dismantle our defensive barriers and establish a space where we could openly share our professional and personal insights. However, as often happens in healthy relationships, these connections organically evolved into something more profound than we initially expected within just a few months. A thirst for meaningful relationships with individuals beyond our immediate circles emerged, as it became evident to each of us that a dormant desire for genuine and profound personal bonds had awakened within. We created a sanctuary, where we could find solace in the fact that our personal and professional triumphs and challenges need not be diminished to fit the mold of the group. Whether we gather once a month or sporadically throughout the week, we enter this space knowing that we could bring not just our authentic self but our complete being.

The unique identity that fuels this group lies in the erasure of ego and the hierarchical lines, and the acceptance of diverse experiences and pedigrees without preconceived expectations. None too great, none too small, but all as equal collaborators of a community that has managed to connect beyond its intellect or social skills. It is founded on the recognition that all bring value, and the various lenses and geographical locations only serve to enrich the Collective. During our times together, we granted ourselves permission to halt the chaotic world surrounding us and to be in the moment with one another. We honor the space as one we can expect transparency and confidentiality. Amidst the overwhelming nature of life and work, we found solace in a space where insightful and supportive Queens were ready to empathetically listen and embrace us. When circumstances prevented us from actively participating with the group, there was never a sense of judgment or perceived lack of commitment. We acknowledge that life happens, and we have to accept when our colleagues need different ways to integrate their daily lived experiences into the work (i.e., child care, mental health days, parental care, etc.), and be flexible to how people can show up.

Whenever a Queen expresses doubt about their commitment due to their absence, we reassure them that our sanctuary differs from the expectations of the outside world. In our sanctuary, we do not evaluate our worth based on the number of meetings attended or participation in group opportunities. Instead, we draw each other closer, and we remind each other that we genuinely understand one's current limitations. Sometimes this has meant dismissing the programmatic agenda to have deep dive discussions to develop actionable short- and long-term solutions, particularly when legislative actions are putting our livelihoods at risk of being erased.

As DEIA+ Professionals, we frequently find ourselves in environments where there is an expectation and pressure to be the epitome of "professionalism" while embodying all facets of equality and justice.

Whether this pressure stems from within or is imposed externally there is minimal room for us to genuinely thrive through expressing our true selves. It is liberating and powerful to have a sanctuary where we can truly be authentic, share accomplishments without any sense of self-promotion, express insights on controversial topics, and openly discuss our most significant professional and personal challenges in detail.

Collectively, we have grown to form a deep understanding to respect the fluctuating rhythms of one another's lives, recognizing that contributions may vary as we navigate through different phases of life. We come together, as the Queen's Collective, united by the shared experiences of these roles, to foster a deep sense of connection and understanding amongst us, and to cherish the whole person for who they are, a Queen.

Principle Five: Professional Development

Often our collective offers us the resources and support that our institutions cannot. We turn to each other for best practices in the work, contacts, and frequent Star Trek references. Perhaps most important to our collective is the commitment to our original call – to make sure that our work, and our lives which cannot be separated from the work, are represented in literature. Since forming, we have presented at conferences internationally and domestically while making sure to document our journey with the goal of publishing our stories.

Conclusion and Recommendations

Despite the challenges (e.g., work isolation, wellbeing, exclusion from scholarship), we've learned a great deal. We forged a mentoring network that reflected the values and characteristics we honor. This mentoring network empowered the group to celebrate our diversity and codified what being a woman of color in this work means to us. We've done so by acknowledging our "whole" self and redefining productivity. And, more importantly the Queen's Collective has become a key component of our professional development. In closing, we offer the following recommendations to WOC starting their journey in the DEIA+ field: 1) Understand your environment, 2) Create a support network through mentorship that centers your experience as a WOC in this work, 3) Acknowledge the complexity of gendered racism, 4) Create time and space for self-care to buffer the emotional toll and isolation of DEIA+ work, 5) Adopt a nimble approach toward your work, as doing so will enable you to address the challenges and growth opportunities presented by constituents.

Finally, remember that it is just, authentic, and courageous to maintain a relentless focus on the people in the organization you serve while not forgetting yourself. It is in the sisterhood of the Queen's Collective that we find solace and community. In the absence of institutions providing this space, we encourage you to build it for yourselves, for your upliftment, for your self-preservation, and for your success.

Key Insights from *A Framework for the Sustainability of WOC DEIA+ Practitioners: A Queen's Collective*

- Melissa Harris-Perry's theory of the "Crooked Room" serves as an apt metaphor for the experiences of women of color in the academy.
- Women of Color equity practitioners engage their work at the triple intersection of race, gender, and gender roles as they navigate the responsibilities of their professional roles.
- Building community is a critical element of the development of WOC DEIA+ practitioners in higher education.
- Career pathing for DEIA+ practitioners has not been given sufficient consideration, and pathways to other leadership positions are inconsistent and unclear.
- When mentoring structures are inadequate to address the distinct journeys of WOC DEIA+ professionals in higher education, create your own.
- While attending to the needs of the institution you serve, don't forget to take care of your self in the process.

Things to Consider:

1 What do Stokes, et al. say about the presence of women of color in the scholarship that focuses on diversity, equity, inclusion, and belonging practices?
2 Many speak of the glass cliff for WOC in leadership in the academy as well as in business. What other challenges do Stokes, et al. speak of in their essay?
3 What is the "Queen's Collective"? How does it help to cultivate community for WOC equity practitioners?
4 What are the factors that adversely affect the success of WOC DEIA+ practitioners as detailed in Stokes, et al. essay?
5 What is compassion fatigue? What are its effects on the people who do the work of DEIA+?
6 What are the "decolonizing approaches" to mentoring that Stokes, et.al speak of that are high impact practices for career growth and well-being for DEIA+ professionals?

References

Alarcón, Jeannette D., and Silvia Bettez. 2017. "Feeling brown in the academy: Decolonizing mentoring through a disidentification muxerista approach." *Equity & Excellence in Education* 50 (1): 25–40. 10.1080/10665684.2016.1250234.

Allen, Amani M., Yijie Wang, David H. Chae, Melisa M. Price, Wizdom Powell, Teneka C. Steed, Angela Rose Black, Firdaus S. Dhabhar, Leticia Marquez-Magaña, and Cheryl L. Woods-Giscombe. 2019. "Racial discrimination, the superwoman schema, and allostatic load: exploring an integrative stress-coping model among African American women." *Annals of the New York Academy of Sciences* 1457 (1): 104–127. 10.1111/nyas.14188.

Arnold, Jeanne, and Marlene Kowalski-Braun. 2012. "The journey to an inaugural Chief Diversity Officer: Preparation, implementation and beyond." *Innovative Higher Education* 37(1): 27–36. https://eric.ed.gov/?id=ED430514.

Ashcraft, Karen, and Brenda Allen. 2020. "How words come to matter: A statement on statements." *Management Communication Quarterly* 34 (4): 597–602. 10.1177/0893318920951643.

Brown, Sarah. 2017. "College diversity officers face a demanding job and scarce resources." *The Chronicle of Higher Education.* https://www.chronicle.com/article/college-diversity-officers-face-a-demanding-job-and-scarce-resources/.

Collins, Patricia Hill. 2004. *Black Sexual Politics: African Americans, Gender, and the New Racism.* Great Britain: Routledge.

Coopwood, Ken D., Sr., and William T. Lewis, Sr. 2017. "From their mouths; The lived experiences of chief diversity officers in higher education." CoopLew. https://www.coopdileu.com/research-and-literature.

DasGupta, Ariana. 2019. *Navigating the Racialized Neoliberal Gaze: Asian American Women Diversity, Equity, and Inclusion Professionals in US Higher Education.* University of San Francisco.

Edwards, Donna F., and Gwen McKinney. 2020. "We are black women. Stop calling us 'women of color'". Washington Post. https://www.washingtonpost.com/opinions/2020/09/14/we-are-black-women-stop-calling-us-women-color/.

England, Jason, and Richard Purcell. 2020. "Higher Ed's toothless response to the killing of George Floyd." *The Chronicle of Higher Education.* https://www.chronicle.com/article/higher-eds-toothless-response-to-the-killing-of-george-floyd.

Felten, Peter, H-Dirksen L. Bauman, Aaron Kheriaty, Edward Taylor, Parker J. Palmer, Angeles Arrien, and Rachel Naomi Remen. 2013. *Transformative Conversations: A Guide to Mentoring Communities Among Colleagues in Higher Education.* Jossey-Bass.

Gaëtane, Jean-Marie, and Jeffrey S. Brooks. 2011. "Chapter 5 Mentoring and Supportive Networks for Women of Color in Academe." In *Women of Color in Higher Education: Changing Directions and New Perspectives*, edited by Gaëtane Jean-Marie and Brenda Lloyd-Jones, In Diversity in Higher Education, 91–108. Emerald Group Publishing Limited.

Gaudiano, Paolo. 2022. "Two years after George Floyd's murder, is your DEI strategy performative or sustainable?". Forbes. https://www.forbes.com/sites/paologaudiano/2022/06/27/two-years-after-george-floyd-is-your-dei-strategy-performative-or-sustainable/?sh=394947fe6aaa.

Harris-Perry, Melissa V. 2011. *Sister Citizen: Shame, Stereotypes, and Black Women in America.* New Haven: Yale University Press.

hooks, bell. 2015. *Yearning: Race, Gender, and Cultural Politics.* 2nd ed.: Routledge.

Johnson, R. 1974. "Vignettes on White Academia." In Johnson, R. (Ed.) *Black Scholars on Higher Education in the 70's,* 1–35. Columbus, OH: ECCA Publications.

Jones, Tamara Bertrand, JeffriAnne Wilder, and La'Tara Osborne-Lampkin. "Beyond Sisterhood: Using Shared Identities to Build Peer Mentor Networks and Secure Social Capital in the Academy." Edited by Brenda L.H. Marina. *Mentoring Away the Glass Ceiling in Academia: A Cultured Critique.* Lanham, Maryland: Lexington Books. 143–159.

Kelly, Bridget Turner, and Sharon Fries-Britt. 2022. *Building Mentorship Networks to Support Black Women: A Guide to Succeeding in the Academy.* Edited by Bridget Turner Kelly and Sharon Fries-Britt. New York, NY: Routledge. 5–18.

Majorana, Jennifer, Kristina Rouech, Elizabeth Ann VanDeusen, and Holly H. Hoffman. 2023. "Building a thriving virtual faculty writing group." *The Journal of Faculty Development* 37 (1): 1–9. https://scholars.cmich.edu/en/publications/building-a-thriving-virtual-faculty-writing-group.

Marana, Jennifer. 2016. "The Lived Experiences of Women of Color Chief Diversity Officers." PhD dissertation, The Claremont Graduate University.

Merriam-Webster. "Collective." In *Merriam-Webster English Dictionary.* Merriam-Webster.com.

Motro, Daphna, Jonathan B. Evans, Aleksander P. J. Ellis, and Lehman Benson Iii. 2022. "Race and reactions to women's expressions of anger at work: Examining the effects of the "angry Black woman" stereotype." *Journal of Applied Psychology* 107 (1): 142–152. 10.1037/apl0000884.

National Association of Diversity Officers in Higher Education. 2021. "A framework for advancing anti-racism strategy on campus." https://www.nadohe.org/resources.

Nixon, M. L. 2013. "Women of Color Chief Diversity Officers: Their Positionality and Agency in Higher Education Institutions." PhD dissertation, University of Washington.

Nixon, Monica L. 2017. "Experiences of women of color university chief diversity officers." *Journal of Diversity in Higher Education* 10 (4): 301–317. 10.1037/dhe0000043.

Núñez, Anne-Marie, Elizabeth T. Murakami, and Leslie D. Gonzales. 2015. "Weaving authenticity and legitimacy: Latina faculty peer mentoring." *New Directions for Higher Education* 2015 (171): 87–96. 10.1002/he.20145.

Pemberton, Andrea, and Jennifer Kisamore. 2023. "Assessing burnout in diversity and inclusion professionals." *Equality, Diversity and Inclusion: An International Journal* 42 (1): 38–52. 10.1108/EDI-12-2020-0360.

Post, Deborah W. 1990. "Reflections on identity, diversity and morality." *Berkeley Women's Law Journal* 6 (1): 136–166.

Ross, Loretta, [Western States Center]. 2011. "The origin of the phrase 'women of color'." February 15, 2011, Video. https://www.youtube.com/watch?v=82vl34mi4Iw

Spranger, Angela. 2018. *Why People Stay: Helping Your Employees Feel Seen, Safe, and Valued.* 1st ed. London: Routledge.

Spranger, Angela. 2022. "The Inclusive Leader's Toolkit." In *Policy and Practice Challenges for Equality in Education,* edited by Theresa Neimann, 279–294. Hershey, PA: IGI Global.

Stanley, Christine A. 2014. "The chief diversity officer: An examination of CDO models and strategies." *Journal of Diversity in Higher Education* 7 (2): 101–108. 10.1037/a0036662.

Stanley, Christine A., Karan L. Watson, Jennifer M. Reyes, and Kay S. Varela. 2019. "Organizational change and the chief diversity officer: A case study of institutionalizing a diversity plan." *Journal of Diversity in Higher Education* 12 (3): 255–265. 10.1037/dhe0000099.

Williams, Damon A., and Katrina C. Wade-Golden. 2013. *The Chief Diversity Officer: Strategy Structure, and Change Management.* Sterling, VA: Stylus.

Wilson, Jeffery L. 2013. "Emerging trend: The Chief Diversity Officer phenomenon within higher education." *The Journal of Negro Education* 82 (4): 433–445. 10.7709/jnegroeducation.82.4.0433.

Word Reference. "Queen." In *Word Reference Dictionary of English.* Word Reference.

7

THE EXTRAORDINARY POWER OF KINDNESS

Reshaping Organizational Culture as a CDO

Yves-Rose Porcena

Chapter Contents

I would not necessarily say that I am a wise person. Instead, I am guided by fundamental principles that I learned in kindergarten. These foundational truths, universally known, require no elaborate repetition, except to say kindness moves me the most. It's a quality I hold dear—both to extend to oneself and to share with others. Kindness occupies a special place in my heart because, in a world enriched by differences, kindness has the extraordinary power to transform strangers into allies and friends.

> *... kindness has the extraordinary power to transform strangers into allies and friends.*

DOI: 10.4324/9781032724881-9

It's the thread that binds us, a constant reminder that our differences don't create divisions but instead contribute to the vibrant tapestry of our collective existence. I have discovered that kindness is not just a personal value, it can be a transformative element in business. Keeping in mind that the practice of kindness in the workplace is not a "one size fits all" and often involves elements of subjectivity, I would posit it as an approach that facilitates the integration of compassion and ethical considerations into the organizational fabric and prioritizes the well-being of all employees. Ideally, kindness should fit perfectly within the benevolent nature of educational institutions. My experience has convinced me that it is a key ingredient in a chief diversity officer's toolkit.

For the past 30 years, I have been fortunate to work as a diversity champion. Despite significant progress in the field of diversity and inclusion, a profound realization emerges — familiar challenges resurface, almost as if time is folding back on itself. It's in these moments that the power of kindness becomes exceptionally significant because kindness is not bound by time; it has served as a timeless tool, allowing me to face each new cycle with renewed energy and purpose. This chapter seeks to unravel the threads in this cyclical journey while illuminating how a commitment to kindness can instigate profound and transformative change by breaking repetitive cycles.

I have had the privilege of holding a number of titles while doing this work. I have been named a Human Resources-Equal Opportunity Officer, a Human Rights Associate, a Human Rights Commission Director, a Director of Institutional Equity, a Chief Diversity Officer (CDO), and a Vice President for Equity and Inclusion. This chapter will draw from the latter position where I also serve as Chief Culture and People Officer for the college. I could have drawn advice from any of the positions above, as there is really nothing novel about the social justice pursued in these various positions. However, working in a setting where the human resources functions report to the division of equity and inclusion's vice president has opened up opportunities for organizational change that I didn't know existed. (see bullet 1 below for further details). Suffice it to say here that this reporting structure came out of college leadership's commitment to align our employee-centered functions to the values of diversity, equity, and inclusion, which we often claim were in our DNA. Knowing that my experience within the human resource realm would provide the leadership guidance needed to move these functions forward was also a plus. Given the uniqueness of this setting and recognizing that everyone's journey is unique, I offer the following six (6) truths imbued with the grace needed to navigate the dynamics of organizational transformation with kindness.

The Organization Drives the Culture

It is not an understatement to say that I experienced real organizational culture change when the president of my current institution renamed the office of human resources as the office of people and culture and moved it from the Business and Finance division to the Division of Equity and Inclusion, which I led. This name change aligned with another project that was tracing the history of Black labor on our campus: the invisible labor initiative that we themed *Every Person By Name.* However, we have not yet found records Of most of the laborers who worked the grounds of the campus in the official college archives. That is primarily because the college was founded after emancipation, during reconstruction, when Black labor was no longer property to be deeded and recorded, but rather a nameless resource to be exploited. In an attempt to learn from our past and reshape the future, the renaming of the office of human resources helped to counter the prevalent paradigm that workers are resources to be managed or exploited. Transitioning to overseeing this additional function brought to fruition learnings from my graduate studies that core behaviors and attitudes of an organization are primarily established by its leadership, policies, and practices. The simple presidential act of relocating the custodians of the college's most prized "assets," its employees, had a transformative influence on shaping the culture unlike any I had witnessed before. This shift also aligned the college's stated mission and values with the way it conducted its business. On a practical level, I was now able to instantly access and approve data that truly mattered, such as employee salaries and selection criteria for hires. I wasted no time in analyzing the data. I needed to ascertain if my beloved college was genuinely what I was proclaiming it to be: the best place I had ever worked because of its unapologetic commitment to diversity, equity, and justice. I promptly formed judgments where I discovered discrepancies. However, my commitment to kindness compelled me to probe deeper into the roots of any discovered inequity. As I did so, I unearthed a reality: individuals weren't inherently malicious, but rather, unconscious biases were rampant—a form of ignorance that even self-proclaimed progressives including individuals of color were not immune to. Such biases were so prevalent that we, the good people, have either learned to rationalize them with anecdotes or turned them into what Gaertner and colleagues (2008) referred to as "aversive racism: bias without intention." These biases, often subtle but cumulatively impactful, manifest beyond conscious awareness, ingrained deeply enough to influence decisions and actions in ways that perpetuate inequality and undermine progress.

Unconscious Bias Undermines Progress

To understand the cumulative effect of biases, we need to first take a detour into our various attempts as a society to remedy them.

To understand the cumulative effect of biases, we need to first take a detour into our various attempts as a society to remedy them.

Our work on addressing bias is not new; Chief Affirmative Action, Compliance, Equity, Minority Affairs, Multicultural or Diversity officers have been addressing biases for decades. In 1965, President Lyndon Baines Johnson signed Executive Order 11246 mandating that contractors not discriminate against any employees or qualified applicants because of race, color, religion, sex, or national origin. Contractors were to take affirmative steps to ensure nondiscrimination in employment practices. During his speech at Howard University's Commencement on June 4, 1965, a few months before signing the order on September 24, 1965, President Johnson proclaimed the following, "Freedom is not enough. ... You do not take a person who, for years, has been hobbled by chains and liberate him, bring him up to the starting line of a race and then say, 'you are free to compete with all the others,' and still justly believe that you have been completely fair. ... Thus, it is not enough just to open the gates of opportunity. All our citizens must have the ability to walk through those gates."

In the early days following the passing of these important civil rights laws, the focus was on compliance and affirmative action. Many institutions hired affirmative action or compliance officers to track their workforce data and write the required annual affirmative action plans that document progress towards outcomes. The plans, which were delivered to the Department of Labor's Office of Federal Contract Compliance Programs, listed affirmative steps taken or made promises to open the gates to recruit, hire, and promote women, minorities, disabled individuals, and veterans. The Equal Employment Opportunity Commission (EEOC) was created in 1965 and could bring class action litigation against employers for discrimination. Employees were also protected from retaliation from having voiced, filed, or taken part in a discrimination complaint or a lawsuit. Violations could put federal contracts at risk. The goal was to ensure everyone was treated fairly but changes were slow to come. Eventually as Thomas (1990) predicted, Affirmative Action "will die a natural death."

To help managers comply with these legislated mandates, training was often provided to help identify biases in hiring practices. The officers in charge of implementing these monumental tasks realized that addressing biases would not be successful if they were perceived as mandates. It became important to help managers grow from the heart and show them how diversity in their teams would benefit them. Hence the rise of diversity initiatives. Whereas AA and EEO are legally driven mandates, diversity is voluntary, intentional, and preemptive change in creating a culture of inclusion. Having been trained as an Equal Opportunity Officer, my initial approach to doing social justice work aligned with that of the EEOC—focusing on outcomes rather than intent. Because of this training, my commitment to doing this work had always necessitated an examination of the impact of systemic inequalities, irrespective of intentions. For me, focusing on outcomes provided a level of accountability that, despite well-intentioned motives, the impact of the actions is what matters. Yet now, to truly drive change, I had to delve into comprehending and hopefully shifting the unconscious driver behind perpetually bad outcomes. This marked a substantial change for me, and frankly, it took me too long to grasp the necessity of addressing both dimensions. I was able to do it by returning to my favorite tenet. Kindness became my vessel for empathy, a kind acknowledgment that unconscious biases exist within all individuals, including myself. Kindness, when extended both to myself and to others, became a beacon that illuminates the dark corners where biases thrive. As CDOs, we must actively confront and mitigate unconscious biases to pave the way for authentic progress, no matter how equitable we think our institutions are. This is particularly crucial in higher education settings because we know that unconscious biases, when unchecked, lead to systemic inequalities in important areas such as admissions, faculty hiring, and academic opportunities. And we also know college and universities directly model and shape the opportunities, experiences, and outcomes for not just their current members but also for future leaders of the world. By actively working to diminish unconscious bias in higher education, we pave the way for a more equitable and harmonious global community. Ultimately, the pursuit of equity in higher education is intimately tied to the collective goal of fostering a more inclusive, enlightened, and kinder future for all.

Ultimately, the pursuit of equity in higher education is intimately tied to the collective goal of fostering a more inclusive, enlightened, and kinder future for all.

Data Tells a Better Story

In the pursuit of change, data emerged as a powerful ally, providing insights that would otherwise remain concealed. My role overseeing the "human resources" functions has afforded me access to a treasure trove of data—a repository I fondly refer to as 'beacons of truth'. This data unveils patterns, trends, and correlations that offer narratives beyond the scope of individual perception.

... data unveils patterns, trends, and correlations that offer narratives beyond the scope of individual perception.

Invoking kindness ensures that every data point is treated and disseminated as a piece of someone's story. Most CDOs can request their institutional data, but true comprehension is attained when we grasp the process behind the final data. Through the back-and forth process of engaging with a manager about why an individual shouldn't receive a pay increase given the conditions of others in the department, one gains a deeper understanding of how bias shows up in intent. And kindness helps to recognize that the evidence gathered is not meant to condemn, but to illuminate areas for improvement. When intertwined with grace, kindness transforms the process of pointing out flaws into a collaborative endeavor.

When intertwined with grace, kindness transforms the process of pointing out flaws into a collaborative endeavor.

Relying on the evidence acquired through that process offers insights that shape understanding and foster more lasting change. So much grace is needed if we are to help managers see their flaws by using data, and maybe a bit of emotions too–though I have never been one to master pathos.

Allies Need Armor

Returning to the chief culture and people officer, this role presented a deliberate opportunity to cultivate a workplace culture that could whole-heartedly embrace belonging, justice, equity, diversity, and inclusion (BJEDI). Without delay, I took measures to equip my human resources, now people and culture, team with the necessary skills and capabilities to effectively leverage the diverse talents of all employees for better institutional outcomes. I provided them with intensive training on BJEDI principles. It is worth noting that effective partnerships between human resources and diversity professionals have always been important, but we generally operated as cousins. As these former human resources "cousins" became "siblings," they found a new level of empowerment in their abilities to shape the culture. They evolved into genuine BJEDI champions. The lesson is clear: for human resource professionals to be meaningful allies to CDOs and contribute to culture change, they must be culturally and inclusively competent. They must know that their work as diversity advocates is sanctioned by their vice president or division head because they often see themselves first as rule followers and enforcers. Furthermore, by investing in their growth, we are not only demonstrating kindness but also fostering a greater sense of belonging and trust for the relationship. We can achieve this by helping institutional leaders understand that ultimately, the institution thrives solely due to the unwavering commitment and dedication of its incredibly diverse workforce. That is a historical truth that human resources personnel must own and promote alongside the chief diversity officers. They must be made to understand that embracing diversity isn't merely a moral or ethical imperative; it's a strategic advantage that will attract top talent, enhance employee engagement, satisfaction, and retention, resulting in a more resilient, productive, and successful organization overall.

Today's Work Transforms the Future

Working as a CDO within a higher education institution often involves navigating a historical backdrop that spans centuries. CDOs may find themselves in institutions with deep-rooted legacies marked by native genocide, slavery, segregation, exploitation, racism, and various other forms of institutionalized prejudices. It becomes imperative to not only comprehend and share these narratives but also to recognize the role of present-day employees in shaping the institution's history and culture. What stories will be left behind about your institution a century from now? How are you actively crafting and preserving that narrative? Are you ensuring that the contributions of today's often invisible workers in dining halls and facilities are duly documented? Many CDOs are taking on this responsibility, and it's a duty that all of us should uphold for our institutions. I am part of a team working on the *Every Person By Name* project to interview and record such stories. One of my cherished stories is about a professional whose grandfather worked as a cleaner in the residence halls decades ago. There is no record of her grandfather's presence at the college, despite the institution being a central aspect of this family's lives. Kindness cannot allow such omissions to occur again. Their work holds significance and deserves recognition. Their work matters. It's grace that enables (this family) and us to persevere in the face of the above recurring obstacles and to tackle familiar themes with a fresh perspective.

Culture Is Both Organizational and Global

I would be remiss if I did not say a word about culture in the global context. One of the roots for the need to promote diversity today is the antiquated notion of a human hierarchy—where certain individuals were deemed more worthy than others based on the color of their skin. This belief serves as the foundation not only for discriminatory attitudes but also for the deeply troubling history of slavery that forcibly uprooted countless of Black lives from the African continent. It's crucial to remind ourselves that the transatlantic and intra-America slave trades involved the transportation of Africans to different regions within the Americas—such as the United States, South America, and the Caribbean—as enslaved people. As a Caribbean-born American woman hailing from a nation once inhabited by the Taino people prior to European arrival, my role as a diversity advocate cannot disregard the connective global thread and the numerous other dimensions of intersectionality that influence our narratives. Kindness is the thread that weaves together these different narratives and encourages us to stand in solidarity with all oppressed people of the world.

In summary, if you were to ask me about the factors that have moved the needle towards progress during my three decades of engagement in this field, my answer would unequivocally be culture and people. Culture stands as the defining force in the realm of organizational diversity efforts. It is both the enabler of positive behaviors and the disapprover of those it condemns. Culture, whether overt or subtle, manifests in behaviors and consequently shapes the collective identity of an institution. The responsibility for us, Chief Diversity Officers, is to mold this culture. And it is the people that serve as catalysts that reshape the culture. Envision, if you would, three interconnected circles: the innermost representing individuals, the second, larger circle symbolizing the organization, and the third, largest circle depicting society. The people, at the core, influence their interactions with one another, subsequently shaping the organization's culture. Yet, no matter their intentions, the second circle—representing the organization—lures in the back and often exerts its influence with its unjust policies and practices. Individuals in the inner circle will struggle against these odds unless culture is made just. The third larger circle underscores why CDOs make their work a calling, a mission to transform societal norms—an expansive subject meriting its own discussion in another chapter. For now, we focus on the first two circles because in a world bustling with hate, the harmonious connection between people and culture serves as a poignant reminder that a person's true strength resides not in authority or titles, but in their capacity to imprint culture with a kindness that leaves an indelible positive mark on the institution.

Key Insights from *The Extraordinary Power of Kindness: Reshaping Organizational Culture as a CDO*

- Kindness is an integral companion to compassion and ethics in the value system of an organization.
- Unconscious bias, while not malicious in some cases, can have a cumulative impact on an organization's business practices. Higher Education is not immune to this cumulative impact.

- To effectively leverage the talent in higher education, and elevate employee engagement and organizational resilience, diversity, equity, and inclusion must be viewed as strategic tools to strengthen operational effectiveness.
- Kindness can serve as the bridge to empathy—a needed skill that enhances one's leadership capacity.
- Culture stands as an enabler or a barrier to achieving inclusive excellence.

Things to consider:

1 Consider the DNA in the culture of your organization. How can you trace the threads of equity, diversity, and inclusion in that DNA?
2 What are the preemptive considerations necessary to create a community culture of inclusion in higher education?
3 Porcena names unconscious bias as an impediment to achieving progress in equality. How does her discussion of former President Lyndon Johnson's Executive Order 11246 shed light on this historic intervention?
4 What does Porcena mean when she states, "embracing diversity is more than just an ethical and moral imperative"?
5 What does Porcena say about the narratives of "invisible workers" in higher education?
6 How should leaders approach the antiquated notion of human hierarchy?
7 What are the three interconnected circles of an organization Porcena describes? What is the impact of these circles on the work of diversity, equity, and inclusion?

References

Gaertner, Samuel L., John F. Dovidio, Jason Nier, Gordon Hodson, and Melissa A. Houlette. "Aversive Racism: Bias without Intention." In *Handbook of Employment Discrimination Research: Rights and Realities,* edited by Laura Beth Nielsen and Robert L. Nelson, 377–393. New York, NY: Springer New York, 2008.

Johnson, L. B. "To Fulfill These Rights." In *Commencement Address at Howard University.* Washington, D.C., 1965. Retrieved from The American Presidency Project: https://www.presidency.ucsb.edu/node/241312.

Thomas, R. Roosevelt, Jr. "From Affirmative Action to Affirming Diversity." *Harvard Business Review,* 1990, 107–117. https://hbr.org/1990/03/from-affirmative-action-to-affirming-diversity.

PART 3
Perfecting the Pivot

8

FROM BOARDROOMS TO BREAKTHROUGHS

Perfecting the Pivot

TaJuan R. Wilson

Chapter Contents

When I reflect on my journey as a diversity, equity, and inclusion practitioner it is not just a professional role; it is an integral part of who I am, and it is only by the grace of God that I can share my story. My path to becoming a Chief Diversity Officer and my current role in executive recruitment was not linear but rather a series of meaningful experiences, life lessons, and personal growth.

Growing up in the small town of Bearden, Arkansas, as the youngest of three children, I never imagined my life or career trajectory to be what it has been. In my small town of 766 people, there were not very many examples of career success. What defined me then and now, however, was consistent exposure to family and a community that operated with integrity, and demonstrated resiliency, and determination—ultimately instilling a belief in me that I could accomplish anything I put my mind to despite very humble beginnings.

My story, like so many others, is not complete without discussing the power and impact that Federal TRIO Programs have had on my life. These programs transformed my life and helped me navigate a world that felt both

DOI: 10.4324/9781032724881-11

foreign and full of possibilities. Thanks to parents who were persistent in their quest to provide me with exposure, I was afforded the opportunity to take part in Educational Talent Search (ETS), Upward Bound, and Student Support Services—all at Ouachita Baptist University. Educational Talent Search was my first exposure to a world beyond my hometown. My first summer camp experience happened to be on the campus of Ouachita Baptist University during my 7th-grade year thanks to Educational Talent Search. In high school, I was afforded the opportunity to participate in Upward Bound. The Upward Bound program gave me hope and instilled in me the confidence necessary to attend college. Upon entering Ouachita Baptist University as a first-generation college freshman, I was afforded the opportunity to participate in Student Support Services. Ouachita Baptist University was a world unlike any I had known before. OBU was academically rigorous, and socially isolating at times, and exposed me to a world of inequity, long before I could name it. Nevertheless, I persisted, completing my undergraduate degree in Political Science and Communications in 3.5 years.

As a first-generation professional, admittedly, I did not fully grasp career planning—I consider myself incredibly blessed. With that context, my journey as a full-time employee in education began in student retention services in Oklahoma City where I was reminded firsthand of the challenges that under-represented students face, this time as a first-generation college graduate myself and now a professional charged with ensuring the academic success of other students with similar backgrounds. It was in this role that I came to understand the immense impact of mentorship and support. I felt a profound connection to the students I was helping. It was here that the seeds of my passion for diversity, equity, and inclusion were sown. It was during this season that I completed an MPA.

I would go on to lead a GEAR-UP program in Wyoming and serve as the Executive Director of TRIO Programs and Multicultural Student Retention at Missouri State University for six years. I saw myself in the students I served daily, and my commitment to their success was unwavering. It was during my six years at Missouri State University that I truly grasped the transformative power of education and the importance of creating equitable opportunities. It was here that I learned to harness the power of working with faculty and staff colleagues beyond my own department to drive success and outcomes for the students I served. It was during this season that I earned my EdD. Shortly after earning my terminal degree, I was encouraged by my network to pursue other opportunities and expand my horizons.

From there, I transitioned into another executive director role in student life and diversity in academic medicine in South Carolina. I continued to champion the cause of inclusion, while also serving all students. This work reinforced my belief that representation matters, and that cultural competency is vital in fostering inclusive environments.

> *This work reinforced my belief that representation matters, and that cultural competency is vital in fostering inclusive environments.*

It was also here that I came to understand systematic work in DEI at the intersection of recruitment, retention, and advancement and embedding the work into the very fabric of institutions and organizations.

After successfully navigating and advocating for students for more than ten years, I would go on to ascend to the position of Chief Diversity Officer twice. It was never my dream. In fact, I fought it. My journey as a CDO was never about climbing a ladder; it was about ascending to a platform where I could amplify the voices of those often unheard. In this role, I navigated the complex terrain of power dynamics and systemic inequalities. My small-town beginnings had provided me with a grounded perspective, but now I was tasked with dismantling structures that perpetuated inequity. It was a formidable challenge, one that called for both thoughtful strategic planning and heartfelt conviction.

In 2019 I accepted my first Chief Diversity Officer role at an institution in Iowa. Seven weeks into my first tenure as Chief Diversity Officer (CDO), I faced a decision that would not only alter the course of my career but also become a defining moment in my journey. It was a difficult choice, one that unfolded in the public eye and carried with it a multitude of lessons. My decision to resign stemmed from a misalignment of values and a fundamental disconnect between the organization's commitment to diversity and the actions it took. I have never believed that my career success was somehow correlated to a number on a paycheck. My departure was confusing to the average person and discussed widely, but it was a choice made in pursuit of authenticity and integrity. It was 100% my choice—and six years later, I can tell you without a doubt that it was the right choice for me. I recognize the privilege of being a single, childless, professional with the financial means to walk away from a job not knowing what would be next. For that, I am grateful and do not want to oversimplify my decision for anyone reading this. It was only by the grace of God that I was able to depart, completely free of financial concerns. In the weeks and months that followed I focused on continued self-development, travel, and of course—job hunting. My singular piece of advice from this season is that you can never go wrong when you operate with integrity—know who you are and establish your core values before going into senior leadership.

Despite the previous challenges, I decided to pursue another CDO opportunity, this time an inaugural, cabinet-level role at a public institution in Georgia. I carried with me the experiences and insights gained from each step of my journey. I understood the unique challenges faced by individuals like me within educational settings, and I was driven to dismantle barriers and foster environments where all could thrive. My approach to DEI work has always been anchored in a strategic, long-term perspective. I firmly believe that true progress in DEI is not achieved through isolated events or superficial gestures but by addressing systemic issues and fostering a culture of inclusivity from the ground up. My approach to DEI emphasizes initiatives like comprehensive professional development and leadership programs, policy review and revisions, and measured structural changes that create a more equitable environment for students, faculty, staff, local communities, and alumni. It is about laying the groundwork for sustained positive change that transcends temporary trends or tokenistic actions. Undoubtedly, I care about the recruitment, retention, and advancement of each community and believe that it requires significant collaboration with other cabinet-level colleagues, particularly those in business and finance, human resources, community engagement, and academic affairs to move the needle in a meaningful way. With the support of a fantastic learning community, I led the institution through the development of our inaugural Inclusive Excellence Action plan, creating measures of accountability as every academic college and central administrative unit was responsible for developing its own quarterly goals. Quarterly goals ensured that our work was prioritized in bite-size chunks that were planned, reviewed, assessed, and made accessible to our learning community. The work and relation-ships were so widespread that our SGA, Faculty Senate, and Staff Council joined us in the development of goals and quarterly reporting by aligning with the plan as well. We developed facilitated and analyzed data from our inaugural campus climate survey, became the first higher education senior leadership team in the country to each complete the Certified Diversity Executive (CDE) credential, created an Inclusive Excellence Faculty and Staff Fellowship program, and became a model across the state and region, ultimately positioning the University successfully to win the Higher

Education Excellence in Diversity Award, ultimately positioning the university to recruit and retain more talented students, faculty, and staff.

Despite the success, I encountered a landscape brimming with complexities and challenges. They included resistance to change, resource constraints, and the need to balance short-term results with meaningful, long-term cultural transformation. It is easy to focus on quick wins and superficial changes that impress the public, but not those within the institution. I am always much more interested in making a lasting, structural, systematic impact that requires a more profound shift in the organization's mindset, which is largely shaped by organizational leadership. Specifically, I have always desired shifts in recruitment, retention, and advancement patterns for students, faculty, and staff along with meaningful resource allocation and measurable outcomes that demonstrate true commitment. Encouraging leaders and employees to embrace diversity and inclusion as integral to our identity in higher education and beyond a moment in time was an ongoing struggle, and it required a delicate blend of persuasion and persistence.

I've encountered situations where there is an expectation that DEI efforts should revolve around planning events, festivals, and inviting guest speakers, often motivated by a desire to showcase diversity without a deep commitment to structural change. In some cases, this can manifest as a figurehead chosen more for optics than for their ability to drive substantive DEI progress. My advice is to choose opportunities wisely and to ask tough questions during recruitment to ensure true commitment exists.

Throughout my career as a dedicated advocate for diversity, equity, and inclusion (DEI), I have faced a series of challenges and decisions that would test not only my professional ethics but also my integrity. These moments, etched into the fabric of my journey, reveal the complex and often disheartening realities of DEI work in the educational sphere.

Throughout my career as a dedicated advocate for diversity, equity, and inclusion (DEI), I have faced a series of challenges and decisions that would test not only my professional ethics but also my integrity. These moments, etched into the fabric of my journey, reveal the complex and often disheartening realities of DEI work in the educational sphere.

One of the earliest experiences that still lingers in my memory is the request to remove the word "diversity" from an event flyer in 2021. It was a subtle but telling indication of the discomfort that can arise when the term itself becomes a source of unease for some. In those moments, it was as if the very essence of DEI was being erased, and I had to grapple with the ethical dilemma of appeasement versus advocacy for the students, faculty, and staff I was hired to support. Ultimately after several conversations and a lot of work spent managing up, the word was allowed to stay. Imagine a Chief Diversity Officer not allowed to use the word diversity. The takeaway is that advocacy and education even for those above us is critical.

Another pivotal moment arrived when a year-long planning effort for a diversity summit was abruptly canceled. The painstaking discussions, community involvement, and excitement that had surrounded this event were silenced by a decision seemingly made in haste. It left me questioning the institution's commitment to DEI, and more importantly, the impact on the communities eagerly awaiting its arrival. I navigated this via a series of conversations around institutional commitment, learning what political interests were at play and most importantly identifying tangible ways to still provide DEI education and exposure to our community.

Accepting fewer resources than my peers was yet another hurdle to overcome. It was a stark reminder that despite the importance of DEI work, it often received less funding and support compared to other initiatives. The inequality of resources challenged my resolve but also fueled my determination to make the most of what was available. To pivot, I began a fundraising campaign to ensure our team had the appropriate unrestricted resources to be effective leaders.

Constant racial battle fatigue, censorship, and disrespectful behavior became familiar companions on this journey. They tested my endurance, my resilience, and my faith in the possibility of meaningful change. Yet, they also underscored the urgency of the work and the importance of persevering in the face of adversity. I maintained my dignity by engaging in serious self-care, lots of talks with God, amazing advice from mentors, and never compromising my integrity for a title. As I often say, I rent my title, but I own my character.

Constant racial battle fatigue, censorship, and disrespectful behavior became familiar companions on this journey. They tested my endurance, my resilience, and my faith in the possibility of meaningful change. Yet, they also underscored the urgency of the work and the importance of persevering in the face of adversity.

I maintained my dignity by engaging in serious self-care, lots of talks with God, amazing advice from mentors, and never compromising my integrity for a title. As I often say, I rent my title, but I own my character.

The tension between a strategic vision for sustainable change and the allure of surface-level initiatives is real. It is essential to recognize that events and speakers can play a valuable role in raising awareness and sparking important conversations. They should be part of a broader, strategic DEI plan, not a substitute for it. Navigating this tension requires clear communication and education about the nuances of DEI work. It means helping stakeholders understand that sustainable change goes beyond appearances and requires deep-rooted structural transformations. It involves highlighting the interconnectedness of individual events with a larger strategy for inclusivity.

As a CDO the work involves advocating for meaningful shifts in policies, practices, and cultural norms. It's about challenging the status quo and championing DEI initiatives that have a lasting impact on the organization. The work of a diversity officer should be to help the institution understand the value of curricular changes, equitable policies and procedures, salary equity, access to scholarships and opportunities, and to cultivate an environment of open dialogue and respect that ultimately yields social mobility for the students, faculty, and staff we serve.

In the face of these challenges, resilience became an invaluable trait. I learned that the path of a DEI advocate is not always straightforward. It's a labyrinth filled with ethical crossroads and moral dilemmas. But it's also a path where the pursuit of equity and inclusion remains a beacon of hope, driving us forward despite the obstacles. My journey is a testament to the enduring commitment to make the world a more just and inclusive place, one decision at a time.

I learned that as a CDO, setbacks were part of the journey. There were times when resistance and politics seemed insurmountable. But I held firm in my belief that our mission was worth the struggle. Each setback served as a lesson, fueling our determination to forge ahead.

Now that you understand the critical junctures of my journey, I would love to offer advice.

Nuggets of Wisdom

As a Chief Diversity Officer, I learned that emotional intelligence is not just a desirable trait; it's a critical skill that underpins success in the role. The work of promoting diversity, equity, and inclusion (DEI) often involves navigating emotionally charged situations, engaging in difficult conversations, and understanding the diverse perspectives and experiences of individuals within the organization. Emotional intelligence allows a CDO to empathize with others, appreciate their feelings and viewpoints, and build bridges even in the face of resistance or controversy. It involves self-awareness, self-regulation, social awareness, and relationship management—qualities that enable a CDO to connect authentically with colleagues, employees, and stakeholders. In the realm of DEI, emotional intelligence equips a CDO to create a safe and inclusive environment where individuals feel heard and valued. It facilitates effective communication, conflict resolution, and the building of trust—a foundation upon which lasting DEI progress can be built. Ultimately, emotional intelligence empowers a CDO to lead with empathy, grace, and the capacity to foster genuine change within an organization.

Adaptation was equally crucial. DEI isn't a one-size-fits-all endeavor. It's about understanding the unique dynamics of your organization and tailoring your strategies accordingly. As the landscape shifted, we evolved our approaches. Flexibility and a willingness to listen and learn were the cornerstones of our resilience. Moreover, I couldn't shoulder this journey alone. Collaboration emerged as a potent ally. Partnering with cabinet-level colleagues, HR, academic colleges, leadership, and various departments was essential in propelling our DEI initiatives forward. We recognized that DEI wasn't the responsibility of a single department but a collective effort that required everyone's commitment and contribution. The cross-functional alliances we formed were rooted in a shared vision of fostering an inclusive workplace. Some of the successes and accomplishments include the development and deployment of inaugural Inclusive Excellence Plans at the University-wide, academic college, and central administrative unit levels and the development of the Office of Inclusive Excellence Faculty and Staff Fellowship program. Additionally, working with the faculty senate and staff council to develop their own inclusive excellence plans, navigating the development of new offices, developing emergency funds for students, community-based economic partnerships in the areas of workforce development and affordable housing, and providing inclusive excellence education to our campus community as well as local communities served. These partnerships amplified our impact, leading to the creation of a more cohesive and aligned organization with increased graduation rates of minoritized populations, and increased employee satisfaction demonstrated by increased retention. While challenges persisted, the collective commitment of various departments became a beacon of hope and progress.

Amidst all the challenges, it was the human element that both motivated and tested me the most. Difficult conversations and personal biases sometimes surface from some of the most interesting places and people. In my experience, it is often the ones you do not expect—many of whom are your colleagues at the top leading the organization. Unearthing organizational biases was a delicate process, and addressing them required patience, empathy, and a willingness to engage in uncomfortable discussions. These experiences underlined the deeply personal and emotional aspects of DEI work. Always remember—this work is not just about policies and programs but about people's lives and experiences. For this reason, it is important to understand the moral imperative along with the business case for DEI. The moral imperative suggests that the work of DEI is simply the right thing to do. I describe it as the "heart" work of DEI. For those of us in the work, we understand that not everyone believes this. However, in my experience, those who do not believe that a firm commitment to DEI met by actions is important, tend to at the very least understand the business case for our work. The business case suggests that for an organization to become or remain financially viable, it must value diverse constituents and issues. For a university, the business case is connected to the recruitment and retention of students, faculty, and staff.

The business case suggests that for an organization to become or remain financially viable, it must value diverse constituents and issues. For a university, the business case is connected to the recruitment and retention of students, faculty, and staff.

It is also connected to advancement and fundraising strategies. It is the reason why many institutions invest in positions including but not limited to multicultural student recruitment, supplier diversity, and divisions of diversity, equity, and inclusion.

I often found myself amid challenging conversations and controversies-in fact, entering my last CDO role on the heels of a book burning that was national news and a month before a global pandemic and a call for racial reckoning. It is vital to recognize that DEI work can sometimes stir discomfort, resistance, or even pushback. Embracing these moments as opportunities for growth and learning is essential. Encouraging open dialogue and providing brave spaces for students, faculty, staff, and alumni to express their concerns or questions can be a powerful way to address controversies. The benefits include a tangible expression of transparency, the ability to hear first-hand the needs and feelings of your community in a way that leaves people feeling valued and heard, and the opportunity to get ahead of challenges that would be pervasive and ongoing.

Active listening, empathy, and patience are your allies in these situations. By approaching these discussions with a willingness to understand and educate, you can transform moments of tension into opportunities for enlightenment. Remember that DEI is a journey of continuous learning, both for you and for those you interact with.

To those aspiring to become Chief Diversity Officers or leaders in the DEI field, I offer some hard-earned advice:

- **People First**: In all things, remember that on the other side of every policy, program, and initiative are people. They matter and should always be prioritized.
- **Build Strong Relationships**: Forming alliances and partnerships within your organization is essential. Collaborate with HR, leadership, and various departments to create a unified approach to DEI. Relationships are the cornerstone of progress in this field.
- **Resilience is Key**: Challenges will undoubtedly arise. Expect setbacks and obstacles but let them fuel your determination to make a difference. Resilience will carry you through the toughest times.
- **Flexibility and Adaptation**: Be prepared to adapt your strategies as circumstances change. DEI is dynamic, and what works today may need adjustments tomorrow. Stay open to new ideas and approaches.
- **Empathy and Active Listening**: DEI work is deeply personal. Empathy and active listening are your most potent tools in fostering under-standing and inclusivity. Cultivate these skills.
- **Lead by Example**: Be an inclusive leader. Your actions and behavior set the tone for the organization. Embrace diversity and inclusion in your daily interactions and decisions.
- **Get it in Writing**: Document your experiences. Plan for the unexpected. From contract negotiations to resource allocation and regular one-on-ones, document everything!

- **Measure and Communicate Impact**: Use data to measure the impact of your initiatives and share your successes. Demonstrating the positive outcomes of DEI efforts can secure ongoing support.
- **Cultivate Patience**: Cultural transformation takes time. Understand that some changes may be gradual. Patience and persistence will be your allies in this journey.
- **Pushback Appropriately**: Pushback is not confrontational; it's a strategic and principled approach to driving change. It involves presenting evidence, sharing personal experiences, and engaging in constructive dialogue to challenge discriminatory practices or attitudes. It's about creating a culture where pushback is welcomed as a means of growth and progress.
- **Continuous Learning**: DEI is a field that is continually evolving. Stay updated on the latest research, trends, and best practices. Attend conferences, read widely, and network with peers.
- **Mentorship and Sponsorship**: Seek mentors and sponsors who can provide guidance and support. Likewise, consider becoming a mentor to others, as mentorship can be a powerful force for change.
- **Stay Committed to Your Values**: Uphold the values of integrity, honesty, diversity, equity, and inclusion unwaveringly. These principles should guide your decisions and actions every step of the way.

A New Chapter: Pivoting to Human Resources Leadership

In 2021 I decided to transition from Chief Diversity Officer (CDO) to Managing Associate in a higher education recruiting firm. I was exhausted by state politics that made lasting change nearly impossible. As a Chief Diversity Officer, you should always position yourself to have other options, whether still in traditional DEI, or adjacent.

Not everyone was happy about my decision to depart. I have learned there will always be voices advocating that you should stay in a job, no matter how tumultuous, to demonstrate stability and commitment. On the other hand, if you are like me, your inner voice will urge you to choose yourself, prioritize your well-being, and be confident in your abilities.

Priority number one was being thoughtful in communicating my departure to all constituent groups, particularly students and my staff. One thing I am particularly proud of is cultivating and mentoring hundreds of team members and supporting thousands of others to continue the work. I desired to minimize the impact of my departure, protect my team, and set them up for success. The same was true for the councils and committees I led. It is for this reason I provided more than 5 months' notice that I would be leaving. It gave us time to identify a plan for interim leadership, answer all questions related to my departure, and stabilize the environment.

The notion of suffering in silence, enduring a challenging work environment for the sake of appearing stable, was a perspective I encountered time and again. It is a viewpoint deeply rooted in conventional wisdom—the belief that enduring hardship is a rite of passage, a testament to dedication, and a marker of professional strength. But as a Chief Diversity Officer, tasked with dismantling systems of inequality and advocating for the well-being of marginalized communities, I recognized the fallacy in this narrative.

My journey as a Chief Diversity Officer has taught me that stability should not come at the cost of self-respect and personal well-being. Advocating for diversity, equity, and inclusion required me to be a beacon of authenticity, not a martyr of silence. It was not only about advocating for the rights and experiences of others but also about recognizing my worth and my ability to effect change. Choosing myself was not an act of selfishness; it was an act of self-preservation and a commitment to the longevity of my impact.

Confidence in my abilities as a professional became my guiding light. It was a belief that the work I was doing had inherent value and that my impact could extend far beyond the confines of a single role or institution. It was a recognition that my dedication to creating equitable and inclusive environments was not dependent on any one job title but was an enduring commitment that transcended specific circumstances.

In choosing myself, I sent a powerful message to those around me—that advocating for diversity and inclusion begins with valuing oneself. It's about being confident in the worth of the work, the significance of the mission, and the ability to effect change, even in the face of adversity. My journey as a CDO had taught me that the pursuit of equity and inclusion required not just resilience but also self-respect. It was a lesson in balancing commitment to a cause with a commitment to oneself. It was a reminder that true stability begins with confidence, authenticity, and an unwavering belief in the power of change, both within and beyond the workplace. My confidence is rooted in my humble beginnings. My authenticity is rooted in my journey. My unwavering belief in the power of change is rooted in the experiences that have shaped me.

This pivot was not a departure from my dedication to diversity, equity, and inclusion (DEI), but rather an expansion of my influence and an avenue through which my previous experiences continue to shape my role in shaping future leaders in education and beyond. My previous experience has illuminated the path forward, guiding me to identify, mentor, and place leaders who will lead with empathy, equity, and inclusion at the forefront. I made the brave decision to return to graduate school for a third time to pursue an MS in Organizational Leadership and Human Resources.

After 17 months at the firm, I received word that I was being promoted to Managing Director. My background as a CDO equips me with a unique perspective on the qualities and competencies required in leadership roles to drive higher education. I understand that leadership goes beyond qualifications; it encompasses values, empathy, and an unwavering commitment to fostering inclusive environments. This understanding has become my compass as I identify and nurture future leaders who lead institutions across the country.

In this new chapter, I remain steadfast in my mission to create more equitable and inclusive organizations. My role is no longer confined to a single institution; it extends across industries and sectors, shaping leadership at the highest levels. My journey continues, driven by the belief that diversity and inclusion are not just buzzwords but essential principles for building a brighter and more equitable future for all (Wilson and Sugin 2023).

As I reflect on my journey, I'm reminded that life's most extraordinary narratives are often woven with threads of determination, compassion, and an unwavering commitment to change. My path, while uniquely my own, embodies the universal truth that each of us holds the power to be architects of transformation and champions of diversity, equity, and inclusion. No matter what you have lived through, you have incredible value and the ability to transform lives via your work. It is a privilege to serve others. Harness the power wisely and always leave others better than you found them.

In the heart of every challenge, I faced and every success I celebrated, I discovered a profound lesson - that the human spirit, when fortified by purpose, can surmount the most formidable obstacles. My journey, marked by humble beginnings and steeped in the values instilled by my upbringing, has taught me that the pursuit of equity and inclusion is not just a professional mission but a deeply personal calling.

The roles of Chief Diversity Officer and Managing Director are more than titles; they are vessels through which I have amplified voices that have long been silenced and ignite change where it is most needed. I have come to understand that our greatest legacy lies not in the titles we hold but in the impact we make, in the lives we touch, and in the doors that we open for others.

My journey serves as a testament that the boundaries of possibility are boundless, that small-town beginnings can lead to far-reaching impacts, and that every individual, regardless of their background, has the potential to be a catalyst for change. I am reminded that our shared humanity transcends the lines of difference, and it is in embracing these differences that we truly find our strength.

I hope that my journey inspires you, as it has inspired me, to embrace your unique path, to champion the causes that resonate with your heart, and to recognize that your actions, however small they may seem, have the power to shape the future. Together, we can build a world where diversity is celebrated, equity is a given, and inclusion is the cornerstone of every endeavor.

I would love to share additional nuggets of wisdom that have been reinforced for me since making the pivot. This list keeps me grounded, reflective, and centered on the most important things.

- *Alignment of Values*: My experience has taught me the paramount importance of alignment between personal values and organizational values. To effect meaningful change, one must be part of an environment that truly embraces integrity at its core.
- *Resilience and Self-Care*: My decision to pivot was a testament to the importance of resilience and self-care. Advocating for DEI can be emotionally taxing, and it's crucial to recognize when one's well-being is at stake. It is not a sign of weakness but a necessity for long-term impact.
- *Authenticity in Leadership*: My experience reinforced the idea that authentic leadership is rooted in unwavering principles. It is about standing up for what you believe in, even when faced with adversity. Authenticity in leadership inspires trust and resonates with others who share similar values. If an opportunity costs you your integrity, it isn't worth it.
- *Continued Advocacy*: Departing from a specific role did not diminish my commitment to DEI. It allowed me to continue advocating for diversity and equity from different vantage points. My journey was a reminder that one's impact can extend beyond the boundaries of a single position.
- *The Power of Public Discourse*: My departure has prompted discussions and reflections on DEI within the broader community. It highlighted the power of public discourse in driving awareness and change. It emphasized that DEI issues should not be relegated to the shadows but should be openly addressed.
- *Respect for One's Journey*: Lastly, my journey taught me the importance of respecting one's own path. Life is a series of experiences, each contributing to our growth and understanding. Even in the face of challenges or unexpected turns, every step has value and can shape us into more effective advocates for change.

The Power of Personal Choice

Throughout my career, I've been fortunate to make interesting and impactful pivots, each driven by a clear sense of purpose and a commitment to personal growth. What sets these transitions apart is that they've always been my own decisions, fueled by a desire to align my work with my values and passions. One thing is also for sure, you should always leave every environment better than you found it, regardless of the duration of your tenure.

In every role I have undertaken, my evaluations have consistently pointed to one clear trend—exceeding expectations. Exceeding expectations is particularly important since the work has always been so highly scrutinized. It was my way of being able to demonstrate undeniable value and organizational commitment. Specifically, I have been evaluated using metrics that focus on the recruitment, retention, and advancement of students, faculty, and staff. I have also been assessed based on employee satisfaction data, education and professional development engagement and satisfaction, fundraising goals, policy, and procedure effectiveness, etc. This isn't just a testament to my dedication and hard work but also to my unwavering commitment to the causes I have championed and the incredible colleagues of teams I have led and campus partners who supported the collective work along the journey. It is a reminder that when we choose paths that resonate with our inner convictions, success naturally follows. The irony is that while I exceeded the expectations of my employers, as I shared with a former supervisor, I did not always feel good about the work we were doing given limitations and political nuances.

Speaking of teams- I have been fortunate enough to cultivate and lead some of the best teams on the planet. The essence of respect and care for teams was demonstrated by first understanding the personal narratives that shaped each team member, recognizing their achievements, encouraging their continued growth and development via promotions, acknowledging personal milestones, and fostering an environment in which mistakes were not fatal, but rather teachable moments. Countless degrees were earned under my leadership and many have gone on to open their businesses, earn tenure and promotion, and hold some of the most incredible leadership positions in the country.

Students have always been the heartbeat of my journey. Their struggles, triumphs, and unwavering commitment kept me going and reinforced my belief that all leadership decisions should prioritize student well-being, safety, growth, and progression. Ultimately, it has always been students who play a pivotal role in steering the course of institutional change. My job has always been to meet them where they are, support them, and ensure they have the very best collegiate experience while minimizing and eliminating institutionalized threats and challenges to their success.

In my career, there has always been a common thread: a deep desire for an environment committed to the work and the opportunity to help institutions understand how critical DEI work is in driving the educational mission of organizations in ways that move from transactional to transformational. What I have longed for, more than anything else is a place where the mission of equity, diversity, and inclusion (DEI) is not just a slogan but a lived reality. It is an environment where DEI is woven into the fabric of the organization, not relegated to a mere checkbox or marketing strategy.

I yearned for an environment where I could deeply invest in building meaningful relationships, nurturing transformative initiatives, and leaving an indelible mark on the organization's culture. It's about creating a legacy of change, one that outlasts any single role or title.

My career pivots have not been a quest for novelty but a pursuit of alignment with my core values. They have been guided by the belief that one's work should be an extension of one's purpose. As I continue this journey, I remain committed to making choices that resonate with my passion for DEI, knowing that when we align our careers with our deepest convictions, we have the power to effect profound change and create lasting impact. I also recognize the profound importance of lifting others as I climb through mentorship, support, and guidance.

I carry with me the invaluable lessons and values instilled by those who have shaped my journey. Their legacy lives on through the work I do, the lives I touch, and the leaders I help nurture. In this narrative, their influence is not just a part of my past; it is the beating heart of my present and the guiding star of my future. It is a testament to the transformative power of love, mentorship, and the enduring impact that individuals can have on the lives of others.

The work of being a diversity practitioner is not just a job; it's a calling. It is about creating a workplace where every individual feels seen, heard, and valued. It's about dismantling systems of inequality and pushing for lasting change. My journey as a CDO is a testament to the transformative power of education, mentorship, and a commitment to equity. It's a reminder that, regardless of where we come from, we can shape a more inclusive and equitable future for all.

But my journey into this role isn't just about reacting to the winds of change. It is about embracing a deeply personal motivation—a desire to be part of something more profound, to shape the narrative of the experiences of all members of learning communities, and to contribute to a future where every individual feels seen, heard, and valued. It's a journey that has tested my resolve, expanded my horizons, and reaffirmed my belief in the transformative power of diversity, equity, and inclusion when appropriately prioritized.

My journey is an ongoing narrative, one that continues to evolve and shape who I am. It is a story of resilience, growth, and integrity. It is a reminder that, as a professional deeply committed to impact, I have the privilege and responsibility to drive change, dismantle barriers, and champion diversity, equity, and inclusion from any seat I inhabit. It is a journey I embrace with open arms, knowing that the path ahead holds both challenges and opportunities to create a more just and inclusive world. I remain steadfast knowing God does ALL things well!

"'Tis so sweet to trust in Jesus, Just to take Him at his word; Just to rest upon His promise; Just to know, Thus saith the Lord ..."

While silence around many parts of my story has always been my strength, I hope you find solace in knowing that you are not alone.

Key Insights from *Boardrooms to Breakthroughs*

- Chief Diversity Officer experiences do not happen in a linear fashion and within traditional academic pathways.
- Federal TRIO programs like Upward Bound, Student Support Services, and Educational Talent Search are high impact interventions for creating access to higher education opportunities.
- Comprehensive accountability measures ensure progress of stated inclusive excellence goals that align with the institution's educational mission of access, inclusion, and community engagement.
- An institution's commitment to diversity, equity, inclusion, and belonging is demonstrated in the resources it allocates to accomplish this work.
- The tension between sustained strategic visioning and tepid surface-level interventions is toggled in the allure of programming involving speakers and events versus measurable structural change.

Things to Consider:

1 What are some of the challenges first-generation college students face in their journey to achieve academic success?
2 What does Wilson say about the importance of other cabinet-level colleagues' participation in this work?
3 What does Wilson say about balancing short-term success with long-term meaningful transformation?
4 What are the ethical dilemmas Wilson speaks of that are a part of the journey of a chief diversity officer?

5 What are the critical skills Wilson notes that are germane to the success of chief diversity practitioners?

6 What are the "pivot moments" that are challenging but promising opportunities for personal and industry growth for DEI professionals?

Reference

Wilson, TaJuan, and Amy Sugin. 2023. *Navigating the Talent Battlefield: Winning the Recruitment Game While Keeping DE&I Front and Center*. Hunt Scanlon Media. Retrieved from https://huntscanlon.com/wp-content/uploads/2023/11/2023_HigherEd_report.pdf.

9
HISTORY OF A CDO'S JOURNEY OVER 50 YEARS

Benjamin D. Reese Jr

As I stood on the stone steps outside of our new, towering three-story house in the Bronx, I was struggling to take it all in. After living my first five years in a five-floor walk-up in Harlem, my grandmother purchased this house, with a grass-covered back yard, in this all-White neighborhood in the Bronx, about five to six blocks from Yankee Stadium. This was my new home. I had certainly seen White people before. Many of the shop owners in our Harlem neighborhood were Caucasian, and living near Harlem Hospital, I regularly saw White doctors entering and leaving the many doors of what seemed like a gargantuan structure. To a four- or five-year-old, anyone with a white coat coming out of that huge hospital building was most certainly a doctor.

To manage the monthly mortgage payments on our new three-story Bronx home, my grandmother had to rent two apartments to various tenants over the years. My grandmother occupied the first floor, the second and third floors were rented, my parents and I lived in the basement. It wasn't what you might think of as a "basement apartment," it was an actual basement. But thankfully, my father was very skilled and handy in terms of woodwork, plumbing, and electrical work. I'm not sure where he learned it all, but he put up plasterboard walls to create three small rooms, and connected piping and electric lines so that we had a bathroom and kitchen. He even hung a thick metal door to muffle the sound from the boiler and to minimize the oil fumes that seeped into our basement apartment. It sure beat our old Harlem tenement apartment. It was my new home.

I don't recall how I met Lenny, who was White, but quickly we became best friends. We never talked about race, but I was always keenly aware of

DOI: 10.4324/9781032724881-12

the stares from other kids and adults ... a sole Black youngster among a group of White kids. During my pre-teen years, Lenny and I would get on our bicycles and ride about an hour and a half to a place in the Bronx called City Island.

A small community of Bronxites who enjoyed living by the water, their boats, as well as the nearby urban area of New York City. As soon as we arrived at City Island, after our long bike ride, Lenny and I would head for our favorite fish and chips stand. I would excitedly run up to the outdoor stand, waving my hand and saying, "I'm next." After several trips to City Island, I realized that although I might have been the first or second customer at the stand, I wasn't served until everyone else was served. I couldn't name the experience, but it certainly felt like it had something to do with my race ... the fact that I wouldn't be served until all the White people were served. Consequently, every time Lenny talked about taking a bicycle ride to City Island, I felt both excitement and anticipation, and that feeling in the pit of my stomach. I knew that I would have to experience that feeling of being ignored, being served last. It was one of several unspoken race dynamics between me and my best friend. Lenny and I maintained a close friendship until we started high school. He went to the elite, Bronx High School of Science. I enrolled at the local high school, William Howard Taft.

In high school, my growing understanding of race in America and racial exclusion formed a springboard for my deepening analysis of the complex politics of racism in America. I read every pamphlet about race issues that I could get my hands on, because there weren't many relevant books in the school library. I attended scores of Civil Rights marches, often during times when I should have been in class or studying for an exam. My grades suffered. When the time came to apply to college, my low grade-point-average and constrained family income made it difficult to get accepted into any college or university. Fortunately, Bronx Community College in New York City, within a tuition-free education system, accepted me as a non-matriculant, part-time student.

After that first semester at Bronx Community College, the governor of New York State, Governor Nelson Rockefeller, announced that he was considering asking the legislature to impose tuition throughout the City University System, including Bronx Community College! I and many of my colleagues, particularly those activist students, were appalled. It would be so difficult to finish our college education if we had to pay tuition. After a planning meeting, a group of us from Bronx Community College, Queens College, and the City College of New York got our sleeping bags and took the subway to the Manhattan office of Governor Rockefeller. We vowed to sleep on the sidewalk outside of his office until he changed his mind. Our protest received coverage in newspapers across New York City. The Governor decided to delay the imposition of tuition, not because of our protest, but likely because of the "push-back" from high-ranking politicians and educators across New York City. Although our protest may not have been successful, I do believe that it highlighted the importance of access to higher education for the widest range of students, an issue I would later focus on in my role as a Chief Diversity Officer (CDO). My parents were so proud when, after two years, I graduated from Bronx Community College.

With my two-year degree in hand, I transferred to the City College of New York to complete the last two years of my bachelor's degree, graduating in 1968 with a major in psychology. My involvement in civil rights and issues of racial equity only deepened during those two years at City College, as well as during my Master's Degree study.

In a sense, it was a bit odd getting degrees in psychology, given I did not really know any psychologists, certainly no Black psychologists. Nevertheless, I developed this deep interest in research about human motivation, particularly motivation related to issues of race, and was an avid reader of books and articles about the subject. I even read "white nationalist's literature" in an effort to gain some insight into what motivated individuals to be attracted to KKK-like organizations. I posed that question to Claiborne Paul Ellis (CP Ellis) in the late 1990s when we met in Durham, North Carolina. CP Ellis was the former Exalted Cyclops (local leader) of the Durham Ku Klux Klan (KKK). I'm not sure I ever got a clear answer from CP, but after spending a Saturday afternoon with one of his children, it was clear that in addition to CP's KKK activities, he was a loving father and struggled with many of the same socio-economic issues as poor Black families, even though his family had the "cushion of Whiteness." My conversations with CP and his family deepened my understanding of the complexity of the human condition. People motivated by what I consider racist ideology could also be individuals committed to loving and meaningful family relationships.

The process of getting a doctorate in clinical psychology was life changing. It wasn't so much the coursework or the interesting professors at Rutgers University, it was the fact that the director of the Greenwich Village mental health clinic (The Fifth Ave. Center for Counseling & Psychotherapy) that served as my clinical externship, asked me to take the role of clinic coordinator ... during my *first month* of placement at the clinic! He felt that despite my young age and minimal experience with mental health services, I had well developed administrative skills. Often holding two jobs at a time, I had accumulated a lot of administrative experience at a relatively young age. I appreciated his confidence in me, but I rejected the offer. I already was working part-time at a not-for-profit community organization. After a number of conversations over the coming weeks, I took a deep breath and finally said, "yes" to his offer. In addition to this major administrative role, I also made time to see my own patients as part of my externship, under the supervision of the director. Over time, as this new job unfolded, I found myself coordinating the schedules of the 80 to 90 part-time psychotherapists at the clinic; supervising the front-desk staff; dealing with frequent crises, including multiple suicide attempts; arranging clinic placements for social work and doctoral students from nearby institutions; and eventually learning to effectively respond to the complex New York State clinic licensing requirements.

After several years of transversing the New Jersey Turnpike, two to three times a week, from New York City to Rutgers University in New Jersey, and running the day-to-day operations of the mental health clinic, I finally graduated in 1978. Although it was certainly gratifying to have a doctorate degree, little changed in my day-to-day administrative responsibilities, other than a change in title from, Clinic Coordinator to Associate Director. But, my new credential, and absence of schoolwork, allowed me to accept the growing number of race and social justice consulting opportunities that came my way. Over the next several years I found myself speaking nationally and internationally about issues of race and the impact of diversity in mental health treatment, education, and workplaces. Sometimes I would make a presentation at a conference, other times I would facilitate workshops, or help an organization examine its culture. One interesting request came from the Rockefeller Foundation. They distributed a request for proposals to provide "diversity training" for their New York staff. After making it to the interview stage, my training proposal was rejected, but they asked me if I would accept the role of Ombudsperson for the Foundation, a new position they were considering creating. I would need to be available 6 to 7 hours per week to mediate conflicts related to cultural, gender, sexual orientation, or racial differences. I accepted the position, surmising that it would be a good use of my counseling and psychotherapy skills, as well as my work on issues of race and diversity. It wasn't until several years later that I realized that the ombudsperson role was a valuable experience in preparation for my CDO at Duke University. The Foundation's staff, like most universities, represented a wide range of cultural, racial, and ethnic backgrounds. Virtually every conflict or disagreement I was asked to mediate had a diversity component. Even when the parties both expressed the same commitment to the Foundation's mission, they brought their own philosophies, work styles, life experiences, and cultural backgrounds. Like in the academy, managing differences requires skill in resolving systemic issues, but also requires a deep understanding and appreciation for the cultural context of individuals, be they students, faculty, or senior level administrative managers of global programs.

*Like in the academy, managing
differences requires skill in
resolving systemic issues, but also
requires a deep understanding
and appreciation for the cultural
context of individuals.*

It was probably the opportunity to observe numerous well-designed workshops and stirring presentations, while at the Foundation, that prompted me to create my own institute. I fashioned The *Institute for The Study of Culture & Ethnicity* located within the mental health clinic. It provided courses and workshops for mental health clinicians, hospital administrators, and not-for-profit organization leaders.

As important as the services it provided, it helped me further my thinking about some of the theoretical underpinnings of racial equity, and diversity in organizations. It was one thing to treat psychotherapy clients or mediate conflicts between individuals, but the Institute challenged me to develop courses for seasoned professionals, many of whom had extensive experience with diversity in organizations. My own professional reading and attendance at lectures and presentations expanded to include business and organizational change topics, helping to prepare me for, not only my CDO responsibilities, but for my current role as a consultant to higher education institutions and organizations across the United States and abroad.

As our four-year-old daughter began to grow, my wife and I thought about the opportunity for her to attend kindergarten in an environment different from the semi-rural area of Carmel, New York, where we were living. I also began to reflect on the notion that I had accomplished so many of my goals in the New York City environment, related to mental health and issues of race and social justice. My wife and I began discussing the possibility of relocating to another part of the country. Our conversations coincided with a couple of magazines articles highlighting the Raleigh/Durham area of North Carolina as one of the best places to live in America. Not knowing anyone in North Carolina, we began to take extended weekend trips to the Raleigh/Durham community. My wife would look at possible housing choices during our visits, as well as opportunities to relocate her own psychotherapy practice. I began networking to explore job opportunities that would use my training as a psychologist, background in race issues and diversity, and my growing competence in organizational change. Before long, I got a couple good job leads and was about to accept an offer, when I met Myrna Adams, who was the current Vice President for Institutional Equity and Chief Diversity Officer (CDO) for Duke University and Duke University Hospital. Her dynamism and sense of commitment to diversity and equity were so very stimulating. Coincidentally, she was looking for someone to help lead the diversity work in her office. The process of interviewing only deepened my excitement about the possibility of working with her and learning from her vast experience. When she made the offer, I gladly accepted the role of Cross-Cultural Relations Specialist in 1996, and in less than a year, I was promoted to Assistant Director.

Not only was Myrna an incredible mentor in helping me better understand the higher education and healthcare environment, but she was critical in guiding me through the complex legal aspects of affirmative action, harassment, and discrimination regulations, which were also the responsibilities of the Duke Office for Institutional Equity. As my responsibilities at the University broadened, she made it clear that she hoped that I would succeed her when she retired in a couple years. I was certainly intrigued by the possibility and so grateful for her confidence in me, but I didn't feel quite ready to oversee a campus and a hospital. The world of higher education still felt like a new environment. Thus, when Myrna announced her retirement and a search committee was formed, I hesitantly applied, just before the close of the application period. A seasoned CDO from another school was chosen. I was both disappointed, but in a sense, relieved.

Two years into the five-year VP/CDO term, the newly hired CDO resigned. The university president called me into her office and made it clear that she, and other university leaders, wanted me to take the role of Interim Vice President of the Office for Institutional Equity. Given that the current university president was stepping down in about 18 months, I would have to understand that a new president might eliminate the position or select someone else. I accepted the offer; I had grown and felt ready for the higher education/healthcare CDO role ... a role that had expanded. Duke Hospital was now part of the Duke University Health System, comprised of three hospitals and a string of outpatient clinics. My area of responsibility included the undergraduate campus, the graduate school, seven professional schools, as well as the Duke University Health System. At the time, I was probably the only higher education CDO in the country who had responsibility for a university as well as an entire health system. Interestingly, there is currently a Duke university CDO, and CDO-like positions in the Medical School, in addition to a senior diversity and inclusion professional for the Duke University Health System, and several other "diversity executives" across the institution.

In 2005, about six to seven months after the new president took office, he contacted me and told me that he wanted me to be his first senior level appointment, Vice President for Institutional Equity/CDO. I would no longer be "Interim." After many individual and group screening interviews and a committee evaluating my accomplishments as Interim VP/CDO, I was appointed.

The expansive role didn't leave much time for outside involvement, but I continued to speak across the country about equity, diversity, and inclusion (EDI) and what had become an area of specialization, implicit bias. In all my speaking engagements, I emphasized the centrality and importance of the CDO role. It was clear to me that equity, diversity, and this new concept of inclusion were everyone's responsibility, but I knew enough about organization structure to realize that without a senior level executive with knowledge, budget, and authority, EDI would flounder within a college or university. It's analogous to a chief financial officer.

It was clear to me that equity, diversity, and this new concept of inclusion were everyone's responsibility

---

... without a senior level executive with knowledge, budget, and authority, EDI would flounder within a college or university. It's analogous to a chief financial officer.

Everyone in an organization should have responsibility and be held accountable for being good stewards of budgeting and fund allocation, but you must have a senior level financial officer to provide leadership, coordination, and alignment across an institution. The CDO, or a similar role, is a critical position in colleges and universities. Although I spoke about the CDO role as I visited colleges and universities across the country, I really didn't think about the need for a national organization. I am deeply grateful for the wisdom of Willian "Bill" Harvey. Bill was an executive with the American Council on Education and a highly respected higher education leader focused on racial equity in the academy.

Bill coordinated a series of meetings, starting in 2003, to explore the viability of forming a national organization of CDOs. The attendance at these meetings was far beyond expectations, suggesting a strong interest in creating such an organization. On February 12, 2006, a "Caretaker Group" met in Los Angeles to formally create an organization, decide upon a name, develop by-laws, and form an initial Caretaker Board of Directors, that would eventually become the first National Association of Diversity Officers in Higher Education (NADOHE) Board of Directors. Drawing "straws out of a cup," I received a three-year term, others received one-year, or two-year terms. NADOHE was officially created.

I was honored to serve on the Board for several years, serve two terms as president, expand the Journal of Diversity in Higher Education, help create the Standards of Professional Practice and the Fellows Program, initiate the first NADOHE International Program, serve as the first Conference Chair, and start the expansion of NADOHE, beyond four-year institutions. I remain involved in NADOHE and recently collaborated with colleagues to create the first NADOHE/Coventry University Global EDI in Higher Education Conference in 2022. As I reflect on the current outstanding leadership that has led the strong growth of NADOHE, playing a role in creating the organization is one of the most important contributions of my career.

I am fortunate to have had parents who helped me navigate the transition from Harlem to the Bronx, supporting me as I slowly ventured into a new racial and cultural environment. Any success as a CDO surely rests on that foundation. It provided me with the security to later venture into the management of a large mental health center and a senior role in a major foundation. I credit those leadership experiences as providing the knowledge and emotional strength to successfully function as a CDO of a university and health system.

In 2019, I stepped down from my VP/CDO role at Duke University and the Health System, although I continue to be engaged as adjunct professor in the Department of Psychiatry and Behavioral Sciences and serve as Co-PI on an implicit bias research grant. I serve on boards of organizations aligned with my life's work in EDI and race issues and am CEO of BenReese, LLC, a global EDI strategy consulting company working with colleges, universities, and not-for-profit organizations across our nation and abroad.

As I think about where CDOs stand in higher education, and the current state of EDI more broadly, several trends and challenges stand out: 1) the shifting and expanding responsibilities of the CDO role as a result of the inclusion of, and focus on, a widening range of complex individual and group identities; 2) the professionalization of the CDO role as a result of ongoing research and the work of NADOHE; 3) the growth in EDI roles/titles and positions to support and collaborate with the institutional CDO and; 4) the conservative trend in our society and its potential impact on the CDO role, and EDI, more broadly.

After almost 60 years of doing this work, and reflecting on the wisdom of my mentors, I regularly remind myself that the struggle towards greater social justice, fairness, and equity benefits ALL of us. In higher education, the CDO is an important leadership role, benefiting ALL students, staff, and faculty.

Key Points from *History of a CDO's Journey over 50 Years*

- Understanding racial exclusion in America leads to a deeper and clearer analysis of the complexities of racism in America.
- Education is a social justice issue too.
- The skills of the ombudsperson role can be transferable to the chief diversity officer and/or other diversity practitioner roles.
- The professionalization and expansion of the CDO role creates an opportunity for organizational realignment with its educational mission and values.
- Psychology provides an alternative lens through which to examine equity, inclusion, and organizational change.

Some things to consider:

1 Reese describes several moments in his leadership journey that were pivotal in helping him to develop a frame of reference for equity work. What were they? How did these moments help to shape his DEI blueprint?
2 Reese's 60-year plus professional career allows us an opportunity to experience personal, communal, and national history through the identity prism. What can we learn from the complexity of that journey?

3 What other forms of diversity and inclusion does Reese elevate in his chapter? What are some unexpected revelations about those discussions?
4 Name three moments in your own leadership journey as a diversity practitioner that have helped you create your leadership compass/blueprint. Has that blueprint changed? Why?

10

NAVIGATING NEPANTLA

Carolyn J. Morales

Within the Aztec language of Nahuatl, there is an Indigenous term—nepantla aptly fitting to the current state of DEI. It refers to being in the middle and existing in a state of in-between-ness. It is "a psychological, liminal space between the way things had been and an unknown future" (Anzaldúa 2015, p. 40). As anti-DEI sentiments and legislation magnify throughout the country, our discipline is in a state of change.

The rapid hiring expansion that occurred across the United States, post-George Floyd, is now in the midst of a national retraction whose end state is unknown. As practitioners, we are navigating nepantla—a change, a "place where different perspectives come into conflict and where you question the basic ideas, tenets, and identities" (Anzaldúa 2015, p. 122).

DOI: 10.4324/9781032724881-13

Essentially, what nepantla advances is a change philosophy. Experiencing in-between-ness represents a transition; an opportunity for change and transformation (Carbajal 2021, p. 1). Anzaldúa suggests that "in nepantla we undergo the anguish of changing our perspectives and crossing a series of cruz calles, junctures, thresholds, some leading to a different way of relating to people and surroundings and others to the creation of a new world" (2015, p. 40–41). Instead of viewing the current DEI landscape from a deficit lens, consider it a reminder of the cyclical and ever-changing nature of life.

Instead of viewing the current DEI landscape from a deficit lens, consider it a reminder of the cyclical and ever-changing nature of life.

We are in the "what-was" and "what-will-be" DEI space. A place that represents "a zone of possibility" (2015, p. 118–119).

The patterns that guide our daily DEI practice will also need to shift and evolve. Kupferberg suggests that "When patterns are broken, new worlds emerge" (n.d., as cited in Taylor 1984). Rather than resist this dynamic, we should lean into it because change inspires and requires innovation. Within this emerging, new DEI reality, I suggest—there is no path; we must make it. Let us embrace this in-between-ness because it provides us with a unique opportunity to reexamine and elevate our discipline.

When looking forward, it is helpful to look back. This offers context to understand what needs to be changed because it provides the capacity to compare and contrast what currently is to what could potentially be. Reengaging the epistemology of why you believe what you believe requires reflection because I can take stock of the victories, both large and small. I can reassess the losses and lessons learned and understand that even when I lost, I won by gaining wisdom.

I can reassess the losses and lessons learned and understand that even when I lost, I won by gaining wisdom.

This is the lens I want us to bring to navigating the application of nepantla to DEI. Reexamining why I chose this career path affords me the ability to see old things with new perspectives and to apply this insight to acquire new life lessons.

Querying Qallariy (The Beginning)

I began my DEI career hiding in a closet. I was in graduate school in Vermont and had joined the People of Color (POC) Support Group. Initially formed as a support system for other graduate students, our role shifted to advocacy once we discovered that our concerns were not new. A letter I found in the student government office, addressed to the board of trustees, played a part of this shift. Written by a former student body president twenty years prior, the memo detailed our current realities—an international curriculum rooted in a Western, Eurocentric lens and a lack of racial, ethnic, or international diversity amongst the students, staff, and faculty.

As a group, we decided that now was the time to pressure the administration to adopt a statement of support for diversity and consider the development of a DEI strategic plan. After conducting a survey of students, staff, and faculty, the data validated our concerns, but proved insufficient for senior leaders. While we were ready for change, the organization was not.

In response to this reality, we hired doctoral students at UMass Amherst to serve as consultants and constructed a series of strategies to move this agenda forward. After reading the letter to members of the board of trustees, they authorized the construction of an institutional diversity statement. Yet, securing the buy-in of senior leaders for the development of a DEI plan proved challenging. After a series of failed negotiations, we reached a stalemate with senior management and moved forward with the next phase of our plan—camping outside of the President's building, beginning a hunger strike, and initiating a phone call tree that brought students from neighboring colleges and universities within Vermont and Massachusetts to campus to support our campaign.

Things changed quickly that last evening of negotiations. When I left the classroom and walked into the hallway, I heard campus security speaking to someone clarifying if we should be arrested. Hearing that word, I quickly stepped into the closest closet. Sitting in the dark, afraid of going to jail, I didn't know if I could continue with the next phase of our plan. It was a pivotal moment for me in ways I couldn't fully fathom at the time because it forced me to question my level of commitment to this work. How far was I willing to go? The irony of seeking illumination while sitting in the dark isn't lost on me.

What compelled me to join my colleagues outside was the possibility that in helping myself I could help others, and that by advocating for change, I could potentially disrupt patterns of exclusion and oppression. Within the People of Color Support Group, I met people who understood my pain because it was their pain. Unbeknownst to me, in walking outside of the closet that evening, I unknowingly embarked upon my future career path.

Our campaign proved successful and several weeks later we had the template for the institution's inaugural strategic diversity plan. To assist with operationalizing the plan, I applied—and was offered—my first DEI job—a diversity affairs associate position, a one-year internship. This position afforded me ability to work with the interim president and graduate school dean and served as a crash course in change management.

After completing the internship, there was no questioning what I wanted to do; I just knew. And, I have been doing DEI ever since 1997 in some capacity or another. As I see the end of my career in sight, I'm inspired by the words:

> … but at the end of the day, it's not about what you have or even what you've accomplished. It's about what you've done with those accomplishments. It's about who you've lifted up, who you've made better. It's about what you've given back. (Hanks 2011)

In sharing lessons learned over the course of 20+ years as a DEI practitioner, I hope that the life and professional experiences of a Latine of Quechuan and Mexican ancestry prove beneficial.

Lessons Learned

As a Quechua Indian, I practice the tradition of giving thanks to Pachamama, Mother Earth. She is a revered deity who not only preserves life on Earth but represents the Andean resistance to sustain Indigenous practices against European colonization. Making an offering to Mother Earth is a way of giving back what has been taken by humanity. In this way, offerings are considered expressions of gratitude known as añaychay or thanks. Extending gratitude to Pachamama is a way to reconnect people to nature so that we can not only learn to live in harmony with the Mother Earth, but with each other.

As diversity scholars and practitioners, we must release what we knew to be DEI and use this in-between stage to step into a creation phase or rebirth of our discipline. According to philosopher Joseph Campbell, "We must be willing to get rid of the life we've planned, so as to have the life that is waiting for us" (Campbell 1991, p. 18). Early career lessons enable me to reframe the current state of DEI into expressions of gratitude and to actively seek out ways to thrive in this environment by crafting and delivering practical and actionable strategies that put añaychay/thanks into practice. For me, this reframe is inspired by knowledge gained from historical patterns and cultural dichos.

Historical Patterns

Lerner (1986) speaks to the capacity of history to reveal cyclical patterns of nature and life—birth, death, and rebirth. She suggests:

> The system of patriarchy is a historic construct; it has a beginning; it will have an end … . What will come after, what kind of structure will be the foundation for alternate forms of social organization we cannot yet know. We are living in an age of unprecedented transformation. We are in the process of becoming. (1986, pp. 228–229)

This idea of becoming illustrates the concept of nepantla in practice. While Lerner references patriarchy, her insight can be applied to other social systems. Implicit to the process of moving beyond in-between-ness is the process of evolving and becoming something else.

When seeking to put añaychay/thanks into practice, my most immediate default is historical inspiration because it serves as a daily reminder that these challenges are longstanding. Truly, when has doing DEI ever been easy? If you choose this work, then you have to accept and come to peace with the reality that this work is hard. Given this fact, it is important to seek comfort in the wins. Remember the wins; share the wins. They become part of your history and serve as professional inspiration to continue to do the work.

Expect to lose from time to time. When a project, program, or practice that I was hoping to advance gets a hard "No," my default is to reflect upon the strategy. Examine what you may have missed or what you could change and use this insight to determine what to do differently. Learn from your losses.

Also, consider that sometimes the "No" isn't about your capacity to do the work, it is about the unwillingness of leadership to support the agenda. If in my analysis, it's about timing with leadership in your organization, then shelve the project. Timing can be everything in this work. Putting a project on hold isn't a loss for me and shouldn't be for you; consider it a timeout. In the interim, continue to build support for your effort in strategic ways, but be prepared to pounce when you believe the timing to be right. When is that? You develop that instinct over time and with practice, so you continue to refine your craft and consult with other trusted colleagues to gain their insight and perspectives. Remember, the best change practices are incremental in nature and are more likely to be sustainable.

Integral to doing DEI is advancing organizational and systems change so as we evolve our work we naturally engage and re-engage the cycle of life—birth, death, and rebirth. In doing so we consistently situate ourselves in the practice of navigating nepantla. Recognizing this pattern is critical because it deconstructs and situates the in-between-ness phase as cyclical in nature. In this way, re-examining history provides us with knowledge on how to best traverse these transitions.

An example of this birth/death/rebirth practice is exemplified at the funeral of my grandmother. When she passed my great-aunts traveled from our family's village of Colcabamba, located in the remote Andes Mountains. Their two-day journey to the capital of Lima was to conduct a traditional ceremony which involved gathering physical possessions like clothing and forming them in the shape of her person on an altar on the ground. These items were then burned as family elders danced in a circle around the altar chanting prayers in Quechua.

This ceremony served as an act of cultural resistance against the traditional velatorio—a Catholic funeral and burial service which has the casket at the family home or church and enables family and guests to pay their respects over a two to three day period. My elders conducted a second funeral that represented a clear departure from the traditional Western-influenced ceremony that had been planned. They did not ask for permission to conduct this Indigenous practice. They just did it. In burning her personal possessions such as her favorite sweater, the elders provided my grandmother's spirit safe passage to the next cycle of life—rebirth. This historical ritual represents how different traditions engage the cycle of change and how Indigenous traditions sustain ancient practices and knowledge.

In this way, Indigenous knowledge provides another pathway of how to navigate nepantla. Sustaining these customs illustrates an inter-generational transfer of knowledge. My Quechuan ancestors maintain this tradition as a mechanism to protect and nurture our Andean identity and culture against oppressive historical colonization. Their sacrifice provides me with inherited knowledge that takes the form of "dichos" (sayings). In sharing these sayings, I give thanks to Pachamama by making intellectual offerings to our DEI community.

Dichos/Sayings

When my father reunited with his Peruvian family after 25 years, there was a large contingent of them waiting for us at the airport. It was a loud, chaotic scene and my limited Spanish made it difficult to understand the discussion. What I do recall was the pull to this stranger in the midst of the 100+ family members who waited for us late that evening. I knew no one, but I remember feeling compelled to walk toward this diminutive woman who I didn't know. Her back was to me, so I stood behind her, and when she turned around we just silently stared at each other.

Her name was Anna Cancan, and she was subsequently introduced to me as my grandmother. Anna shared with me the dicho/saying *La sangre llame a la sangre*/Your blood calls out to my blood. And, it has always evoked the memory of when I first met her as an adult. While this proverb speaks to the links that connect us as families, I extend its usage further to apply it to the links that bind us as humans. More specifically, I share this dicho with fellow practitioners, because it speaks to the unspoken dynamic that unites us as a community in the institutions we serve and extends beyond us to Pachamama/Mother Earth. Every day we practice our discipline we make an offering to humanity. This offering takes the shape of programs, policies, and practices we craft, execute, and assess that seek to redress persistent and long-standing social and structural inequities.

I give gratitude to Pachamama by expressing añaychay/thanks to the wisdom shared to me by my elders and creating avenues to pass it forward to others. As DEI challenges continue to evolve, we must actively create avenues of support for one another both professionally and personally. Our fears, our hopes, our anger necessitate safe avenues for expression. A reframe to the current local, state, and national dynamics is to use this time to reinforce your/our community. Rather than allowing the current culture to fracture our community, we must utilize this transition as a space to reinforce our professional practice as we shift from this middle, in-between space to the next cycle of our practice.

The offering I make to us as a community is that we should seek opportunities to integrate Indigenous wisdom within our practice. Within DEI, we have yet to create a formalized mechanism that models the inter-generational transfer of knowledge found within Indigenous practices. In a State of the CDO Survey Report published by the National Association of Diversity Officers in Higher Education (NADOHE) in August 2023, only 1.53% of the 261 chief diversity officers who participated were Native American or Alaskan Native. We suspect the representation of Indigenous leaders within the discipline is nominal, but there is no validated national data to provide insight on Native representation within DEI leadership.

Representation matters because without Indigenous perspectives, then our discipline crafts and sustains a DEI leadership prototype that self-perpetuates the marginalization of Indigenous identities.

Representation matters because without Indigenous perspectives, then our discipline crafts and sustains a DEI leadership prototype that self-perpetuates the marginalization of Indigenous identities.

It also limits the capacity for this knowledge transfer, like dichos, to be shared within our discipline. Battiste (2005) suggests:

> Indigenous knowledge has always existed .... The task for Indigenous academics has been to affirm and activate the holistic paradigm of Indigenous knowledge to reveal the wealth and richness of Indigenous languages, worldviews, teachings, and experiences, all of which have been systematically excluded from contemporary educational institutions and from Eurocentric knowledge systems. (p. 1)

The wisdom exists; it just needs to be shared. As DEI practitioners, we have the capacity to do this. While I reference US and Peruvian Native knowledge, there are Indigenous communities throughout the world that are untapped wells of wisdom. As we navigate nepantla, dichos are useful offerings that provide a pathway to enhance our professional practice as we work to create more equitable, inclusive, and just campus communities.

Hatun kayqam ichikpitam qallan—*Greatness Begins from the Little Things*

This Quechuan proverb reminds me of our potential for greatness as a community. Every day I advance change, little or big, I honor Pachamama. This practice takes expression in a myriad of ways. While my work focus is strategic planning, I am cognizant of the fact that change occurs slowly. This focus is important to remember because large, lofty plans can lose focus, and well-intentioned strategic plans often collect dust. I prefer to begin the work with a narrowed focus in order to acquire buy-in and support for future areas of development so I start small with "little things" with the hope and expectation that greater things will evolve.

Starting small enables me to build momentum because integral to this process is gaining trust from community stakeholders and illustrating how this work benefits everyone and in what ways the needle is being moved. It also allows me the flexibility to pivot when assessment mechanisms reveal what is and what isn't working. Integrated into this strategy is also amassing early wins. I do this by seeking out the community leaders within staff and faculty to gain a sense of the history and culture of an organization. I learn from them what is on their "wish list," and what institutional legacies I must contend with.

With any new position, you are under a microscope. People are watching to see what you can deliver so actively seek out getting something that's tangible from the wish list accomplished early. This strategy buys you time to evolve other long-term strategic goals and objectives and to develop relationships with stakeholders from all levels of the organization. Once you scratch something from that list, they become vested in your success because it becomes "our" success and by default the communities' success. Collectively, these small strategies create space for larger strategies to evolve. And, with each victory, you collectively expand the circle and culture of belonging. This is where and how your community can achieve hatun/greatness.

Llaqtakunaq atipayninwan, teqrimuyuta kuyuchisunchis

When the Villages Work Together, We Will Turn This World Around

Village is synonymous with community so I will use these terms interchangeably. These incremental wins that lead to *"hatun"*/greatness do not happen in a vacuum. The work of belonging is about something larger than you. It's about leaning into a collectivist orientation of "we above me." It's a delicate balance that you continually struggle to achieve. You need to develop an awareness of who you are and what you need from community.

You will find in your organization that there are villages, but they sometimes exist in silos. While the silo space is important it is equally valuable to create opportunities for the varying villages to be reminded of the larger institutional connections.

While the silo space is important it is equally valuable to create opportunities for the varying villages to be reminded of the larger institutional connections.

Villages are created for multiple reasons but within them, members often seek a space of safety and belonging. Other social identity groups will likely have these same outcomes in mind so it's important to find ways to connect the villages from time to time and remind them of what connects them rather than what separates them.

When these communities work together the capacity to effect change increases. It requires mobilizing them around common experiences and utilizing the wisdom they've gained from their respective identities to advance larger institutional goals. When you are able to harness this energy and this institutional knowledge you increase the ability to advance strategic plans, organizational transformations, and systems change.

When you are able to harness this energy and this institutional knowledge you increase the ability to advance strategic plans, organizational transformations, and systems change.

When villages within your organization work together everybody wins because you expand the scope of belonging and with it the culture of your respective institutions. As a DEI practitioner, fortifying the village and advancing humanity is the offering you make to Pachamama. And, ultimately reflects how we will achieve teqrimuyuta kuyuchisunchis/we will turn this world around.

Putting Añaychay into Practice

Every day we step into our space to do this work we give back to Mother Earth what has been taken by humanity. Our DEI offerings are our hearts, our minds, and our skills—all precious items that deserve to be honored, recognized, and valued. The gratitude we extend to others we must also extend to ourselves. In this way, these expressions of appreciation reconnect us to our motivation for doing this work. Staying centered and clear about our sources of inspiration, whatever they may be, provides a daily practice in clarity.

This sustained well-spring of remembrance has served me well and may do so for you. It reminds us that we are instruments and that our calling is to be of service to others. It grounds us with the prompt that our time with Pachamama is also limited. It also reiterates to us that our work rectifies the wrongs perpetuated against humanity. In nourishing ourselves through the practice of añaychay, we can nourish others. This cyclical pattern of giving establishes a legacy of change because it situates the practice of gratitude as a bi-directional process. While our practice is to extend it outwards to the communities we serve, it must also extend inward to us as agents of change, advocates, and allies. This process reinforces our universal connection to each other and Mother Earth.

Beyond applying añaychay to ourselves, how do we extend it to others within our organizational practice? Understanding how to operationalize gratitude within organizational behavior is experiencing an expansion of research interest (Locklear, Sheridan, and Kong 2023). This research, however, is often framed within a Eurocentric, often Western lens.

Were one to trace a history of scholarly work on gratitude to modern day, it would begin with philosophers (e.g., Seneca, Adam Smith, Thomas Aquinas, and David Hume), followed by sociologists (e.g., Blau 1964; Gouldner 1960) and social psychologists (e.g., Algoe 2012; Algoe and Haidt 2009; Wood, Froh, and Geraghty 2010; Fredrickson 2004; McCullough et al. 2001), who variously noted the importance of gratitude to moral behaviors, social relationships, and personal wellness. (Locklear, Sheridan, and Kong 2023)

While these intellectual contributions are commendable, it is important to acknowledge that excluded from the research on gratitude are Indigenous epistemologies. Raining, a member of the Sault Ste Marie Tribe of Chippewa Native Americans, contends that gratitude is "the bedrock of many indigenous cultures such as Native Americans" (Raining 2021, p. 315).

Putting añaychay into practice is beneficial because it validates both our standpoint and capacity as knowers. Empowering Othered perspectives and ways of knowing, whose historical traditions are rooted in nature—Mother Earth is essential to enhancing organizational culture. Because all life, inclusive of culture, flows through Pachamama and into us, as members of organizations, and, more importantly as members of humanity. This epistemological stance is supported by Victor et al. (2016) who contend:

Many Indigenous philosophies arise through a relational epistemology where understandings of the world are constructed through the lens of interconnectivity with our social and physical environments (Goulet and Goulet 2014; Healy and Tagak 2014). This recognition of our inter-connectivities translates into a relational accountability where the implications of all activity are considered so that actions honour individuals, the community, the spiritual world, and the environment. (Absolon 2011; Wilson 2008, p. 424)

How then is an offering to Pachamama useful in an organizational context? As diversity practitioners, we must invite and engage all members of our respective organizations with the ability to both extend and receive gratitude. If marginalized perspectives are not afforded the ability to illustrate their respective cultural context for gratitude, then the production of knowledge is compromised as is the organizational culture. Acknowledging and addressing this epistemological miss is important in our work because if your culture excludes stakeholders from being the recipients and producers of knowledge, then your capacity to advance your agenda through efforts like strategic planning is impacted by these limitations. Teasdale (2002) suggests that "[c]ulture, eats strategy for breakfast" (p. 195). This stance does not diminish the importance of strategic planning, but rather notes the superseding value of the individuals that make up your institutional culture.

Gratitude is considered "the secret sauce of company culture" (Globoforce 2021). Science helps support this assertion by demonstrating the positive benefits of experiencing gratitude in the workplace. Using functional magnetic resonance imaging (fMRI), neuroscientists have the ability to assess how individuals experience gratitude (Burton 2020). These images monitor brain activity and reveal that experiencing gratitude releases neurochemicals like oxycotin, serotonin, and dopamine which "activates multiple regions of the brain, including those for moral reasoning, fairness, empathy, economic decision-making, taking the perspective of others, and psychological well-being" (Burton 2020, p. 216). Sawyer et al. (2022) note that promoting opportunities for employees to experience gratitude is "an important imperative in modern organizations" which are dependent on advancing organizational objectives through teamwork (p. 256).

Inspired by the work of Kimmerer (2013a), Schutt (2023) offers a gratitude model which I believe is helpful for us to consider within DEI. It captures the varied ways in which the Potawatomi Nation defines gratitude as a cycle that recognizes the value of diversity and productivity (Schutt 2023). He utilizes nature to articulate how the practice of gratitude occurs:

> Gratitude understands that the world is uneven. We as humans cannot honour berries by giving berries, and even if we could that would not serve the berry bush which has berries aplenty. In a cyclical gratitude economy, each participants contribution is unique and different. Therefore, gratitude honours diversity. (p. 11)

Gratitude can also serve as a vehicle to improve productivity. When applied to our work, relationships with colleagues, and our job efforts, practicing gratitude can enhance our relationships with co-workers and how we perceive our work (Schutt 2023). Sharma adds: "Gratitude drives happiness. Happiness boots productivity. Productivity reveals mastery. And mastery inspires the world" (Sharma 2014).

Embedded within the various definitions that encompass this model is the idea that we can use nature as a vehicle to express gratitude. This notion is supported by the definition of gratitude which suggests "that the object of gratitude is other-oriented, including human and nonhuman sources (e.g., God or nature)" (Sawyer et al. 2022, p. 242). In this way, nature like organizations is in constant states of change and evolution. Embracing an epistemology that enhances our understanding of how to engage the collective perspectives within our organizations provides us with the ability to recognize how the diversity of nature (e.g., berry) extends to the diversity of humanity and our capacity to be productive in different ways. This practice offers another way of knowing that is beneficial to us as we consider the benefits of gratitude in shaping and reshaping organizational culture. According to Kimmerer (2013b),

> But we carry gifts of our own, which the Earth urgently needs. Among the most potent of these is gratitude. (para. 2)

> Gratitude may seem like weak tea given the desperate challenges that lie before us, but it is powerful medicine, much more than a simple thank you. Giving thanks implies recognition not only of the gift, but of the giver. (para. 3)

As DEI practitioners, utilizing Indigenous knowledge to put añaychay into practice to feed ourselves and our organizations gratitude offers our community another way of knowing and doing our work. As the challenges related to doing DEI work continue to expand, be reminded that we are in the midst of navigating nepantla. And, in this space of change and transformation we can seek and find gratitude in everything around us.

Key Insights from *Navigating Nepantla*

- Change offers an opportunity for us to innovate in the space of diversity, equity, and inclusion by embracing Indigenous principles of nepantla.
- The field of diversity, equity, and inclusion is not immune to change.
- Institutional legacies help to shape the work of DEI by highlighting organizational gaps and opportunities for change.
- In the change cycle, gratitude is a ready tool to help us find common ground for the work of DEI.

Things to consider:

1 What does the change philosophy of nepantla portend?

2 Leaning into the current dynamic affecting and effecting the fields of diversity, equity, and inclusion will cultivate what opportunities for evolutionary change?

3 How does advocacy reveal itself in Morales' narrative? What is its import in shaping her professional DEI career?

4 What does rebirth look like in the space of diversity, equity, and inclusion, according to Morales?

5 What are the historical patterns Morales speaks of within the tradition of Pachamama that provide insights for a path forward for future work in DEI?

6 What does Morales say about well-intentioned strategic plans?

7 How is wisdom deployed in Morales' narrative? How does it help to undergird her understanding of her professional DEI role?

References

Absolon, Kathleen E. [Minogiizhigokwe]. 2011. *Kaandossiwin: How we come to know*. Fernwood.

Algoe, Sara B. 2012. "Find, remind, and bind: the functions of gratitude in everyday relationships." *Social and Personality Psychology Compass* 6 (6): 455–469. 10.1111/j.1751-9004.2012.00439.x.

Algoe, Sara B., and Jonathan Haidt. 2009. "Witnessing excellence in action: the 'other-praising' emotions of elevation, gratitude, and admiration." *The Journal of Positive Psychology* 4 (2): 105–127. 10.1080/17439760802650519.

Anzaldúa, Gloria. 2015. *Light in the dark/Luz en lo oscuro: Rewriting identity, spirituality, reality*. Edited by Ana Louise Keating. Duke University Press.

Battiste, Marie. 2005. "Indigenous knowledge: foundations for first nations." *WINHEC: International Journal of Indigenous Education Scholarship* 0 (1): 1–17. https://journals.uvic.ca/index.php/winhec/article/view/19251.

Blau, Peter. 1964. *Power and exchange in social life*. John Wiley & Sons.

Burton, Linda Roszak. 2020. "The neuroscience and positive impact of gratitude in the workplace." *The Journal of Medical Practice Management* 35 (4): 215–218. https://www.proquest.com/scholarly-journals/neuroscience-positive-impact-gratitude-workplace/docview/2504871067/se-2.

Campbell, Joseph. 1991. *Reflections on the art of living: A Joseph Campbell companion*. Edited by D. Osbon. HarperPerennial.

Carbajal, Marcy. 2021. "What does 'nepantla' mean?" *Ofrenda*.

Fredrickson, Barbara L. 2004. "Gratitude, like other positive emotions, broadens and builds." In Robert A. Emmons and Michael E. McCullough (Eds.), *The psychology of gratitude* (pp.145–166). Oxford University Press. https://doi.org/10.1093/acprof:oso/9780195150100.003.0008.

Globoforce. 2021. "The science of happiness: How to build a magnetic culture in your company." https://www.workhuman.com/resources/reports-guides/the-science-of-happiness.

Gouldner, Alvin W. 1960. "The norm of reciprocity: A preliminary statement." *American Sociological Review* 25 (2): 161–178. 10.2307/2092623.

Goulet, Linda M., and Keith N. Goulet. 2014. *Teaching each other: Nehinuw concepts and indigenous pedagogies.* UBC Press.

Hanks, E. 2011. "Denzel on mentoring: 'We are all extraordinary.'." Huff Post. https://www.huffpost.com/entry/denzel-on-mentoring-we-ar_n_81867.

Healy, Gwen, and Andrew Tagak, Sr. 2014. "PILIRIQATIGIINNIQ 'Working in a collaborative way for the common good': A perspective on the space where health research methodology and Inuit epistemology come together." *International Journal of Critical Indigenous Studies* 7 (1): 1–14. 10.5204/ijcis.v7i1.117.

Kimmerer, R. 2013a. *Braiding sweetgrass: Indigenous wisdom, scientific knowledge and the teachings of plants.* Milkweed Editions.

Kimmerer, R. 2013b. "Returning the gift." Humans Nature. https://humansandnature.org/earth-ethic-robin-kimmerer/.

Lerner, G. 1986. "The creation of patriarchy." Oxford University. https://gepacf.files.wordpress.com/2015/03/women-and-history_-v-1-gerda-lerner-the-creation-of-patriarchy-oxford-university-press-1987.pdf.

Locklear, Lauren R., Sharon Sheridan, and Dejun Tony Kong. 2023. "Appreciating social science research on gratitude: an integrative review for organizational scholarship on gratitude in the workplace." *Journal of Organizational Behavior* 44 (2): 225–260. 10.1002/job.2624.

McCullough, M. E., S. D. Kilpatrick, R. A. Emmons, and D. B Larson. 2001. "Is gratitude a moral affect?" *Psychological Bulletin* 127 (2): 249–266. 10.1037/0033-2909.127.2.249.

National Association of Diversity Officers in Higher Education. 2023. *State of the CDO survey report. (NADOHE).* https://nadohe.memberclicks.net/assets/2023/State-of-the-CDO.pdf.

Raining, Hillary. 2021. "Miigwech and blood memory: gratitude as a multi-lineage spiritual practice." *Anglican Theological Review* 103 (3): 311–325. 10.1177/00033286211023898.

Sawyer, K. B., C. N. Thoroughgood, E. E. Stillwell, M. K. Duffy, K. L. Scott, and E. A. Adair. 2022. "Being present and thankful: a multi-study investigation of mindfulness, gratitude, and employee helping behavior." *Journal of Applied Psychology* 107 (2): 240–262. 10.1037/apl0000903.

Schutt, Vince. 2023. "Gratitude as a systems-wide values-based approach to enhance sustainable consumption choices." *YU-WRITE: Journal of Graduate Student Research in Education* 2 (1). 10.25071/28169344.31.

Sharma, R. [@RobinSharma]. 2014. "Gratitude drives happiness. Happiness boosts productivity. Productivity reveals mastery. Master inspires the world." Twitter.

Taylor, Marvin J., (Ed.). 1984. *Changing patterns of religious education Abingdon Pr.*

Teasdale, Sheila. 2002. "Culture eats strategy for breakfast!" *Journal of Innovation in Health Informatics* 10 (4): 195–196. 10.14236/jhi.v10i4.259.

Victor, Janice M., Linda M. Goulet, Karen Schmidt, Warren Linds, Jo-Ann Episkenew, and Keith Goulet. 2016. "Like Braiding Sweetgrass: Nurturing relationships and alliances in indigenous community-based research." *International Review of Qualitative Research* 9 (4): 423–445. 10.1525/irqr.2016.9.4.423.

Wilson, Shawn. 2008. *Research is ceremony: Indigenous research methods.* Fernwood.

Wood, Alex M., Jeffrey J. Froh, and Adam W. A. Geraghty. 2010. "Gratitude and well-being: a review and theoretical integration." *Clinical Psychology Review* 30 (7): 890–905. 0.1016/j.cpr.2010.03.005.

11

CODA

We Can Build the World We Want to
See: Reflections on the Roots, Branches,
and Future of DEI Work

Anneliese Singh

Chapter Contents

No one I know in diversity, equity, and inclusion (DEI) leadership dreamed of growing up to do DEI work. Yet, everyone I know who currently serves as a Chief Diversity Officer or is engaged in DEI leadership describes their DEI work as a "calling" of sorts. We felt (and often still feel) deep in our bones that higher education can meet its potential to be accessible to people from all cultural backgrounds, lived experiences, and social identities. We come from different disciplines—social sciences, STEM, and yes, the humanities. We in many cases describe "falling" into the work because we were already advocating for change within our professions. We were likely the ones early in our academic careers who were raising our hands to lead the faculty or staff search committees and serving as that sounding board for students from historically marginalized backgrounds. Throughout all of these experiences, we could see a pathway forward for our universities that did not leave anyone behind.

However, as this book goes to press, there has been a palpable tension in our field as the encroaching attacks on DEI that we have known were always there are now at our doorstep and intensifying. In addition, there have been many long days for CDOs and DEI leaders after the Hamas-sponsored attack on Israeli civilians October 7, 2023 and the continuing Israel-Palestine conflict as we supported campus community members

DOI: 10.4324/9781032724881-14

through geopolitical crisis after crisis on and off campus. There is also a presidential election looming. There are states where using "DEI" has been banned in K-12 settings, and there are public universities in states like Texas, Florida, Tennessee, South Carolina, and Louisiana (amongst others) that have quietly or loudly repurposed their central DEI offices and replaced "DEI" with words like "community engagement" and "access" (e.g., Hicks, 2023). I have sat many hours with mentors, colleagues, consultants, and community members who have had a weariness in their eyes I have not seen … . ever … really. On some of my long walks or after, I'll wonder myself, "How did we get here?" Just four short years ago, it was May 25, 2020 when white Minneapolis police officer, Derek Chauvin, murdered George Floyd—a Black man—as the world was watching. Minneapolis, the United States, the world—and certainly campuses—promised a cultural transformation uprooting anti-Black racism. What happened?

This question—"how did we get here?" can encourage us as CDOs and DEI leaders to reflect on the origin story and resulting branches of DEI work so that we can build a compass for what the future can hold for our field. In attempting to answer this specific question, we can remember our progress moves forward because of and despite backlashes and other attacks on DEI. Our shared DEI origin story includes the work of abolitionists, Civil Rights activists, and other change makers across time who dreamed of a world that could exist beyond what they could see in their own contemporary settings at the time.

Landing Back in Yourself and the World as a CDO

I am a relatively recent Chief Diversity Officer (four years at the time of this writing), but I am "long in the tooth" as they say as a community organizer. I cut my teeth in community organizing as a teenager growing up in New Orleans, working in the environmental justice, reproductive justice, and the HIV/AIDS movements in the late 80s and early 90s when people were more dying of AIDS than living with HIV. As the child of an Indian, Sikh, immigrant professor who worked in an HBCU and a white, Southern mom who dared to marry him despite her family's wishes, I learned very early on in my life how race and racism worked. When I was with my white mom in public, it was not assumed that I "belonged" to her as a light-skinned person. When I was with my dark-skinned dad (who wore a turban as part of his Sikh faith), I would see him called a "terrorist" and feel the embedded idea that there was something "foreign" about us that did not belong in this country. My parents did the best they could to raise my younger brother and me in the city of New Orleans that they loved. They made sure to surround our family with the few Indian and Sikh families in the city, as well as with Black and Jewish Americans who gave our family community no matter how well we "fit" into the racial demographics of New Orleans.

I share my story before I dive into ten strategies we can use to chart our paths forward as CDOs and leaders because I know you have a story that predates your DEI work too. Your story and journey to your role is often a beautiful and tragic one—like most stories of being human. In a time where efforts to erase teaching Black history and the history of race and racism in our country, we need to remember our intergenerational stories more than ever at this moment. In academia and in the larger world, we are often urged to forget our stories to function in the C-Suites and other offices across campus in order to be treated with respect and dignity. But the truth is, when we are disconnected from our stories, we are more vulnerable. We get disconnected not just from ourselves, but from the deep inner knowing we have that is our strategic vision of equity for our universities and for the world. Because of the embedded disconnecting forces we encounter each day and because our DEI work is intergenerational, our first step in taking root through any storm is to land back inside of ourselves and remember our purpose in the world. So, if you haven't done this in a minute, I invite you to take out an old-fashioned pen and a paper and answer these questions:

- Who am I?
- Why am I here?
- Where am I going?

These questions were posed to me by my yoga teacher, Aadil Palkhivala, a student of B.K.S. Iyengar. Aadil advocates that we ask these questions of ourselves regularly in our meditation and asana practice. I have found that my "answers" to these questions are remarkably consistent over time. What are your answers? Try snuggling these questions (or other questions that remind you of who you are, truly) into an auto-alarm on your phone each day. I have a feeling that your answers will also be strikingly similar over time, and I have a pretty strong hunch that when you are connected to those answers your clarity for the DEI work ahead is unshakeable. And that is what we need right now—CDOs and DEI leaders who are so rooted in our own ground that the winds of attacks that shake the branches and trees flow over and between us, not through us diminishing us. Now that you remember your own beautiful soil and roots, let's talk about ten ways we can recommit to moving our DEI work forward.

1 **The language we use is crucial ... and it also does not matter.** A first step of our DEI work involves helping our university communities develop a shared vocabulary. I love that our profession has so many acronyms (e.g., DEIB, EDI, JEDI, IDEA) to reflect the evolution of different DEI vocabularies (often originally called "minority affairs") that guide the work forward at the very different types of institutions that exist within higher education. For those unfamiliar with our long history in DEI, people can critique the words (e.g., "Diversity is not enough," "I don't want to just be 'included' in academia—I want to belong," "We need to talk about access more," "Where is antisemitism and Islamophobia in DEI work?"). But a huge truth we need to remind people of in our use of a shared DEI vocabulary is that we need these words as umbrella terms that give our community a broad idea and understanding of our work and why it matters (e.g., to cultivate bias-free environments for our learning, living, and working communities on campus). And, these words are also ... well, just ... words. The words are to be *lived*—and that has always been the point in DEI work. If the political winds in your university have threatened to batter the work, change the words to umbrella terms that keep the purpose of DEI work (e.g., to ensure our research, teaching, and service missions are accessible to people from all backgrounds) moving forward. If you are more protected from the political winds, use this moment! Make sure to gather in groups to collectively identify if the common DEI vocabulary and related aims of your overall strategic DEI work you are using is *still* working. We have the right to grow and evolve as a DEI field—we always have, and we always will. This is the power of cultural humility, change, and addressing power differentials in our universities. We should not abandon our creativity and vision in the process.

2 **Teach our DEI history—from abolition to current day.** One of the challenges we have faced in our DEI work is teaching our history. Our offices are called to do DEI education, consultation, and advocacy work with high expectations that we will "solve" our university's most inextricable problems—individual bias, prejudice, and harassment and systemic inequities. But we also labor regularly under the critique that we are not doing enough for our minoritized communities, and we are often working at such a fast pace that we have not slowed down enough to help people understand the historical moments that have led to our work. Many trace the roots of our DEI profession to the Black students who sued universities all over the country to gain admission to these historically white universities (Williams, Wade-Golden, & Emmert, 2013). After Black students gained access to historically white universities, Black student activism continued across campuses through

Black student unions calling for equitable treatment in the classroom, for internships, the professoriate, and more (Franklin, 2003). Their calls to address anti-Black racism within the academy resulted in the building of offices of multicultural affairs (Patton & Hannon, 2008), and one might even say had a significant influence and escalation of resources and support for offices of disability services, LGBTQ+ students, international students, and more. These are all crucial parts of our DEI origin story. And we must also do a more consistent job of teaching the DEI history before this. Black and white abolitionists called for universities to uphold the promise of Reconstruction and to challenge the brutality of Jim Crow. These calls formed the basis for the Civil Rights movement and help us understand also how to not just weather and withstand the political attacks of the day, but how to also gain clarity from the strategic visions of these earlier racial justice movements.

3 **Use popular education techniques to make the personal political.** As we teach the origin story of our DEI profession, we have the opportunity to help our university community members understand "why" DEI matters to them. Popular education techniques that are grounded in the work of Freire (2000) and other justice scholars (e.g., Wong, 2007) provide tools CDOs can use to make DEI personal. Some popular education (also called "pop ed") techniques are more global in their intent—the dismantling of the hierarchy between teacher and learner and the assumption that everyone is teaching and everyone is learning so there is a continual emphasis on collective, participatory efforts that generate new knowledge and collective action (Wiggins, 2012). One of the most effective pop ed techniques is to draw a timeline for a certain period in history with a start and end date and then to map onto this timeline university and personal events that were going on during this same time period. For instance, you can take the date of the beginning of the Civil Rights movement to now (1954–2024) and share major historical events at the university (e.g., admission of first Black students, establishment of various multicultural and DEI offices) during this time period. On this timeline, university community members are invited to reflect on the meaning of these historical moments in DEI history and also to "map" their own personal family history during this time. DEI work is some of the most personal work we can do, and its effectiveness is intricately connected to the uptake and personalization of the work no matter our role in the university.

4 **Refocus on cherished values and reimagine the DEI work ahead.** In a famously titled *Time* magazine article ("DEI is not the monster

here"), Princeton Professor and public scholar Eddie S. Glaude advocates for "seeing diversity as a value to cherish ... We begin with a recognition that diversity is constitutive of who we are, and our aim is to reflect it in our institutions and civic arrangements ... fundamental to who we are that becomes a critical part of how we assess whether we are fulfilling the overall mission of the institution" (2023). Glaude's reminder is right on time as the attacks on DEI seek to intentionally obfuscate and distract larger society into seeing ourselves as the source of the problem. The truth is that when you look at demographic trends, higher education is a year away from the dreaded "enrollment cliff" where we will see declining enrollments (Matthews, Warner, & Stokes, 2023); however, we are also at the doorstep of students of color being the majority of high school graduates (51%) in 2026 (American Council on Education, 2019). With the Supreme Court reversal of consideration of race in university admissions, we also expect to see universities enroll more first-generation college students and Pell grant recipients. In addition, no matter how we analyze the impact on university campuses that the October 7 Hamas invasion of Israel and the resulting Israel-Palestine had, we know that antisemitism and Islamophobia have been rising over the last few years in the United States and DEI leaders have and will play important roles in challenging hatred through our overall DEI efforts. We need strong, comprehensive DEI programs that don't—as Glaude reminds us—see DEI as a challenge, but rather as the cherished values that make universities thrive. Amidst many choices, students and their parents will continue to look for universities where they believe students will be safe and supported no matter what their cultural backgrounds, lived experiences, and social identities are. Larger industry, innovation, and class mobility rely on diversity—we know we are more effective problem solvers when diversity is present in class-rooms, research labs, board rooms, and companies.

5 **Sharing the impact of DEI work through data.** Since the inception of our DEI work, data has been a critical component of our work to show the influence of DEI efforts over time. In the origins of our work, the use of data was primarily tracking demographic changes—how much racial and gender diversity we saw increase as a result of, for instance, student recruitment efforts (e.g., pre-college and other pathway programs), faculty and staff equitable search trainings and more. Conducting DEI climate surveys and evaluations of our DEI professional development efforts followed as our profession matured, allowing us to track the influence of our efforts over time. As our field has grown, again so have the critiques—how can we "really" know that DEI efforts make a difference? As we reimagine and recommit to our

DEI efforts, we should lean into our most pressing data questions about our effectiveness, collaborate across similar and different university types on large-scale studies and help bolster the research that demonstrates the need for and the impact of our DEI infrastructure. In addition, thinking more broadly about different ways to use data-driven interventions (e.g., LGBTQ+, disability, religious minorities, veterans) to support underrepresented and underserved communities on our campuses.

6 **Be maladjusted.** As I write this afterword reflecting on the future of our DEI profession, it is King Day in 2024. I am a psychologist, so I am particularly reminded of Dr. King's speech to the American Psychological Association in 1967 (1968): "You who are in the field of psychology have given us a great word. It is the word maladjusted. This word is probably used more than any other word in psychology … But on the other hand, I am sure that we will recognize that there are some things in our society, some things in our world, to which we should never be adjusted … We must never adjust ourselves to racial discrimination and racial segregation … to religious bigotry … to economic conditions that take necessities from the many to give luxuries to the few" (pp. 221–222). The work we do as CDOs each day demands that we are maladjusted—that we feel empathy for those who have the least amount of power on our campus and that has historically been who we have served. One of the dangers there, however, is that when we serve and advocate for those who have less power (as I believe we should), we also can look away from power structures that drive inequities. We become seen as the "safe" people minoritized communities can go to for support and resources (again, this is a good and important thing), but another danger lurks here because we can neglect to work with those who have the most power to make changes and create more equitable policies, procedures, and practices. We must regularly pause to make sure we are working with those in power as much as we are working with those on the ground leading DEI efforts.

7 **Pull all the levers for DEI culture change.** When I sit with campus constituents who are impatient for change, I am reminded to listen *deeply*. Sometimes this impatience (or flat-out attack) is politically motivated. Left-leaning faculty, staff, and students may critique us for not doing enough for our minoritized communities, while right-leaning community members say we are encroaching on their views of society as a meritocracy and say DEI efforts should not exist at all because they privilege certain groups over others. These days in our field, the left and the right leaning communities have sounded more and more like one

another—easy to lob attacks and slow to participate in culture change that would lead to our universities being bias-free and more equitable places of learning, living, and working for all. This is, in many ways, to be expected in the "divided" sociopolitical times we are living in currently. However, at your core, you as a CDO and DEI leader know what DEI work is truly about culture change - and that takes time. Right now, we are living with the culture that was produced up to 30 years ago, and through our DEI initiatives we are changing the culture that future generations will live with on our campus and in our communities (Kim, Toh, & Baik, 2022). Stay focused on culture change and pull all the levers we typically do to change culture and be clear that our efforts are cross-campus collaborations to ensure prejudice, discrimination, and harassment have no place at our universities so that all community members find an environment where they can grow and thrive

8 **Make good trouble, see no stranger.** Many people called the quote from Representative John Lewis about good trouble as a rallying call to action to dismantle anti-Black racism in universities after the murder of George Floyd: "Speak up, speak out, get in the way. Get in good trouble, necessary trouble, and help redeem the soul of America" (Lewis 2020). But the thing is that Representative Lewis didn't just see his call for good trouble as some "performance." When you saw him in-person within his Atlanta district, he would ask you directly about what kind of "good trouble" you were getting into—it was his expectation that we were actively working for a world of racial and other intersectional justices. At the heart of our work as CDOs and DEI leaders is making good trouble. We are consistently called to speak truth to power in our roles in order to be effective. There is also a mini-trap set when we are truth-tellers—a trap that might trick us into thinking there are only two audiences for our DEI efforts, those who are DEI supporters and those who are DEI resisters. As with #7 ("Pull all the levers for DEI culture change"), the truth is that transforming university culture so it is more diverse, equitable, and inclusive means to consistently reach for those we have not worked with as closely. Typically, these are our community members in athletics, campus services, facilities, investment officers, and our research enterprise. The future of our DEI profession demands we continue to deepen our work, seeing all campus community partners as crucial partners in moving DEI efforts forward, and as voices who can help us in the reimagining of DEI change initiatives. As Valarie Kaur says, "When we choose to wonder about people we don't know, when we imagine their lives and listen for their stories, we begin to expand the circle of those

we see as part of us. We prepare ourselves to love beyond what evolution requires" (p. 26).

9 **We are the ones we've been waiting for.** Let's tell the truth here. DEI work is tough. It is intergenerational work. Culture change takes time. It demands resources we often do not have enough of to accomplish our institutions' strategic visions. Sometimes we look around the rooms we lead and see the faithful DEI champions that continuously show up for the work, and we wonder how effective our messaging is. Some days, we wonder ourselves if the work is authentic, substantial, and … real. I remember a couple of summers ago I visited a powerful mentor of mine, Dr. Robert Sellers (former CDO at the University of Michigan). Like any good DEI mentee, I was bemoaning the daily grind of DEI work where I was starting to feel like "damned if I do, damned if I don't" as a CDO. I was struggling in that place of, "I miss my faculty life. Why do I always feel like I am hitting my head against an unmoving wall of resistance to DEI. Where were the allies now that it was the second summer after George Floyd was murdered? Is anything ever going to change?" Sellers turned to me and said, "Who do you want to do this work, Anneliese? If not you, then who?" It was a simple exchange, but it was one that stopped me in my tracks. I remembered the words of Alice Walker, who reminded us of the futility of waiting for "other" leaders to step up into the work of building the light of justice in the world. She reminded us, as Sellers was doing with me, that it is our own inner light that we need and not some savior outside of us. The work of racial and intersectional justice has been built over generations and time intentionally brick by brick, stone by stone, and tree by tree—and we live with the fruit of that intergenerational work today. We can always opt out of DEI work—it is a choice that I believe we must each wrestle with asking ourselves, "Are we the right ones to lead right now?" At the same time, I want that answer we give to be a true and authentic one emerging from the core of what we know deep in our bones about our purpose (what we call "dharma" in my culture) in this world.

10 **Cultivate your rest, self-care, and community care—and protect these at all costs.** CDOs know intimately that the draw on our resources, time, and personhood is endless. We can clearly see the signs of burnout in others, and we support people in identifying all of the opportunities for them to draw boundaries within academia, protect their wellness, and follow their inner wisdom on the life they want to lead. We, too, need this same medicine. Audre Lorde reminds us long after her death about the importance of self-care in long-term, organizing work: "Caring for myself is not self-indulgence, it is self-

preservation and that is an act of political warfare" (p. 130). Tricia Hersey (2022), Nap Bishop and author of *Rest is Resistance*, further reminds us: "You were not just born to center your entire existence on work and labor. You were born to heal, to grow, to be of service to yourself and community, to practice, to experiment, to create, to have space, to dream, and to connect" (p. 122) I want our CDO community and DEI leaders across campus to be well. I want us to heed the words from Lorde and Hersey, especially at this sociopolitical moment, to prioritize our rest and connection to self and community care so we can look back at each day with gratitude and awe of the time we get to be alive in and the history-making DEI work we have the honor to lead. You, my CDOs and DEI leaders, have precious lives. Thank you for gifting a part of your lives as a DEI leader to our movements of abolition, Civil Rights, and human rights. Now, as Hersey says, rest. That rest will keep you centered, clear of mind and heart, and focused on your own personal dharma.

References

American Council on Education. *Race and Ethnicity in Higher Education: A Status Report.* (2019). Retrieved from https://www.equityinhighered.org/wp-content/uploads/2019/02/Race-and-Ethnicity-in-Higher-Education.pdf.

Franklin, V. P. "Introduction: African American Student Activism in the 20th Century." *The Journal of African American History* 88, no. 2 (2003): 105–109. 10.2307/3559059. http://www.jstor.org/stable/3559059.

Freire, Paulo. *Pedagogy of the Oppressed.* Continuum, 2000.

"DEI Is Not the Monster Here." 2023, Retrieved from https://time.com/6458406/dei-campus-speech/

Hersey, Tricia. *Rest Is Resistance: A Manifesto.* Little, Brown Spark, 2022.

Hicks, Maggie. "Diversity Chief at U. Of South Carolina Has 'Diversity' Stripped from His Title." *The Chronicle of Higher Education* (2023). Retrieved from https://www.chronicle.com/article/diversity-chief-at-u-of-south-carolina-has-diversity-stripped-from-his-title.

Kim, Yeun Joon, Soo Min Toh, and Sooyun Baik. "Culture Creation and Change: Making Sense of the Past to Inform Future Research Agendas." *Journal of Management* 6 (2022): 1503–1547. 10.1177/01492063221081031.

King, Martin L., Jr. "The Role of the Behavioral Scientist in the Civil Rights Movement." *American Psychologist* 23, no. 3 (1968): 180–186. 10.1037/h0025715.

Lewis, John. *Representative John Lewis Speech at the Commemoration of the 55th Anniversary of 'Bloody Sunday'.* 2020. Retrieved from https://www.youtube.com/watch?v=Vb5Hw6t2e3o

Lorde, Audre. *A Burst of Light and Other Essays.* Ixia Press, 2017.

Matthews R., Warner B. & Stokes P. "Managing the Demand Cliff." Inside Higher Ed, 2023, Retrieved from https://www.insidehighered.com/opinion/views/2023/10/16/managing-other-enrollment-cliff-opinion.

Patton, L. D., and Hannon, M. D. "Collaboration for Cultural Programming: Engaging Culture Centers, Multicultural Affairs, and Student Activities Offices as Partners." In *Creating Inclusive Campus Environments: For Cross-Cultural Learning and Student Engagement* edited by S. Harper, pp. 138–154. National Association of Student Personnel Administrators, 2008.

Wiggins, N. "Popular Education for Health Promotion and Community Empowerment: A Review of the Literature." *[In eng]. Health Promotion International* 27, no. 3 (Sep 2012): 356–371. 10.1093/heapro/dar046.

Williams, Damon A., and Katrina C. Wade-Golden. Contributed By Mark A. Emmert. *The Chief Diversity Officer: Strategy Structure, and Change Management.* Stylus, 2013.

Wong, Angelina T. "Popular Education: Engaging the Academy – International Perspectives." *Canadian Journal of Education* 30, no. 3 (2007): 969–972.

ADDITIONAL MATERIALS

LEADING WITH CONVICTION

Conversations with Paulette Granberry Russell and William B. Harvey

Carol E. Henderson

Dr. William B. Harvey

Dr. William B. Harvey started his career in education as a high school teacher.[1] He was recruited to teach at Brookdale Community College in New Jersey by a college professor and mother of a high school student who noticed his talent for engaging students in English and History. He would go on to have a distinguished career in higher education, serving as full professor at University of Virginia, and North Carolina A&T State University, among others. A renowned equity practitioner in the field of equity, diversity, and inclusion (EDI), Dr. Harvey helped to co-create the National Association of Diversity Officers in Higher Education (NADOHE) and served as its founding president. He was recently appointed rector of Danubius University in Galati, Romania in January 2021, becoming the first African American to head a European university. After recruiting his successor as the Rector at Danubius, he returned to his position as Distinguished Scholar at the American Association for Access, Equity and Diversity in Washington, DC.

CH: **Name an incident that was pivotal in helping to lead you to the work of justice, equity, diversity, and inclusion.**
WH: Well, one of these incidents certainly occurred when I was at the University of Pennsylvania where I was director of a program in Penn's residential community called the W.E.B. DuBois Program. At that time, University of Pennsylvania was 98% white. The program housed 100 Black students in a living-learning center. In 1975,

someone, whose name has never been revealed to me, decided that having a program for 100 Black students in a residential learning program somehow violated the tenets of that academic institution and decides to file suit against that program for racial discrimination to, in fact, eliminate the program. This suit actually resulted in the Office of Civil Rights sending a team from Washington to visit the program on our campus.

CH: **What was that experience like?**

WH: It was like insanity. I couldn't even understand the rationale of what was being brought to bear. Understanding Penn's history and environment—a very prestigious university serving White elite students and faculty, why having 100 Black students in one place on that campus should be such a danger to those individuals who saw the institution as a pillar in the American academic community.

But the suit was filed, and not only just filed, but was filed with such concern to somebody in Washington that the Office of Civil Rights decided they had to pay a visit and spend three days with us, going through all the things that were inherent to the program. There were interviews with institutional officials, the provost, and myself who was responsible for directing the program, and reported to the Provost. Now, eventually, I believe, because I never did see the written report, and I understand that there were not enough statements of concern by OCR that the program was caused to have any significant change. In fact, it's still in existence to this day and was recently highlghted by the university, but just thinking about the incredible reverse kind of application of the idea of getting people who have been excluded intentionally from this institution for hundreds of years now being sued just for being there.

CH: **Wow. The power of that visit. That was a pivotal moment in helping lead you to this justice, equity, diversity work. You saw, as you mentioned, the imbalance and the inequities of who was allowed on the campus, and who wasn't. And to see this replicated in the services given, I can only imagine what those students experienced daily. So that house—that home—had to become their affirming community so they could have a sense of belonging as they went out to experience what they experienced in classrooms and other parts of the campus.**

WH: You make a particular point. Penn, of course, is located in West Philadelphia, which is a heavily Black community. We were located, we, being my facility, was located at 39th and Walnut Street, which is almost at the far end of the campus. The campus starts at about 30th Street. And there's a big train station at 30th street. If you come in on the train and then walk the nine blocks to the residence halls, it was not unusual, literally, for Black students to be followed by police as they walked down campus at that point in time. That gives you a sense of what the overall ambiance was at that time.

CH: **Switching gears, who were some of the leaders that influenced how you approach this work?**

WH: I can interweave the answer to that with some of the rest of my experiences in the academic community. When I left Penn, I went to the Midwest, where I spent two years in Indiana as an associate dean at a small private Quaker institution, Earlham College. It was an interesting place for me. One of the meaningful things I really took away from that experience is the process of consensus, which is basically what the institution used to establish and review policy matters. It really gave me an understanding about the necessity of listening to people and hearing what they have to say, and giving their point of view reasonable consideration before you move into negating it and trying to shut it down.

After a couple of years there, my family and I moved back to the East coast, and I took a position at Stony Brook University where I took over a program that was called the Educational Opportunity Program. These programs are designed to identify and support students from underrepresented backgrounds and help them matriculate and be successful in the academic environment. I led one of largest programs in the State of New York at that particular institution for six or seven years, eventually moving into a more specialized mainstream position when I became an Assistant Vice Provost. It was also at that point in time that I began to understand the significance of having a faculty appointment and what that could do for career enhancement. Stony Brook did not have a school of education, so I taught part time in the school of social work and was subsequently nominated for and received an American Council on Education fellowship. The ACE fellowship placed me at North Carolina State University, and upon completion of my ACE fellowship, I returned to Stony Brook as a senior researcher for a year, then returned to North Carolina State as an associate professor of education policy. That's where I received and earned tenure and received full professor status for the first time which allowed me the opportunity to move back and forth between the academic side and the administrative side of the academy.

When I was at Stony Brook, I came under the tutelage of one of the most extraordinary people in the academic world, Homer Neal. He is not with us anymore, but he was one of the most well-known and successful physicists in the country, if not the world. Homer was a great mentor. He was the person who was most helpful for me in getting my materials to ACE to qualify to receive that fellowship. And he in turn, when I received the fellowship, introduced me to John Slaughter, who was just an incredible person --academician, leader, and a great human being. John was the first African American to head the National Science Foundation. He was the first African American to lead the University of Maryland and thus became the first African American Chancellor in the ACC; and then became the first African American to lead both public and private institutions when he took the Presidency of Occidental College in California. He just passed last week, and I want to make sure I give the right amount of credit to him and Homer.

Let me get back to Homer for a second. As I mentioned before, Homer Neal was just an outstanding academician, one of the greatest theoretical physicists of his time. He also was an extraordinary administrator, and for a time, as few people know, served as the interim President of the University of Michigan.

So, as you can see, I have had some extraordinary exemplars who have helped me to get a sense of who I am and what I can do in this space.

CH: **Based on that, what led you to co-create the professional organization NADOHE? Can you share lessons learned along the way?.**

WH: I mentioned the ACE fellowship because that was important in the long term. When I was at NC State as a faculty member, I was then recruited to the University of Wisconsin, Milwaukee, to be the Dean of their School of Education, which was a wonderful experience for me. I began to really understand the significance of what somebody in that position is able to do in terms of outreach to communities. Milwaukee was, even at that time, a majority, minority city. I came in as the Dean of the School of Education for a public school system that had 100,000 students, which was approximately 20% of the popula- tion in the city. Of those 100,000 students, a large majority of them were African American, and many of them came from households where the family income was below the poverty line. So, I had a wonderful landscape to go out and do some things in schools and in the communities that demonstrated how universities can carry out their responsibility to the communities that they're a part of.

This work gave me some additional level of national recognition, such that when the Vice President's position became available at ACE, I was asked if I would come back and assume that role, thus becoming the first African American ever to hold the title of vice-President at ACE. It became quite a platform and enabled me to do a lot of things that I would not otherwise have been able to do, including going around talking to people on the various member campuses around the country as well as bringing people together through my convening responsibility and authority. I ran a national meeting every other year called "Educating All of One Nation." And it was in those meetings that I began to connect individually with people on various campuses across the country who were involved in activities that we would now call DEI activities. I began to understand, from my perspective, how useful and even important it might be to begin to bring those people together in some kind of functioning organization. So that's where the idea for NADOHE was born.

CH: **I love that, Educating All of One Nation.**

WH: It's really interesting, Carol, because I inherited that set of meetings from my predecessor, Reginald Wilson. At that point in time the title of it was called "Educating One Third of a Nation." I was encouraged to change the title of it and to also broaden the outreach efforts of those meetings.

To give you a sense of how different things are today, at that point, the last meeting that Reggie organized called "Educating One Third of a Nation," the honorary co-chairs of that meeting were Gerald Ford and Jimmy Carter.

CH: **Wow.**

WH: That's where things were at that point in time to show you how much of a transposition we've had in terms of attitude and the political environments that we're working in.

CH: **Gerald Ford and Jimmy Carter, who sit on opposite sides of the isle.**

WH: Exactly! So, we organized those meetings—Educating One Third of a Nation—every other year. They were enormously successful. We would bring people in, obviously who had interests and concerns about diversity, all the way from Presidents to people who worked specifically in DEI related fields, faculty members, student representatives—it was just a tremendously diverse, literally diverse, group of academic practitioners and people who had a place in the academic communities.

And it was from those meetings that I begin to get a real sense of people, about how they, even in situations where they were successful relative to their specific campuses, still experienced isolation in terms of any kind of national opportunity to engage and reinforce their activities and events with people who are doing the same things in similar settings. At one of my national meetings we put out a call, to see who might be interested in coming together to form a national organization. We expected, I think, about 35 people. I think there were close to 100 people who came to that meeting. Out of that group, I asked for people who would be interested to volunteer their service so that we would have kind of a think tank which would in turn lead into an advisory committee, and those began the steps that we took in order to establish the National Association of Diversity Officers in Higher Education and to put it on a footing where it would have national recognition, and just as important, an appropriate financial base.

That was the start of the organization. There are several people, including Paulette, who was a member of the original board, and several other people who have gone on to very important positions in higher education, including presidencies, who were a part of that original Advisory Committee. And I would have to say we got tremendous, advice and support from the ACE.

CH: So, if you had to do a SWOT analysis of what you see in the field, trends, strengths, weaknesses, opportunities, threats, what would you say about that.

WH: The trends are obvious. They are going in the opposite direction of what we would like and hope to see. I think in some ways it is not surprising. Whenever there is movement forward for people of color in this country, there is always reaction. I think the reaction is more organized and more vicious now, from what I see, and we need to acknowledge and recognize that. It's clear that we need to be as strategic and thoughtful as our adversaries are.

CH: In thinking of the weaponization of the language, is that new?

WH: I don't think it is new. I think it is more overt, in some instances. I think we must, again, be very strategic and use some of the same tactics that are being used against us.

I've been writing a series of articles for *Diverse Issues in Higher Education*. In one of these articles, I talked about positive pluralism as a term that might work in some places and situations. If we can't use affirmative action or DEI, let's create terminology that conveys what, in fact, is important to us and what we're trying to do. In another article I talked about using the term historically white colleges and universities. We talk about HBCUs, let's also talk about HWCUs, because that's what the origin of these institutions are. They're intended to serve white populations. And we need to put that on the table and talk about how we change that perspective. In one of the most recent articles I wrote, I talk about, what I'm calling, hypocritical race theory because some people have weaponized CRT by distorting what it is and what it means. So, I'm saying that what they are doing in attacking a legitimate academic mode of analysis is exercising hypocritical race theory. I think we must be intentional about framing the conversation in ways that suit our needs and interests, and provide some clarity for the circumstances we find ourselves in.

We must be focused and flexible in order to make the positive changes that must be made in these institutions.

CH: **What are you most proud of?**

WH: I think one of the most important accomplishments that I'm particularly proud of is when I got to the University of Virginia, I initiated a program which is still in place. It's called the Virginia-North Carolina Louis Stokes Alliance for Minority Participation. It brought together four HBCUs and four historically white research institutions in partnership. These institutions could help one another to increase diversity and access, not only in their own institutions, but in the communities they serve. We were able to fund that initial program with a $5million grant from the National Science Foundation. I've always argued that institutions that want to become more diverse have to be as willing to invest resources in those processes and programs just as they are willing to do so in other areas that they consider to be important.

CH: **So, pearls of wisdom for those leaders doing this work? What is the grace they need for each day to do this work?**

WH: Well, no matter how successful you are or unsuccessful you are, people are going to come at you. So, I used to tell people do not beat yourself up, no matter how bad you feel about something because there are lots of other folks who are willing to do that for you.

CH: **Any final thoughts?**

WH: We've gone through different iterations [of this work] before, we're going to go through it again and other new nuanced iterations in the future. We must be really cognizant of the fact that the success that we have is going to be met by folks who do not wish us well. And we have to understand that reality and to contextualize it. Part of what's important for us in terms of the energy that we bring to these jobs is a recognition that there are lots of other folks who made tremendous sacrifices for us to be in these positions. So, let's draw from their strength. Let's recognize that, they, too, had tough days, just like we did. And they were able to come back to reinsert themselves into the fight and continue to press on. We have to do the same thing.

Paulette Granberry Russell

Attorney Paulette Granberry Russell is the current president of the National Association of Diversity Officers in Higher Education. She spent over two decades as a senior diversity officer and equity practitioner at Michigan State University, prior to this role. Granberry Russell's expertise in gender equity in STEM, affirmative action, and inclusive leadership makes her a sought-after speaker in countries across Africa, the UK, and the US. Her research and practice centers on dismantling structural barriers that prevent US higher education from reaching its identified mission, values, and goals that include advancing diversity, inclusion, and being regarded as equitable environments of change.

CH: Name a person that has helped to influence your work in justice, equity, diversity, and inclusion?

PGR: My grandmother, who was raised by her grandparents who were formerly enslaved in the South (Tennessee). She told me the story of our ancestor, brought to this country as an enslaved African, and her grandfather, who tried to swim the Ohio River to freedom, and fought for his freedom in the Civil War. I learned about John Brown, Nat Turner, and Harpers Ferry, Virginia, and the slave revolt through her storytelling—not through history books. She aspired to attend college and growing up in the South she didn't anticipate that she could go any place other than an HBCU, or what we call HBCUs today. And while she did not realize that dream for herself, because she married young, began a family, and they made the Great Migration to the North, she understood the doors that would open as a result of my going to college, and she supported my goals. My mother, who was brilliant, graduated from high school at 15, but never really had the opportunity to go to college for a lot of different reasons. Both, my mother, who was a voracious reader, and my grandmother, who understood what it meant to be a Black woman in America would be very proud of my successes.

CH: What moment and/or experience helped to shape your trajectory in this career?

PGR: In K-12 I was driven to succeed. I was probably driven for a lot of reasons, including, [what today] would be called racial discrimination/harassment and bullying that I experienced in K through 12 at a predominantly white parochial school and a community public high school. At that time, we, and certainly I didn't have the words to define what I experienced, but I knew from the stories I was told by my grandmother and living through the early efforts of the civil rights movement, that what I was experiencing was not right. I was also a very empathic child, which I attribute to my upbringing—if someone was targeted because they were "different" I was quick to step in and defend them—which wasn't also respected coming from a girl. I never would have said then that I was equity-minded, but I was. I grew up in the 1960s and early '70s. I was influenced by what was the "counterculture" movement and the anti-Vietnam protests. I was also influenced by Dr. King, the Black Power movement, and the rise of the Black Panther Party. All were significant influences in my life at the time. The "younger generation" was instrumental in giving voice to change. We did not necessarily refer to it as a social justice movement, but we were fighting for equality.

That is basically what led to my trajectory [in this work]. I [also] had a cousin who was in college at the time and she invited me to the university for what [was called] little sister weekend. I did not know how it would happen, and it's not that I had been introduced to any other colleges, other than my grandmother encouraging me to go to an HBCU in Tennessee, but I said to myself, "this is where I want to go."

CH: **Were there moments for intra or intercultural engagement with other groups? What I'm sensing, and what I think you're telling me is because it was the sixties and seventies, people were reticent to cross certain lines.**

PGR: There were white students who would be "friendly" and a few that crossed racial boundaries, but few who actually, absent an event engaged with Black students in or outside the classroom. I was 17 years old at the time, and I had very few white friends when I attended college as an undergraduate student. It was very difficult to cross into white spaces. The Black community there at the time was very, very close. We were Black students who were being admitted into a predominantly white institution and we had to form a sense of community among each other. There were very few social support systems that existed as they do today and very few faculty and staff of color. And there was not a lot of cross-cultural experiences that were deliberately created for students.

CH: **So, I took this from you, and from the conversation we had at our 2023 NADOHE annual meeting where you encouraged us to spell out the acronym DEI. In defining these terms, what do you think is important for leaders, practitioners, and readers to know?**

PGR: As I've said to people, particularly when they use the acronym "DEI," which I don't use any longer, each [term]represents something very different. And the work associated with creating a more diverse environment is very different from creating an environment that is intended to be a more equitable environment. We have to acknowledge the differences and the lived experiences of people and the two-impact success. When you consider inclusion, it requires a different set of skills in order to create what we hope is not only a more equitable environment, but one that is regarded as inclusive as well. That, in turn, can create a sense of belonging for all of us.

I think about the issues that we're confronting now. And how the acronym has been demonized and weaponized. Politicians refer to "DEI" as discrimination, exclusion, and indoctrination. For those who mischaracterize the efforts that support the mission and values of institutions who have invested years of effort and funding for progress, albeit incremental, my fear is returning to an era where "justice for all" and diversity's promise will be set back 50 years, if not greater.

CH: **What is it like to lead a professional organization like NADOHE in this current moment? How are we being stretched as leaders?**

PGR: Let's start with, what is it like? I started with a particular goal in mind. And that goal in 2019, when I ran for the office of President, was to build an infrastructure [having watched the organization grow] that could better support our present membership [and] move us into the future.

There were some who felt that maybe we needed to wait to start investing in the infrastructure, but others of us felt the time was right for the near- and long-term viability of the association. A paid executive would manage the day-to-day operations and allow the Board to govern and set policy. We envisioned a more robust membership strategy and innovative support for the professional development of our members. The association was positioned to consider ways in which funded research would enhance the future of diversity, equity, and inclusion not only in higher education, but other industries as well, and forming coalitions with other industries and organizations with similar objectives as NADOHE's.

NADOHE became aware in mid-2022 of legislation that was being drafted and introduced in a number of states attacking academic freedom in higher education, portraying certain curriculum, including critical race theory as a form of indoctrination, and legislation being drafted and introduced on so-called "divisive concepts." The attacks were well orchestrated, well financed, and appeared to be based on a publication developed by the Manhattan Institute, a conservative think-tank's publication entitled "Abolish DEI Bureaucracies and Restore Colorblind Equality in Public Universities." The legislative efforts were having a chilling effect on institutions that were in states where the bills were being introduced. Few, including institutions and higher education associations, were speaking out in opposition to the efforts. As an organization, it was the work of our members that was being misrepresented and demonized, and whose jobs, in many of the bills, were intended to be eliminated. We had no choice. We had to speak up and we had to speak out in opposition to what was in play.

At different times it was a balancing act—what to say and how to say it—and then it became clearer that the bills being introduced where being taken seriously by states and being passed with at least two states at the time, defunding "DEI" offices. Members were fearful, campus leaders were faced with potential budget cuts and loss of state funding, accreditation threats were possibly looming, and the bills themselves were being vetted, debated, modified, and too often with terms that were vague and ambiguous. The uncertainty of outcomes was being debated across the country. As a result, for some members who could afford to find other opportunities, they began to pursue them. Others had to adjust their efforts, offices, and programs within their offices and institutions to comport with the new laws. The work among various campus leaders, including legal counsel where there is a lack of clarity in the implementing regulations, has been daunting and the stress has been tremendous. For some the stress has impacted their health and well-being.

CH: **Yes, you had to fill that void because silence is its own language. What were the responses to your messages?**

PGR: You know it's interesting. There is a consistency in the legislative strategy that is being played out, and those who are advocating the dismantling of "DEI" have been effective. However, I also believe that our pushing against it has had an impact as well. Our mindset is clear—there can be no going back. We have had to be thoughtful on how as diversity leaders we both support our institutions that are under attack, and faculty, staff, and students who are as well. We better appreciate the need to help a broader audience understand what is meant by academic freedom and diversity, equity, and inclusion—we need consistency in messaging and an accurate counter narrative. It is academic freedom that helps to reinforce the ways in which we do our work to create a more diverse, equitable, inclusive campus. When we advocate for inclusive pedagogy; when we talk about inclusive leadership; when we talk about inclusive curriculum; and the impact of recruiting for greater diversity; we have to break it down so the broader community outside the academy understands what is at stake and can be advocates for higher education.

Is it true that there are individuals and groups that do not feel included, or feel silenced based on their values, or political ideologies? How do we respond to their concerns? We have a responsibility to assess the impact of our efforts on students, the culture and climate of the institution, and outcomes associated with the policies, programs, and practices that are intended to serve the campus and broader community.

I believe that organizations who value academic freedom and free speech and their preservation, are increasingly understanding the necessity of supporting diversity, equity, and inclusion as well. It has required work on our part to avoid an outcome where the threats are prioritized with "DEI" placing third behind academic freedom and free speech. The threats truly are threats against the role higher education plays in a democracy, especially, a democracy that at its founding was not colorblind (or gender blind)—a democracy that viewed education as something for elite, white men.

CH: **What trends do you see in the field? Opportunities and challenges? I think we've spoken about what some of those challenges are: the weaponization of the language, lack of funding, lack of support for the role, lack of career pathing in the role? From your national view, what do you see in the field?**

PGR: I think about this in the context of the professionalization of the field. To be successful, it requires understanding the depth and breadth of the profession, the past and future of higher education and the role diversity has played in shaping the experiences of students, faculty, and staff, the research that informs practice, inclusive curriculum and pedagogy, the role of alumni, K-12, and more broadly, how we influence our present democracy, and the impact globally. As a daily practitioner you are called upon to respond to any situation that might arise that impacts the campus—and that includes situations that were not originally a result of events on a campus, but can be, or are manipulated to impact a campus, and those responsible for leading its efforts (e.g., a pandemic, global conflicts, worsening economy, etc.).

We anticipated resistance because this work was borne out of resistance from its beginning.

CH: **What are you most proud of? And is there something you wish could be done differently?**

PGR: I am proud of both our members and people who have dedicated themselves to advancing diversity, equity, and inclusion in K-20 and that includes students who have always insisted that our campuses do more to enhance their learning and experiences. If I were to wish for something that could be done differently, it would be that we had done more to communicate to the broader community how we all gain from this work that is still in its infancy. The reality is we've been pushing against resistance before the ink was dry on the 1964 Civil Rights Act.

CH: **What pearls of wisdom can you offer to those leaders doing this work now? What is the grace they need for each day in staying the course?**

PGR: It's always understanding why we chose to do what we do. My commitment, and I believe it is true for others, is deeply embedded in my personal values, but also with a profound commitment to justice.

I also think there are those times when leaders have to pull back to preserve themselves—their health. The stresses associated with change are tremendous. Pulling back doesn't necessarily mean that you walk away, just remember to put self-first.

I know when my journey leading this organization is done that I will always believe in equity. I will always recognize and reject injustice, and I will always be aware that there are people in this world that if they could dismantle all of the work of those before me, including my ancestors, they would. We must prepare a place for the next generation of those who will do this work.

Note

1 I had the esteemed honor to interview two leading practitioners in the field of higher education: current president of the National Association of Diversity Officers in Higher Education (NADOHE), Attorney Paulette Granberry Russell, Tuesday, December 19, 2023, and co-creator of NADOHE, Dr. William B. Harvey, Monday, December 18, 2023, via Zoom. These interviews were edited for clarity and length to be included in this collection.

ADDITIONAL RESOURCES

Courtesy of Lisa Fenn and Erica Bruchko

Associations | Alliances | National Conferences

1. African American Policy Forum—AAPF
2. American Association of Colleges & Universities—AAC&U
3. American Association of Community Colleges—AACC
4. American Association of State Colleges and Universities—AASCU
5. American Council on Education—ACE
6. Association for the Study of Higher Education—ASHE
7. Association of American Universities—AAU
8. Center for Antiracist Research—Antiracism Center Boston University
9. Business School DEI Collaborative—BUSDEIC
10. College & University Professional Association for Human Resources—CUPA
11. Faculty Women of Color in the Academy—FWCA—Virginia Tech
12. Higher Education Recruitment Consortium—HERC | Toolkit
13. Hispanic Association of Colleges & Universities—HACU
14. International Ombuds Association—IOA
15. Martha's Vineyard Chief Diversity Officer's Summit
16. National Association of Blacks in Higher Education—NABHE
17. National Association of Diversity Officers in Higher Education—NADOHE
18. National Association of Independent Colleges & Universities—NAICU
19. National Association of Student Personnel Administrators—NASPA
20. National Association of Women in Higher Education—NAWHE
21. National Conference on Race & Ethnicity—NCORE
22. National Council for Faculty Development and Diversity—NCFDD

23. National Diversity Council—NDC | Annual Conference
24. Race & Equity Center—RACE—University of Southern California
25. Society for Human Resource Management—SHRM
26. The Conference Board | Annual Conference
27. University Industry Innovation Network—UIIN | Certification Programs, Annual Conference
28. Workhuman
29. Women of Color in the Academy—WOCIA—Northeastern University

Books

1. Allen, Antija M. and Justin Stewart, eds. *We're Not Ok: Black Faculty Experiences and Higher Education Strategies.* Cambridge: Cambridge University Press, 2022.
2. Brooms, Derrick R., Jelisa Clark and Matthew Smith. *Empowering Men of Color on Campus: Building Student Community in Higher Education.* New Brunswick, NJ: Rutgers University Press, 2018.
3. Byrd, W. Carson. *Behind the Diversity Numbers: Achieving Racial Equity on Campus.* Cambridge, MA: Harvard Education Press, 2021.
4. Byrd, W. Carson, Rachelle J. Brunn-Bevel, Sarah M. Ovink, eds. *Intersectionality and Higher Education: Identity and Inequality on College Campuses.* New Brunswick, NJ: Rutgers University Press, 2019.
5. Crenshaw, Kimberlé, Neil Gotanda, Garry Peller, and Kendall Thomas, eds. *Critical Race Theory: The Key Writings That Formed the Movement.* New York: The New Press, 1995.
6. DiAngelo, Robin. *Nice Racism: How Progressive White People Perpetuate Racial Harm.* Boston, MA: Beacon Press, 2021.
7. ———*White Fragility: Why It's So Hard For White People to Talk about Racism.* Boston, MA: Beacon Press, 2018.
8. Dowd, Alicia C. and Estela Mara Bensimon. Engaging the *"Race Question": Accountability and Equity in U.S. Higher Education.* New York: Teachers College Press, 2015.
9. Fasching-Varner, Kenneth J., Katrice A. Albert, Roland W. Mitchell, and Chaunda M. Allen, eds. *Racial Battle Fatigue in Higher Education: Exposing the Myth of Post-Racial America.* Lanham, MD: Rowman & Littlefield, 2015.
10. Fenwick, Leslie T. Jim Crow's Pink Slip: *The Untold Story of Black Principal and Teachers Leadership.* Cambridge, MA: Harvard Education Press, 2022.
11. Hale, Frank W., ed. *What Makes Racial Diversity Work in Higher Education: Academic Leaders Present Successful Policies and Strategies.* Sterling, VA: Stylus, 2004.

12. Graham, John. *Plantation Theory: The Black Professonal's Struggle Between Freedom & Security*. Atlanta, GA: Mynd Matters Publishing, 2021.
13. Jack, Anthony Abraham. *The Privileged Poor: How Elite Colleges Are Failing Disadvantaged Students*. Cambridge, MA: Harvard University Press, 2019.
14. Johnson, Royel M., Uju Anya, and Liliana M. Garces, eds. *Racial Equity on College Campuses: Connecting Research and Practice*. Albany: State University of New York Press, 2022.
15. Kaepernick, Colin. *Our History Has Always Been Contraband: In Defense of Black Studies*. Chicago, IL: Haymarket Books, 2023.
16. Karabel, Jerome. *The Chosen: The Hidden History of Admission and Exclusion at Harvard, Yale, and Princeton*. Boston, MA: Houghton Mifflin, 2005.
17. Kendi, Ibram X. *How to Be an Antiracist*. New York: One World, 2019.
18. Love, Bettina L. *Punished for Dreaming: How School Reform Harms Black Children and How We Heal*. New York: St. Martin's Press, 2023.
19. Magolda, Peter Mark, ed. *Contested Issues in Troubled Times: Student Affairs Dialogues on Equity, Civility, and Safety*. Sterling, Virginia: Stylus, 2019.
20. Maltbia, Terrence, and Anne Power. *A Leader's Guide to Leveraging Diversity: Strategic Learning Capabilities for Breakthrough Performance*. Oxford: Routledge, 2008.
21. McNair, Tia Brown. *From Equity Talk to Equity Walk: Expanding Practitioner Knowledge for Racial Justice in Higher Education*. Newark, NJ: John Wiley & Sons, Incorporated, 2020.
22. Messer-Davidow, Ellen. *The Making of Reverse Discrimination: How Defunis and Bakke Bleached Racism from Equal Protection*. Lawrence, KS: University Press of Kansas, 2021.
23. Museus, Samuel D. *Creating Campus Cultures: Fostering Success Among Racially Diverse Student Populations*. New York: Routledge, 2012.
24. Neely, Teresa Y., and Margie Montanez, eds. *Dismantling Constructs of Whiteness in Higher Education: Narratives of Resistance from the Academy*. New York: Routledge, 2023.
25. Nichols, Laura. *The Journey Before Us: First-Generation Pathways from Middle School to College*. New Brunswick, NJ: Rutgers University Press, 2020.
26. Noel, James Gerard. *Safe Space Rhetoric and Race in the Academy: A Reckoning*. Lanham, MD: Lexington Books, 2023.
27. Okechukwu, Amaka. *To Fulfill These Rights: Political Struggle over Affirmative Action and Open Admissions*. New York: Columbia University Press, 2019.

28. Park, Julie J. *Race on Campus: Debunking Myths with Data*. Cambridge, MA: Harvard Education Press, 2018.

29. Park, Julie J. *When Diversity Drops: Race, Religion, and Affirmative Action in Higher Education*. New Brunswick, NJ: Rutgers University Press, 2013.

30. Parker III, Eugene T., ed. *Becoming a Diversity Leader on Campus: Navigating Identity and Situational Pressures*. New York: Routledge, 2021.

31. Phelps-Ward, Robin, and Wonjae Phillip Kim, eds. *The Power of Names in Identity and Oppression: Narratives for Equity in Higher Education and Student Affairs*. New York: Routledge, 2023.

32. Pinkett, Randal. *Data-Driven DEI: The Tools and Metrics You Need to Measure, Analyze, and Improve Diversity, Equity, and Inclusion*. Hoboken, NJ: Wiley, 2023.

33. Posselt, Julie R. *Inside Graduate Admissions: Merit, Diversity, and Faculty Gatekeeping*. Cambridge, MA: Harvard University Press, 2016.

34. Rosenberg, Marshall B. *Nonviolent Communication: A Language of Life*. Encinitas, CA: PuddleDancer Press, 2015.

35. Smith, Daryl G. *Diversity's Promise for Higher Education: Making It Work*. Baltimore, MD: Johns Hopkins University Press, 2009.

36. Stulberg, Lisa M, and Sharon Lawner Weinberg, eds. *Diversity in American Higher Education: Toward a More Comprehensive Approach*. New York: Routledge, 2011.

37. Sue, Derald Wing. *Race Talk and the Conspiracy of Silence: Understanding and Facilitating Difficult Dialogues on Race*. Hoboken, NJ: Wiley, 2015.

38. Williams, Damon A. *Strategic Diversity Leadership: Activating Change and Transformation in Higher Education*. Sterling, VA: Stylus Publishing, 2013.

39. ——*The Chief Diversity Officer: Strategy, Structure, and Change Management*. First Edition. Sterling, VA: Stylus Publishing, 2013.

40. Willie-LeBreton, Sarah. *Transforming the Academy: Faculty Perspectives on Diversity and Pedagogy*. New Brunswick, NJ: Rutgers University Press, 2016.

Journals | Magazines | Newspapers | Newsletters | Blogs

1. *The Chronicle of Higher Education*
2. *Diverse Issues in Higher Education*
3. *DiversityGlobal*
4. *Diversity Officer Magazine*
5. *Higher Ed Today*

6. *Inside Higher Ed*
7. *Insight Into Diversity*
8. Journal of Diversity in Higher Education
9. Russel Reynold's Leadership Newsletter, *NEXT*
10. *Savoy Magazine*
11. *Strategic Management Journal*

Selected Articles

1. Arnold, Jeanne, and Marlene Kowalski-Braun. "The Journey to an Inaugural Chief Diversity Officer: Preparation, Implementation and Beyond." *Innovative Higher Education* 37, no. 1 (February 1, 2012): 27–36.
2. Davis, Tangier M., Martinque K. Jones, Isis H. Settles, and Paulette Granberry Russell. *"Barriers to the Successful Mentoring of Faculty of Color."* Journal of Career Development 49, no. 5 (October 1, 2022): 1063–81.
3. Gravley-Stack, Kara, Chris M. Ray, and Claudette M. Peterson. "Understanding the Subjective Experiences of the Chief Diversity Officer: A Q Method Study." *Journal of Diversity in Higher Education* 9, no. 2 (June 2016): 95–112.
4. Hancock, Merodie A. "Equity, Inclusion, and Beyond: Today's Urban Chief Diversity Officer." *Metropolitan Universities* 29, no. 1 (February 2018): 53–63.
5. Harris, Jessica C., Ryan P. Barone, and Lori Patton Davis. "Who Benefits?: A Critical Race Analysis of the (D)Evolving Language of Inclusion in Higher Education." *Thought & Action*, 2015.
6. Harvey, William B. "Chief Diversity Officers and the Wonderful World of Academe." *Journal of Diversity in Higher Education* 7, no. 2 (June 2014): 92–100.
7. Jones, S. Renée, Christina Cobb, Jeremiah O. Asaka, Chandra R. Story, Michelle C. Stevens, and Michaele F. Chappell. "Fostering a Sense of Community among Black Faculty through a Faculty Learning Community." *Adult Learning* 32, no. 4 (November 2021): 165–74.
8. Nixon, Monica L. "Experiences of Women of Color University Chief Diversity Officers." *Journal of Diversity in Higher Education* 10, no. 4 (December 2017): 301–17.
9. Nzinga-Johnson, Sekile. *Laboring Positions: Black Women, Mothering and the Academy.* Bradford, ON: Demeter Press, 2013.
10. Stanley, Christine A. "The Chief Diversity Officer: An Examination of CDO Models and Strategies." *Journal of Diversity in Higher Education* 7, no. 2 (June 2014): 101–8.

11. Stanley, Christine A., Karan L. Watson, Jennifer M. Reyes, and Kay S. Varela. "Organizational Change and the Chief Diversity Officer: A Case Study of Institutionalizing a Diversity Plan." *Journal of Diversity in Higher Education* 12, no. 3 (September 2019): 255–65.
12. Stevenson, Michael R. "Moving beyond the Emergence of the CDO." *Journal of Diversity in Higher Education* 7, no. 2 (June 2014): 109–11.
13. Sue, Derald Wing, Sarah Alsaidi, Michael N. Awad, Elizabeth Glaeser, Cassandra Z. Calle, and Narolyn Mendez. "Disarming Racial Microaggressions: Microintervention Strategies for Targets, White Allies, and Bystanders." *American Psychologist* 74, no. 1 (2019): 128–42.
14. Sue, Derald Wing, Annie I. Lin, Gina C. Torino, Christina M. Capodilupo, and David P. Rivera. "Racial Microaggressions and Difficult Dialogues on Race in the Classroom." *Cultural Diversity and Ethnic Minority Psychology* 15, no. 2 (2009): 183–90.
15. Thompson, Sherwood. *Campus Diversity Triumphs: Valleys of Hope. Diversity in Higher Education. Volume 20. Diversity in Higher Education.* Emerald Publishing Limited, 2018.
16. Williams, Damon and Katrina C. Wade-Golden. What is the Chief Diversity Officer? *Inside Higher Ed* (April 18, 2006).
17. Wilson, Jeffery L. "Emerging Trend: The Chief Diversity Officer Phenomenon within Higher Education." *Journal of Negro Education* 82, no. 4 (2013): 433–45.
18. Wong, Kathleen. "Diversity Work in Contentious Times: The Role of The Chief Diversity Officer." *Liberal Education* 103, no. 3-4 (2017).
19. Worthington, Roger L., Christine A. Stanley, and William T. Lewis. "National Association of Diversity Officers in Higher Education Standards of Professional Practice for Chief Diversity Officers." *Journal of Diversity in Higher Education* 7, no. 4 (December 2014): 227–34.
20. Worthington, Roger L., Christine A. Stanley, and Daryl G. Smith. "Advancing the Professionalization of Diversity Officers in Higher Education: Report of the Presidential Task Force on the Revision of the NADOHE Standards of Professional Practice." *Journal of Diversity in Higher Education* 13, no. 1 (2020): 1–22.

Major SCOTUS Cases

1. Plessy v. Ferguson, 163 US 537 (1896)
2. Brown v. Board of Education of Topeka, 347 US 483 (1954)
3. Regents of the University of California v. Bakke, 438 US 265 (1978)
4. Grutter v. Bollinger, 539 US 306 (2003)

5. Fisher v. University of Texas, 576 US (2015)
6. Students for Fair Admission v. President and Fellows of Harvard College, 600 US (2023)

Initiatives | Frameworks

1. Truth, Racial Healing & Transformation—TRHT

Search Firms

1. Academic Search
2. DiversifiedSearch Group
3. Wittkeiffer

Coaching Services

1. Columbia Coaching Certification Program—3CP
2. International Coaching Federation—ICF
3. Korn Ferry Leadership University

Legal

1. Asian Americans Advancing Justice—AAJC
2. Center for Intersectionality and Social Policy Studies
3. Southern Poverty Law Center—SPLC

DEI Legislation Trackers

1. The Chronicle of Higher Education
2. The Education Trust

Democracy Dialogues

1. America Civil Liberties Union—ACLU
2. Free Speech at Universities—Miller Center—University of Virginia

Lists

1. List of HBCUs—Historically Black Colleges & Universities
2. List of MSI—Minority Serving Institutions

Models / Tools For Fostering Tough Conversations

1. Allen, Antija M. We're Not Ok: Black Faculty Experiences and Higher Education Strategies. Cambridge: Cambridge University Press, 2022.
2. DiAngelo, Robin. White Fragility: Why It's So Hard for White People to Talk about Racism. Boston, MA: Beacon Press, 2018.
3. Fenwick, Leslie T. Jim Crow's Pink Slip: The Untold Story of Black Principal and Teacher Leadership. Cambridge, MA: Harvard Education Press, 2022.
4. Graham, John. Plantation Theory: The Black Professional's Struggle Between Freedom and Security. Mynd Matters Publishing, 2021.
5. Kaepernick, Colin. Our History Has Always Been Contraband: In Defense of Black Studies. Chicago: Haymarket Books, 2023.
6. Love, Bettina L. Punished for Dreaming: How School Reform Harms Black Children and How We Heal. New York: St. Martin's Press, 2023.

Dissertations and Theses

1. Allen, Brandon C. M. "Using Critical Race Theory to Examine How Predominantly White Land-Grant Universities Utilize Chief Diversity Officers." Ph.D., Purdue University, 2020.
2. Edwards, O'Juan Durante. "The Experiences of Black Chief Diversity Officers at Predominantly White Institutions During the Anti-Critical Race Theory Movement." Ph.D., The Florida State University, 2023.
3. Griffith, Matthew. "Chess, Not Checkers: How Chief Diversity Officers Navigate the Political Terrains of the University Leadership Structure." Ph.D., University of California, Los Angeles, 2023.
4. Parker, Eugene T. "Exploring the Establishment of the Office of the Chief Diversity Officer in Higher Education: A Multisite Case Study." Ph.D., The University of Iowa, 2015.
5. Smith-Morris, Micaiah. "Re-Conceptualizing the Role of Chief Diversity Officer within Small, Private, Four-Year Colleges." Ph.D., Immaculata University, 2018.

INDEX